Building A L

A Listener's Guide to Record Collecting

by arrangement with the British Broadcasting Corporation

Edited by JOHN LADE

London

OXFORD UNIVERSITY PRESS

New York   Melbourne

1980

Oxford University Press, Music Department, Ely House, 37 Dover Street, London W1X 4AH

OXFORD   LONDON   GLASGOW   NEW YORK
TORONTO   MELBOURNE   WELLINGTON
IBADAN   NAIROBI   DAR ES SALAAM   CAPE TOWN
KUALA LUMPUR   SINGAPORE   JAKARTA   HONG KONG   TOKYO
DELHI   BOMBAY   CALCUTTA   MADRAS   KARACHI

ISBN 0 19 311327 9

Collection © Oxford University Press

First published 1980

British Library Cataloguing in Publication Data

Building a Library.
  2: A listener's guide to record collecting.
  1. Music – History and criticism – Addresses, essays, lectures.
  2. Sound recordings – History and criticism – Addresses, essays, lectures.
  I. Lade, John   II. British Broadcasting Corporation.
  789.9'131   ML160
  ISBN 0–19–311327–9

*Printed and bound in Great Britain by
Ebenezer Baylis and Son Limited,
The Trinity Press, Worcester, and London*

Preface

JOHN LADE

In the early days of Radio 3's *Record Review* it was introduced as a 'programme for all record enthusiasts'. I hope that even though those words long ago disappeared from our opening announcement the enthusiasm still remains, not only among our listeners, but also in the choice of works for our weekly 'Building a Library' feature and in the presentation of the comparisons. From the letters I receive, and from the scripts that make up this second collection, I believe it does. More importantly, perhaps, I hope we shall never forget that small word 'all', and I like to think that the widely different works included here show that it is still our aim to provide something for everyone, music ranging, in this instance, from Bach and Handel to Bartók and Prokofiev. It is also important not to overlook composers who, although quite well represented in the catalogues, have no one work recorded a sufficient number of times to justify a comparative review; it is almost unbelievable that Delius should be one of the composers in this category. The present collection includes a survey of his works that *are* available on record and a similar consideration of the music of Edmund Rubbra and Percy Grainger.

Record Review has been running for many years now, and organizing 'Building a Library' is not unlike painting the Forth Bridge: new listeners join us all the time, many of them just beginning to build up a collection from scratch. This means that certain standard works need from time to time to be reconsidered. It is all too easy to become *blasé* and to forget that there is always someone anxious to acquire the finest recording of Beethoven's Fifth or Brahms's First. So during the last season we compared all the current versions of the symphonies of Beethoven and Brahms, not in thirteen programmes, one to each symphony, but in four. Two were devoted to each composer, boxed sets and single versions treated separately. This was a daunting task, as the reviewer had to familiarize himself with some two-hundred-and-fifty versions of the Beethoven symphonies and very nearly a hundred of the Brahms.

As in the last collection, I have had to take certain liberties in adapting the broadcast scripts in an attempt to make them just as informative, even when deprived of their all-important musical illustrations. It will be evident from the texts that the reviewers' recommendations are primarily based on judgements of musical and recording quality, but we are also well aware of the importance of economic factors and, wherever possible, try to give more than one recommendation covering the different price ranges. Sometimes we are lucky and the quality of the performance solves this problem for us, as in the case of Haydn's 'Clock' Symphony. It is also true for Mahler's *Lieder eines fahrenden Gesellen*, for although both first and second choices involve two records (the songs being a fill-up on the fourth side of a Mahler symphony) in neither case does the financial outlay greatly exceed the price of a single full-priced record.

Finally, I would like to thank again all the contributors, the staff of the Oxford University Press, and friends at the BBC for their kind co-operation and patience.

Note on the Lists of Recordings

Each review in this collection is supplemented by a complete list of recordings discussed, together with their numbers. In the main, the recordings are arranged in chronological order according to date of issue, the reviewers' recommendations being marked with an asterisk; for the three articles on composers, however, the recordings are listed in alphabetical order according to title. Every effort has been made to keep the reviews up to date since the time of the broadcasts, and to see that all the numbers are accurate at the time of going to press.

Contents

Contents

CHORAL MUSIC

CHAMBER MUSIC

SOLO INSTRUMENTAL

SOLO SONG

COMPOSERS

Mozart   *Così fan tutte*

CHARLES OSBORNE

There are seven complete recordings of *Così fan tutte* currently available, and three of those seven are conducted by Karl Böhm. Three out of seven: that is rather surprising, I suppose, although, having heard Böhm conduct the opera many times during the past quarter of a century, in London with the Vienna State Opera in 1954, and in Salzburg and Vienna in the '60s and '70s, I must say I think he has a very special relationship with this particular opera, over and above his experience and expertise as a conductor of Mozart in general. In Karl Böhm's earliest recording of *Così fan tutte*, with the Vienna Philharmonic (Decca: Ace of Diamonds), the cast consists entirely of singers who appeared in that Vienna Opera London season of 1954, either in this opera or in *Figaro* or *Don Giovanni*. It is far enough in the past for us to look back on that time as a golden age, with singers of the calibre of Lisa della Casa, Christa Ludwig, Anton Dermota, Paul Schoeffler, Erich Kunz, and Emmy Loose. Having admitted my partiality to Karl Böhm's way with *Così fan tutte*, I am going to delete from my list for further consideration his earliest performance, though with very great reluctance. Some of the available performances take four records to perform the opera, while some, including this Karl Böhm version of the '50s, take only three. Needless to say, the three-record sets are somewhat less than complete. Böhm makes heavy cuts in the recitative, which I do not mind all that much, but he omits four numbers completely and truncates one other. The characters most affected by this are Ferrando and Dorabella. At least three of these numbers are regularly cut in stage performance, but that is no reason not to include them in a studio recording. Another three-record set has two numbers missing from it – the little duet for Ferrando and Guglielmo in Act I, and Ferrando's aria, 'Ah, lo veggio quell' anima bella' in Act II. However, it has at least one great asset: the beautiful and youthful voice of Kiri Te Kanawa as Fiordiligi. The performance comes from Erato, with the Strasbourg Philharmonic Orchestra competently conducted by Alain Lombard. The women in the cast are distinctly better than the men: Kiri Te Kanawa does not bring a great deal of personality or individuality to Fiordiligi, but Frederica von Stade and Teresa Stratas characterize Dorabella and Despina much more successfully.

For sheer beauty and individuality of voice combined with superb acting, that celebrated sister-act which dominated the Salzburg performances of *Così fan tutte* in the '60s cannot be bettered. I refer to Elisabeth Schwarzkopf and Christa Ludwig. They head the cast of Karl Böhm's second recording of *Così fan tutte*, made in London with the Philharmonia Orchestra in the early '60s (HMV). This is on three discs, and only two numbers are omitted – the same two that are missing from the Strasbourg Erato performance. They are also missing from a 1955 recording with the Philharmonia conducted by Herbert von Karajan, which is now available from World Records on three discs. Schwarzkopf again is Fiordiligi, Leopold Simoneau sings Ferrando's arias most beautifully, Sesto Bruscantini is an authoritative Don Alfonso and I especially like Nan Merriman and Rolando Panerai as Dorabella and Guglielmo. Vocally, I find this set a most attractive proposition, but I miss in Karajan's overall direction the affection and warmth which Böhm finds in the score and conveys so unfussily. That particular quality is also missing from the next version I turn to, which is a Decca set of four records conducted by Solti, and this time absolutely complete. Solti gets quite lovely playing from the London Philharmonic Orchestra, but somehow the performance as a whole lacks shape and direction, and the cast, which on paper promises well, is generally disappointing. I must qualify that. The singers are mostly excellent: Pilar Lorengar, Teresa Berganza, Tom Krause, for instance, but they are not so interesting first time round that one wants immediately to hear them again. This is rather a defect in a recorded performance intended for repeated hearing, even though the first act Finale goes happily enough.

Of the remaining performances one is complete, on four discs, and is conducted by Sir Colin Davis for Philips. I think this is one of Davis's most successful Mozart recordings, firmly shaped but by no means lacking in warmth and sensitivity. The cast includes some very starry names like Caballé, Cotrubas, Janet Baker, and Nicolai Gedda. The Guglielmo, Vladimiro Ganzarolli, sounds somewhat rough in this company, and the Alfonso, Richard Van Allen, is just a shade dull, but the great moments of the score come across beautifully, with Montserrat Caballé a rich-voiced Fiordiligi and Gedda a strong Ferrando.

The remaining set to be considered is Karl Böhm's most recent recording of the opera (DG). It is rather a special case: the recording was made at a performance during the 1974 Salzburg Festival, on Karl Böhm's eightieth birthday. I was present in the audience on that occasion, and I thought it an absolutely superb performance. But, although I treasure the recording as a memento, I do not think I can recommend it as a recording of *Così*. Minor inaccuracies which are hardly noticeable in the opera house would become noticeable with repeated hearing; also, the usual theatre cuts are made – numbers 7, 24, 27, and 28 of the score – and one or two of the cast seem less impressive when they are only heard but not seen. I think I must regard this three-disc set as somehow above the battle. The orchestra, incidentally, is the Vienna Philharmonic.

I think the three performances of *Così* I have not already ruled out in my own mind are the HMV Böhm, Colin Davis on Philips, and Solti on Decca. I like Solti's dramatic thrust in the accompanied recitatives, he has an excellent Ferrando in Ryland Davies and he includes the aria 'Ah, lo veggio quell' anima bella', one of the numbers usually omitted from stage performances of the opera. Ryland Davies gives a fluent and mellifluous performance of it, but none of the other members of Solti's cast sounds so convincing. What about Böhm's cast in his HMV recording with the Philharmonia? There are no weak links there, and Böhm's tenor is Alfredo Kraus, in the days when his voice was young and fresh, and before he had begun to succumb to that narcissistic style which overcomes so many otherwise fine tenors.

Colin Davis's cast, for Philips, includes a number of justly admired singers, but they are not all caught at their best. I have already mentioned that Ganzarolli, as Guglielmo, seems to me distinctly inferior to the others. But I am very much drawn to the way Colin Davis conducts the opera. This is a very natural performance, unmannered, not as elegant as Karajan, perhaps not as lively as Solti, nor as calmly authoritative as Böhm, yet to steer a middle course is not necessarily negative, and Davis makes it seem absolutely the right thing to do. His is one of the really complete recordings, containing even the Act I duettino for Ferrando and Guglielmo which is usually the first number to be cut.

I have narrowed my first choice down to two recordings, Colin Davis on Philips and Karl Böhm on HMV. Davis is complete on four discs, and Böhm not quite complete on three. In a way, these two performances complement each other, though in other respects they are similar in approach. In general, Davis's singers place singing before characterization, and Böhm's do the reverse. But that is a generalization, and, as such, can easily be challenged. I am certainly not implying that Elisabeth Schwarzkopf and Christa Ludwig in the Böhm version do not sing beautifully, or that Ileana Cotrubas, Nicolai Gedda, and Janet Baker in the Davis recording are not able to act with the voice. Janet Baker's Dorabella indeed, is marvellously sung and acted, and if I allow myself two recommendations, this would certainly be one of them. But if I have to narrow it down to one, then I think that, even though two numbers are missing, the tenor-baritone duettino and the tenor's Act II aria, 'Ah, lo veggio', my choice would be Karl Böhm's HMV recording. Böhm conveys to me, more clearly than any other conductor, the extraordinary ambiguity of mood at the heart of this comedy, and at the heart of so much of Mozart's music. Sunlight and shadow are both there, and where the shadow enhances the sunlight, where it casts a certain chill across it, one cannot always be absolutely certain. What one can be certain of is a first-rate performance from each of the singers, and an extra radiance in the interplay between the two sisters, as portrayed by Elisabeth Schwarzkopf and Christa Ludwig.

4 *Opera*

Recordings discussed

Della Casa, Ludwig, Loose, Dermota, Kunz, Schoeffler/Vienna Philharmonic Orchestra Böhm	Decca, Ace of Diamonds GOS 543–5
Schwarzkopf, Ludwig, Steffak, Kraus, Taddei, Berry/Philharmonia Orchestra/Böhm	HMV SLS 5028
Schwarzkopf, Merriman, Otto, Simoneau, Panerai, Bruscantini/Philharmonia Orchestra/ Karajan	World Records SOC 195–7
Lorengar, Berganza, Berbié, Davies, Krause, Bacquier/London Philharmonic Orchestra/ Solti	Decca D56D4
Caballé, Baker, Cotrubas, Gedda, Ganzarolli, Van Allan/Orchestra of the Royal Opera House Covent Garden/Davis	Philips 6707 025
Janowitz, Fassbaender, Grist, Schreier, Prey, Panerai/Vienna Philharmonic Orchestra/ Böhm	Deutsche Grammophon 2709 059
Te Kanawa, von Stade, Stratas, Rendall, Huttenlocher, Bastin/Rhine Opera Chorus/Strasbourg Philharmonic Orchestra/ Lombard	Erato STU 71111

© Charles Osborne

Mozart   *Don Giovanni*

RODNEY MILNES

No less than four sets of *Don Giovanni* are on the Decca label. The earliest was first released just over twenty years ago, and for the playing and conducting alone it still deserves its place in the catalogue. There is nothing to take exception to in Josef Krips's direction: every tempo seems exactly right, every nuance you feel is just as Mozart must have imagined it, never over-pointed, never driven. The Vienna Philharmonic Orchestra's playing is sublime. In the second-act trio, for instance, where Giovanni and Leporello tempt Elvira down from her balcony, the first violins play as one person, and, after the modulation into C major, their sweet portamentos are again unanimous, very alluring, very Viennese. The singers include Cesare Siepi, a classic Giovanni in the bass mould, imposing and authoritative, Lisa della Casa a coolish Elvira, and Fernando Corena very much a buffo Leporello. Apart from Siepi the cast is fair enough, save for a poor Zerlina and Commendatore, but the singers are not the point: it is the playing and conducting that count, and we haven't really heard much to match it since. Yet, for reasons of age if nothing else, this could not be a first choice, nor can two others from the Decca stable. The problem about the one conducted by Erich Leinsdorf is the casting. The Anna and Elvira are Birgit Nilsson and Leontyne Price. Neither are Mozart singers, though both try very hard to persuade us that they are and Miss Price succeeds rather better; but these are not interpretations to live with. The best things about this set are Siepi and the Vienna Philharmonic who, in any case, are on the earlier Krips version, and I am not too sorry to jettison a dim Ottavio, an ordinary Commendatore, and a very obtrusive production full of irritating sound effects. Another Decca set, issued in 1970, is too eccentrically conducted by Richard Bonynge for serious consideration. He double-dots the opening of the overture, introduces all manner of decorations in dubious taste, and there are so many *appoggiaturas* that it is hard to tell which are the notes that are being *appoggiatur*-ed on to. There are all sorts of rallentandos and changes of tempo, too, that Mozart did not write; and while I am sorry to lose Gabriel Bacquier's aristocratic if dryly sung Giovanni, I am less so to lose Marilyn Horne's extremely unlikely Zerlina.

I hope I am not being too wilful in rejecting the Deutsche Grammophon version conducted by Karl Böhm, but it is a special case. It was recorded live at Salzburg three years ago, with all that that implies: resonant acoustic, sudden changes of level, stage noise, and some faulty intonation that the singers would obviously correct in a studio. Nor is the cast unexceptionable, with Sherrill Milnes a monochromatic Giovanni, Edith Mathis a disappointingly unsteady Zerlina, and Peter Schreier a detached Ottavio. Even if we were building a library of live performances, I am not sure how high this would rate, as in contrast to the theatrical atmosphere we have Dr Böhm's decidedly slow tempos. This is true, for example, in the opening of the first-act quartet: purely musically it is lovely, but I can find little indication of the danger underlying the dramatic situation, of Giovanni being exposed by Elvira's accusations. Böhm's approach, here as elsewhere, is dangerously leisurely. Also in the cast are Anna Tomova-Sintov and Teresa Zylis-Gara, both good. A special case then, and not strictly comparable with studio recordings. Another reject, sadly, is the CBS version conducted by Lorin Maazel. This, too, is a special case: it is the soundtrack of the film directed by Joseph Losey; those who have seen it will know whether or not every scene really *is* set in a huge, empty aircraft hangar, which would explain the horribly over-resonant sound quality. There is a good two-second reverberation period, which may sound very impressive at the end of numbers but plays havoc with the audibility of the notes within them. Instruments come and go at the whim of knob-twiddlers, and the singers are placed far forward at the expense of the orchestra. For example, after the entry of Anna and Ottavio at the opening of the sextet in Act II, I defy you to hear what the first and second violins are playing, if, in fact, you can hear them at all. In the same number Leporello gives little suggestion that he is frantically trying to find his way out of a dark courtyard. The Leporello in question is José van Dam: he sings very well but finds little of the character. The rather gusty Anna is Edda Moser, the forceful Ottavio Kenneth Riegel, who certainly creates a positive character but at the expense of Mozartian line in both his arias. The Elvira, though, Kiri Te Kanawa, gives the best performance on the set, dramatically vivid, technically absolutely secure, and much improving on her previous attempt at the role on record. Her 'Mi tradi' is really marvellous, and I wish this outstanding interpretation could have been heard in worthier surroundings. For the rest, the Giovanni is Ruggero Raimondi, very Italian, very bass-orientated, very forceful, but at times he forgets he is singing Mozart, not Verdi, and unfortunately one of those times is in 'La ci darem la mano'. The Leporello and Masetto are also very dark basses, and the Zerlina is a none-too-comfortable Teresa Berganza, so there is a lack of light and shade in the overall tone picture. Maazel, as is his wont, tends to over-point the music.

That ruthless weeding out leaves three versions for serious consideration: the one on Philips under Sir Colin Davis, the Giulini recording from HMV, and the recently released Solti version on Decca. Comparing just one passage is instructive; the duet after the death of the Commendatore, when Anna fiercely rejects Ottavio's attempts at comforting her, then softens, and Ottavio answers that she has both father and husband in him. Martina Arroyo and Stuart Burrows are the Anna and Ottavio on Philips, and Davis takes it very fast and energetically and gives a real sense of the crisis in their relationship. But I wonder if it is not perhaps too fast for the consoling oboe and bassoon phrase to make its full effect. The second violin figure is prominent, as it should be, to give the feeling of unease; it is less prominent on Decca, where the singers are Margaret Price and Burrows again. Solti's tempo is gentler, the mood less hysterical, but the oboe and bassoon phrase much more compassionate. The sound is more spacious, after the manner of today, with the danger of a corresponding lack of clarity. The Giulini recording was produced in 1960 by Walter Legge, and the sound is more forward and immediate after the manner of those days. The Anna and Ottavio here are Joan Sutherland and Luigi Alva. Sutherland appears less distraught than the other two ladies, but her tone is much brighter than on most of her other recordings, and although Alva's voice is on the dry side, I like the urgency of his characterization and his idiomatic Italian. It is hard to choose between the two Ottavios on these three sets. Burrows is more honeyed, and his Italian is better for Solti, where he also turns in a virtuoso 'Il mio tesoro' with that notorious coloratura passage all in one breath, like McCormack. But his first-act aria is unsteady, and I do think Alva is slightly the more positive character. When it comes to considering the opening of 'La ci darem la mano' one needs to ask one simple question: which is the most seductive Giovanni, which the most seduceable Zerlina? On Philips, with Ingvar Wixell and Mirella Freni, it is a bit fast, I think, with the linking woodwind phrase very baldly stated. Wixell does have an insistent, fast beat in his voice, and by the highest standards Freni is a little unsteady. On Decca there is lovely singing from Lucia Popp, that woodwind phrase is more lovingly caressed, and Bernd Weikel is smoother of emission. Giulini on HMV has Eberhard Waechter as Giovanni and Graziella Sciutti as Zerlina. Sciutti sounds to me eminently seducible, and Waechter's charm is positively poisonous. Of the three Zerlinas, Popp's is the most accurate in the arias, but her voice is not quite so lissome, her phrasing not quite so winning as Sciutti's. Freni, developing into a heavier soprano when she made the recording, does not always get right into the centre of the notes. As for the Giovannis, few lady's maids would bother to come down from the balcony for Wixell, more would for Weikl, more still for Waechter, whose singing has an unsettlingly hypnotic quality. All three sing the so-called Champagne Aria very well. It is at this stage, I fear, that the Davis recording has to drop out, for Wixell's singing is unvaried in colour, his characterization peremptory rather than charming, hectoring rather than authoritative, and the beat in his voice does get wearing after a bit. For all Arroyo's passion and clarity of enunciation – her narration of the attempted rape is spell-binding, the best I have heard yet – she does have trouble with the arias, especially 'Non mi dir'. Te Kanawa's Elvira is heard to much better advantage on the new CBS version even if her accompaniment is not.

While I like the drive and impetus that Davis brings to his reading, and the wonderful clarity of the Philips sound, there are moments, like the one mentioned in 'La ci darem', that lack love. Still, it is really a case of Don Giovanni without the Don.

Now, the two remaining Donna Annas. Margaret Price is very good for Solti, the voice beautiful in quality and hardly ever over-strained by Mozart's technical demands, though she *is* tested by Solti's very slow opening speed for 'Non mi dir', and in the *allegretto* section of the same aria. Sutherland's expression and diction may not be so vivid as Price's, but what marvellous singing it is technically. I think this Anna is one of her best recorded performances, and as such it is treasurable – after all, there have been some pretty poor ones since. By now you will have sensed which way my choice is falling. Gabriel Bacquier, Solti's Leporello, is inventive, funny, coarse, and a little dry of voice. But to my mind this is the one role in the opera that has to be sung by an Italian, which Giuseppe Taddei on HMV is. From his sarcastic enunciation of 'Ah che caro galantuomo' at the very opening, he is alive to every facet of the character: the class resentment, the earthy humour, the cruelty of the Catalogue Aria, and, most important, the real terror in the graveyard and the supper scene, which merely funny Leporellos cannot quite bring off.

As Giovanni, Weikl on Decca is good: there is plenty of variety of vocal expression, less of tone colour, but a lively response to the text. I find his characterization rather lacking in dramatic weight: he is an obvious bounder, what Evelyn Waugh would call 'not quite a gentleman'; you feel he gets his way by bullying or pulling rank rather than by natural authority. In a word, his Giovanni lacks stature. Waechter's interpretation, on the other hand, I find constantly fascinating: he is naturally commanding, funny, volatile, dangerous, switching from charm to menace in a flash, in general so vivid as to present a pathological case-history in sound.

When we come to conductors, Solti's reading, strangely enough, is on the cool side. The overture is an overture to a comedy, not an overture to the nineteenth century, and he responds to the sunny rather than the dark elements in the score. The Catalogue Aria, for one, is witty rather than nasty. At the entry of the Statue he underplays the relentless dotted figure throughout and adopts an almost casual tempo; added to this, his Commendatore, Kurt Moll, sounds less like a statue coming to a last supper to extract retribution than Sarastro dropping in for afternoon tea. This Solti version, on eight sides, includes the rarely performed duet written for the first Vienna performance in which Zerlina threatens Leporello with a razor. I do not think it adds anything to the opera; indeed it holds the action up where it least needs it, and it is not on the same musical level as the rest of the score. Solti's Elvira, Sylvia Sass, is disappointing: her Italian is cloudy, there are one or two dangerously raw notes above the stave, and she can only manage the passage work by taking it very, very carefully and quietly. Giulini also has a notable Masetto in Piero Cappuccilli, inky of voice, properly bloody-minded of character.

Lastly, the orchestras. The London Philharmonic Orchestra for Solti is very alert and lively, but the Philharmonia (vintage 1960) was an outstanding orchestra, and it shows. In contrast to Solti's generally relaxed reading, Giulini's tense conducting grabs you by the scruff of the neck with the first chord of the overture and never lets go: it is as full of impetus as Davis's, but more generous of shading and nuance; the well defined 1960s sound may lack the spaciousness of Decca 1979, but you can hear just as much orchestral detail as on Philips, and rather more than on Decca.

Furthermore, Giulini is on three records at medium price. If you insist on full price and the razor duet, then the Decca will do nicely; if you do not, then I recommend Giulini's as the most satisfying all-round version of the opera, as well as costing less.

Recordings Discussed

Siepi, Danco, Dermota, della Casa, Corena, Böhme/Vienna Philharmonic Orchestra/Krips	Decca GOS604–6
Siepi, Nilsson, Price, Valletti, Corena, van Mill/Vienna State Opera Chorus/Vienna Philharmonic Orchestra/Leinsdorf	Decca D10D4
*Waechter, Sutherland, Alva, Schwarzkopf, Taddei, Frick/Philharmonia Chorus/Philharmonia Orchestra/Giulini	HMV SLS 5083
Bacquier, Sutherland, Krenn, Lorengar, Gramm, Grant/Ambrosian Singers/English Chamber Orchestra/Bonynge	Decca SET 412–5
Wixell, Arroyo, Burrows, Te Kanawa, Ganzarolli, Roni/Covent Garden/C. Davis	Philips 6707 022
Milnes, Tomova-Sintov, Schreier, Zylis-Gara, Berry, MacCurdy/Vienna State Opera Chorus/ Salzburg Mozarteum/Vienna Philharmonic Orchestra/Böhm	Deutsche Grammophon 2740 194
Raimondi, Moser, Riegel, Te Kanawa, van Dam, MacCurdy/Paris Opéra/Maazel	CBS 79321
Weikl, Price, Burrows, Sass, Bacquier, Moll/ London Opera Chorus/London Philharmonic Orchestra/Solti	Decca D162D4

© Rodney Milnes

Verdi   *Otello*

ALAN BLYTH

Shall we, I wonder, ever hear the ideal *Otello* on record? I doubt it. The piece is so demanding. The title part calls for a powerful presence, an heroic tenor, an intelligent vocal actor. Desdemona must be a full yet pure-voiced soprano and a positive personality; Iago a subtle baritone and a plausible villain. Over all three must rule a conductor aware that this opera has perhaps the most varied and remarkable orchestral writing of any Italian score. Yet it is, as a whole, a grand concept, a through-composed work that moves forward inexorably from first to last. Toscanini realized that better than any in his classic set, at present unavailable and demanding reissue, but, of course, in terms of recorded sound his version is no match for more recent ones. Among these James Levine, with the National Philharmonic, Britain's own specialized recording orchestra, in the most recent, RCA issue, comes closest to Toscanini. At the very start he gathers us up into the drama, sweeps us into the storm music, and throughout gives us a taut, forward-moving interpretation. Rhythmic alertness – sometimes taken to excess – and the clarity of the instrumental colouring, less than ideally registered in the tight RCA recording, are other constant and admirable features of his conducting.

Placido Domingo is Levine's Otello. His voice has tonal glamour, and he discovers the strength, the passion, and pathos of Otello's character, even if they are not always expressed in ideally individualized phrasing or very specific verbal accents. We note at once in his account of the notoriously difficult 'Esultate' that he attends to note values and even places the awkward *accacciatura* on the high B accurately; and he is just as successful at portraying the anguish of the role, as in the gloriously lyrical second half of Otello's third-act monologue.

The Iago in this set is Sherrill Milnes. Like Domingo, he is scrupulously muscial, obeying note values, accentuations, and most dynamic markings. Although he is not the most vivid Iago on disc, he is nonetheless a credible engineer of Otello's downfall, and is subtly successful in suggesting Cassio's supposed Dream. The third of Levine's soloists is Renata Scotto, quite the most individual, indeed the most convincing Desdemona on any set. The intensity of her utterance is Callas-like, the feeling truly Italianate, even if the higher notes discolour occasionally. She makes us believe in

Desdemona's wrongful suffering.

For Solti, on the Decca set issued in 1977, the part of Desdemona is taken by Margaret Price. She has the edge – perhaps not quite the appropriate word – over Scotto in vocal perfection, in clean intervals, and serene vocalization but the result is cooler, less personalized, a characteristic of Solti's own reading. As one American critic has put it, 'everything is shipshape, but somehow the guts are missing'.

Decca had earlier recorded the work in a spacious yet lucid acoustic that has not, I think, been surpassed in terms of sound, a version, incidentally, that includes the wholly superfluous ballet music. Karajan was the conductor, his Desdemona the reigning Verdi diva of that day, Renata Tebaldi. She and her conductor epitomize their set's approach, strong, poetic, but not always as passionate as one might wish. Tebaldi is not as lustrous as Price nor as involving as Scotto, but she does exhibit a kind of *spinto* quality neither of her rivals matches. In Karajan's later recording, for HMV, based on his Salzburg production of the early 1970s, Mirella Freni is an affecting though slightly over-parted Desdemona. Unfortunately, Karajan chose to cut a substantial section of the big third-act ensemble, so for me ruling this version out of consideration. We can, in any case, do without his dull dog of an Iago, Peter Glossop. I am more regretful at putting aside Jon Vickers's highly-charged, psychotically unhinged depiction of Otello, a powerful if idiosyncratic reading of the part. Vickers had earlier recorded the role in a more restrained but still eloquent enough manner for Tullio Serafin, by then in his eighties. There is a quiet authority in Serafin's reading with Rome forces but something less than the requisite fire for such a tempestuous score. In the grand sections such as Otello's farewell to arms, he and Vickers go to the heart of the matter. Unlike some rushed, modern accounts, it is possible to understand here the dignity as well as the sorrow of this passage in Act II. A great man is here beginning to fall. This, the earlier of RCA's two currently available versions, is also adorned by Tito Gobbi's many-sided portrayal of Iago, more convincing in suggesting Iago's pliable, quickwitted treachery than any of his recorded rivals. When, also in Act II, he sets the trap for Otello, his pointed asides as Cassio approaches Desdemona, a scene soon to be overlooked by Otello – and his call for Satan's help – are an object lesson in fusing words and tone.

Gobbi has one rival in this kind of vocal finesse. He is Gabriel Bacquier, Solti's Iago. Bacquier is an insinuating, very individual villain, consoling us with verbal pointing for his no longer full-toned voice. All intelligence can do, he achieves. Cossuta, his Otello, does not have Vickers's tortured approach nor Domingo's unfettered tone, but he compensates by the patent honesty of his portrayal. This Otello, one feels, is all the more believable because he would certainly be taken in by Iago's machinations. The Otello and Iago in Decca's and Karajan's earlier recording are Mario del Monaco and Aldo Protti. Del Monaco commanded the title role during the 1950s and early '60s, and by the time he came to make this, his second recording of the part, he had considerably refined his portrayal, tempering the steely voice to moving effect. Yet, as I remember, it was the sheer physical impact of his trumpet-like tenor that made such an effect in the theatre. Protti had a rather routine baritone, yet returning to this old, but still very competitive set, after a break, I was surprised at how much character he brought to the role. This Karajan set is a grand, central performance as a whole with Tebaldi very fine in the last-act Willow Song and Ave Maria, but I do not think it offers as many specific insights or such individual interpretations as those of Solti or Levine.

The RCA Serafin set is seriously weakened by Leonie Rysanek's Desdemona. This artist, always so telling in the theatre, seldom does herself justice on disc. Here, good intentions are too often vitiated by imperfect control and by cloudy tone. Yet there are facets of Serafin's set I would be loth to part with, particularly Gobbi's deceptively genial Iago and much of Vickers's acute declamation. But as a whole it cannot be recommended above the versions conducted by Solti and Levine. Between these two choice is hard. Both have much to commend them; both have limitations. One good reason for preferring Solti would be the superior supporting cast, including Peter Dvorsky's supple Cassio. Another might be the refulgent yet splendidly lithe playing of the Vienna Philharmonic Orchestra and the full-blooded singing of the Vienna State Opera Chorus, all firmly controlled by Solti and spaciously recorded by Decca.

Where Levine's set scores over Solti's is not only in his more dramatic, more involving direction but also in the interpretative accomplishments allied to vocal mastery of its principals. Its greatest asset is Scotto's Desdemona. In the Ave Maria, for example, Decca's in many ways laudable Margaret Price gives us beautiful vocalization and careful phrasing, but not much inward feeling. Scotto, on the other hand, in the Ave Maria seems more inside the role, aware, and able to convey to us that this may be Desdemona's last prayer. She is also even more obedient than Margaret Price to Verdi's markings. She takes the opening, as he requests, truly *sotto voce*, then within the *cantabile* of the prayer proper manages to encompass the significance of the staccato marking over certain notes. The total effect is moving beyond words.

However, Levine's RCA set is not without its drawbacks. The supporting singers, mostly American, leave something to be desired, the recording has not the range of presence of Decca's, and at the time of preparing this review I had difficulty in finding a set with clean surfaces. So if you want recording, as opposed to interpretative truth, go to Decca and Solti, who give perhaps the more carefully prepared version. But I think that the RCA's assets are more decisive in making it my first choice. Levine, by his vigour, intensity, and feeling, brings us closest to the heart of Verdi's most searing music drama. Scotto is undoubtedly the most convincing and moving Desdemona. Milnes, as always an intelligent singer, may not match Gobbi or, indeed, Solti's Bacquier in care over verbal detail, but his is a bluff, believable characterization, sung in firm voice. As the Moor himself, Domingo does not utter the text with the detailed accents of some of his predecessors in the part, or even with the touch of pathos found in Cossutta's singing for Solti. Yet he, more than his rivals, catches the tragic stature of the part, that of a powerful general and a generous heart struck down by a fatal and unjustified jealousy.

Recordings discussed

Del Monaco, Tebaldi, Protti/Vienna State Opera Chorus/Vienna Philharmonic Orchestra/Karajan	Decca D55D3
Vickers, Rysanek, Gobbi/Rome Opera/Serafin	RCA SER 5646–8
Cossutta, Price, Bacquier/Vienna Boys' Choir/ Vienna State Opera Chorus/ Vienna Philharmonic Orchestra/Solti	Decca D102D3
*Domingo, Scotto, Milnes/Ambrosian Opera Chorus/National Philharmonic Orchestra/ Levine	RCA RL 02951

© Alan Blyth

Beethoven

The Nine Symphonies (boxed sets)

RICHARD OSBORNE

Complete Beethoven cycles have often appealed to conductors and concert promoters. Nonetheless, it is one thing to attend a Beethoven Festival; it is quite another to settle down for life with one man's view of the nine on record. Before the war, the performances of one conductor, Felix Weingarter, did tend to hold the field, partly because he had few effective rivals, partly because his readings quickly won the trust of an increasingly discriminating musical public. His great potential rival was Arturo Toscanini; but Toscanini did not complete a cycle of the symphonies until the early 1950s by which time Walter Legge, with his world-beating Philharmonia Orchestra, was embarking on what were to be two great Beethoven projects, first with the young Herbert von Karajan, later with the still indestructible Otto Klemperer. So successful were the Karajan performances that by the mid-1950s the authoritative *Record Guide* was suggesting that collectors might seriously consider investing in the complete Karajan cycle, which had already produced outstanding recordings of the Sixth and Seventh Symphonies, and an 'Eroica' which, in its turn, was preferred to all rival versions.

Four years ago HMV reissued this complete Philharmonia cycle under Karajan as a bargain box, with the mono recordings reprocessed for stereo listening. It is one of the cheapest sets of those now available and remains highly competitive – though it is now decisively challenged by Schmidt-Isserstedt's admirably consistent 1960s Vienna Philharmonic cycle on Decca Jubilee.

Cheapest of all, though, is another collection from the late 1940s and early 1950s. Like his great teacher Gustav Mahler, Bruno Walter conducted Beethoven with fire and eloquence. Like Mahler, he was not wholly averse to eccentric spur-of-the-moment gestures; but at best he was one of the more imaginative and incisive Beethoven conductors of his time. The old New York recordings do not always cope very well with the orchestra, but the ardour and eloquence of Walter's interpretations almost invariably shine through.

If you are on a very tight budget, this Bruno Walter set on CBS Classics is most welcome. Smart friends with stereo will no doubt make derisive remarks about the recordings, but if you acquire the set you can rest assured that in Bruno Walter you have a fine Beethoven conductor and a generous personality.

It was not until 1962 that a record company, Deutsche Grammophon, conceived the idea of a totally integral cycle: all nine symphonies recorded over a comparatively short period of time and issued together as a boxed set at a special subscription price. It was a move which had interesting musical and economic repercussions. Indeed, so attractive was the economic concept of the heavily-discounted subscription set that it became, and has remained, a major feature of the record scene.

The conductor of that 1962 DG cycle was, once again, Herbert von Karajan, who left us in no doubt whatsoever that, musically, the cycle had taken on something of the character of a quest – Karajan and his Berlin players moving inexorably across the great peaks of the Third, Fifth, and Seventh symphonies towards a performance of the Ninth which did, indeed, prove to be the set's crowning glory. As a result the set had tension and an inner consistency which had often eluded cycles recorded over longer periods of time.

All of which raises the point of what are we looking for when we choose a complete Beethoven cycle. Do we, in fact, see it as an exploration, a search for truths which, in the very nature of things, can only be provisional ones? Or are we looking for the stamp of a very great musical personality, a conductor fit to confront Beethoven? Or are we, after all, looking for what one might call 'central' performances – sane, literate readings to which we can return over the years with the minimum of fuss? As it happens, it is possible to meet all three criteria from among currently available cycles. And no prizes for guessing who is the larger-than-life personality. Though his tempos often strain credibility, no conductor conveys more vividly than Klemperer the sheer reach, in harmonic and rhythmic terms, of Beethoven's musical thinking.

In the Fifth and Seventh Symphonies of this stereo cycle Klemperer's tempos are often mind-bogglingly slow. In the 'Eroica', though, his shaping of rhythm and accent is wonderfully astute; the first full E flat major climax is gloriously arrived at. Curiously, one of our outwardly more fiery conductors, Sir George Solti on Decca, follows Klemperer's approach in the 'Eroica', quite successfully, even if he does not have all Klemperer's variety of emphasis or quite such compelling brass playing at the climax itself. There is also less impeccable wind intonation from the Chicago Symphony Orchestra. In a sense, it is odd to hear so dynamic a conductor treating in so stately a fashion a movement marked 'Allegro con brio'. Clearly Solti's primary aim is structural coherence – though you may think him rather bland in matters of dynamics and phrasing, those vital elements which define for us the very contour of Beethoven's thought.

But at least with Solti the contour is retained. Lorin Maazel, with the Cleveland Orchestra on CBS, launches the principal theme of the 'Eroica' not *piano* but *mezzo forte* and proceeds to make a sudden unmarked decrescendo to the crucial C sharp in bar 7. It may be very exciting, but it is not actually what Beethoven wrote. Frequently the performances are direct to the point of literalness. It is the approach of Maazel's predecessor in Cleveland, George Szell, without always Szell's own inimitable brand of tension, and without Szell's incorruptibility in the face of the text. Even if you are prepared to overlook what is a distinctly bizarre account of the Finale of the Ninth Symphony, I rather doubt whether you will be much impressed by Maazel's somewhat meretricious blend of private whimsy and obsessive rigour.

To hear what Beethoven really wrote at the start of the 'Eroica' and as one eminent conductor has recently observed, 'if you can conduct the ''Eroica'' you can conduct almost anything in this genre' – we must turn to an orchestra and conductor whose wonderfully acute shaping of the opening bars gives their interpretation the undeniable stamp of authenticity: Karl Böhm and the Vienna Philharmonic on DG.

Listening to over a dozen sets of the Beethoven symphonies has certainly confirmed my view that no orchestra rivals the Vienna Philharmonic in its intuitive grasp of the Beethoven style. Couple this with Karl Böhm's shrewd, alert detailing of the scores, and you have a sequence of performances which offers a good many central insights into Beethoven's music.

Nonetheless, the Leipzig Gewandhaus Orchestra has an equally long and distinguished Beethoven tradition. What is more, their present principal conductor, Kurt Masur, though he may lack something of Böhm's flair, is an excellent Beethovenian. At their best, his readings are distinguished by a natural rhythmic motion touched, at key points, by a certain strength and urgency which is vital if Beethoven's music is to make its full impact. Also from Philips we have Bernard Haitink and the London Philharmonic Orchestra in a set which is close to the Masur in its general musical intention. Yet in the odd-numbered symphonies Haitink is never quite as tough. There is a lack of dramatic and psychological penetration in his readings which I find disappointing. At critical moments in the 'Eroica' Beethoven achieves a terrifying mingling of nobility and pain: moments which demonstrate beyond doubt the creative possibilities of dissonance. Yet at the height of the development, Haitink either fails to register, or chooses to turn aside from, the awful splendour of Beethoven's vision. Characteristically, Karl Böhm's performance has much more presence, both in the climax itself and in the plaintive E minor lament which follows. Karajan, in his 1977 Berlin recording, is thrilling in the climax; though I do not much care for the slithery accents in the strings or the slightly attenuated woodwind sound in the important E minor theme which follows. Once again this extraordinary music teases out weaknesses which can, in a sense be made to speak for the whole cycle. What is exciting about Karajan's new 'Eroica' is its exploratory, questing spirit. Like Toscanini and Erich Kleiber before him, Karajan, in his third Beethoven cycle, now treats the first movement as a fierce *allegro con brio*, at a pace which comes within hailing distance of Beethoven's own very fast metronome. At best, this produces an exhilarating sense of forward motion, with Beethoven's beloved inner string voices radiating energy like the pulse of a bright star. Eugen Jochum has also recorded the symphonies three times. Jochum's name will crop up quite a lot when I come to consider 'single discs' for he is a Beethoven conductor of great experience and integrity, more emotional, less austere, than Klemperer but sharing with Klemperer a certain old-fashioned pragmatism of approach. In the coda of the 'Eroica's' first movement in this latest cycle for HMV, Jochum uses the re-written trumpet line but does not miss the climax which follows as many conductors seem to do. This is certainly an interesting cycle and I shall be mentioning it again later.

Leaving aside Antal Dorati's rather expensive and to my mind musically uncompetitive set, and the reverberantly recorded Cluytens cycle which is best approached through one or two individual discs, I am left at this point with an imposing shortlist of half-a-dozen stereo sets for final consideration, conducted by Böhm, Karajan, Masur, Solti, Klemperer, and Jochum. I have already referred to the fact that Klemperer's readings of the Fifth and Seventh Symphonies are highly idiosyncratic in matters of tempo, putting him some way behind, say, Karajan, who conducts glorious accounts of both works. Yet Klemperer conducts glorious accounts of the Fourth and Sixth Symphonies, and contrary to general expectation adds fine recordings of the First and Eighth, performances full of architectural strength and mordent wit, qualities which when translated into a tragic, ironic key give his reading of the first movement of the Ninth Symphony a quite special authority.

Although Sir George Solti's 'Eroica' is quite successfully cast in the Klemperer mould, his account of the Ninth offers some revealing musical failures. Discussing the performances some years ago in *Record Review*, Robert Philip drew attention to Solti's over-indulgence of the lyrical episodes. I would go further and suggest that he too often treats rhythm, melody, and harmony as independent units, robbing his readings of that integrity of line and texture which conductors like Klemperer, Böhm, and Karajan can so thrillingly provide. There are also some characteristic rhythmic lapses. For example, the famous two-note figure which launches the Ninth Symphony is clearly iambic in character. Once the dynamic level begins to rise, though, we find Solti punching out the unstressed upbeat with a crude emphasis which runs quite contrary to the letter and spirit of Beethoven's music. Throughout Solti's cycle I sense an uncertainty in his own mind as to what constitutes a proper Beethoven style. In an interview which accompanies the set, he talks about arbitrating between the Beethoven styles of Toscanini and Furtwängler. Not only is this in itself an impossible task, it clearly draws the conductor's attention away from finding his own solutions to the formidable difficulties the symphonies present. A Beethoven interpreter must be his own man, for to some extent these symphonies are about the individual confrontation of difficulty.

Midway through the first movement of the Ninth Symphony – in the great D major crisis – Beethoven presents the conductor with significant problems of balance. Here, Solti rather surprisingly falls back on a dubious old German tradition of adding steep crescendos and decrescendos in the timpani. Jochum does it, too, but at least with Jochum there is a measure of consistency, for he plays the middle-period symphonies which precede the Ninth with a certain old-fashioned truculence: slowish, sonorous performances, played with tremendous thrust and frequent orchestral retouchings. The Seventh is particularly fine and though the latest reading of the Ninth is in no way *Urtext* at least it carries with it the force of strong personal conviction. Though I do not care for Jochum's re-interpretation of Beethoven's text nor for the sour-toned woodwinds in the lead away from that crisis, I do admire the passion and honesty of his Beethoven. This passage midway through the first movement does present major problems of orchestral balance, for the strings especially. Play it literally, as Maazel does, and it can sound very tame indeed. It is here that we have to turn to Klemperer, Böhm, and Karajan, men who have solved these great problems not by external means but in terms of Beethoven's own score. It takes persistence, even perhaps genius, to do this; but once achieved the results are truly awe-inspiring. Karajan's newest Ninth is one of the finest ever recorded, not only in that first movement but in the Finale which is truly an Ode to Joy, a spellbinding response to Schiller's great Ode, where joy is the daughter of Elysium, and to Beethoven's music: players and singers truly 'feuertrunken', 'drunk with fire'. Klemperer, too, is magnificent, narrowly avoiding those moments of portentousness which do occasionally mar Böhm's reading of the Finale. Between them, Klemperer, Karajan, and Böhm meet the various options I mentioned earlier. If you are seeking performances of incontrovertible grandeur and reach, then Klemperer is probably your man, though you will have to put up with some deadening tempos in the Fifth and Seventh Symphonies. By contrast, the latest Karajan set is something of an adventure, a musical quest that goes, ambiguously, in several directions. In the Ninth Symphony I have no doubt that the quest is, indeed, a moral and spiritual one. But Karajan is also a man of his time, fascinated by technical challenges. To play the Finale of the Eighth Symphony at the speed requested by Beethoven's metronome marking is a *tour de force* which few orchestras other than the Berlin Philharmonic could even contemplate. Yet like many technical achievements of our time it can, in retrospect, seem curiously pointless, strangely detached from the needs of living, breathing humanity. Beecham played the Finale of the Eighth at half the speed and made twice as much musical sense of it. Make no mistake, Karajan's is a brilliant and accomplished set, but the aims are complex and many of the findings, as I know Karajan himself is the first to admit, tantalizingly provisional.

Which leaves Karl Böhm presiding over the incomparable Vienna Philharmonic Orchestra, and conducting performances which are wonderfully sane and alert. Conservative without in any sense being conformist, his performances often begin quietly yet blaze to climaxes which at the outset we never quite envisaged. This is the real Böhm whom many of us know from the concert hall and opera house, rather than the rather sober Kapellmeister figure which records have sometimes made him out to be. Except in the first movement of the Fifth Symphony, there is a tension and an electricity in the set which gives it an edge even over such distinguished rivals as Masur and the Leipzig Gewandhaus Orchestra. What is more, this is a set which I suspect appeals to a broad spectrum of English musical taste. For unlike his great rivals, Klemperer and Karajan, Böhm almost invariably achieves authenticity of musical response without in any way appearing to strive for it; and that, to an Englishman's taste, is a mark of true style.

Note

In the most recent addition to the catalogues, Leonard Bernstein conducts the Vienna Philharmonic Orchestra on DG. As his earlier CBS set demonstrated, Bernstein is an unusually gifted Beethoven conductor, exuberant and intelligent. Thus, with the Vienna Philharmonic at his disposal as well as up-to-date engineering, Bernstein's new set has been eagerly awaited. In the event, the set is alert, thoughtful, almost consciously responsible. In the First, Fourth, and Sixth Symphonies Bernstein has moderated some of his tempos whilst retaining the readings' energy, wit, and lithe orchestral lines. Conversely, the first movement of the Fifth Symphony now has a stronger dramatic profile as a result of typically sparer, more disciplined orchestral texturing. Though in the Finale of the Ninth Symphony Bernstein does not quite catch the transcendent joyfulness of the latest Karajan set, the symphony as a whole receives a reading which requires and rewards serious contemplation. The 'Eroica' is very fine, a shade less ardent, perhaps, than the famous New York performance. The Seventh is again glorious, a reading of great character which confirms Bernstein's place as one of the most literate and compellingly musical conductors of our time. In practice, the set stands somewhere between the authoritative Böhm cycle and the more questing, exploratory 1977 Karajan cycle: one of a remarkable trio of sets from a single company.

Recordings discussed

Walter/New York Philharmonic Orchestra	CBS 77511 (5 records)
Karajan/Berlin Philharmonic Orchestra	HMV SLS 5053 (7 records)
Klemperer/Philharmonia Orchestra	HMV SLS 788 (9 records)
Cluytens/Berlin Philharmonic Orchestra	CFP 48999 (8 records)
*Böhm/Vienna Philharmonic Orchestra	Deutsche Grammophon 2721 154 (8 records)

Masur/Leipzig Gewandhaus Orchestra	Philips 6747 135 (9 records)
Solti/Chicago Symphony Orchestra	Decca 11BB 188–196 (9 records)
Haitink/London Philharmonic Orchestra	Philips 7699 037 (6 records)
Karajan/Berlin Philharmonic Orchestra	Deutsche Grammophon 2740 172 (8 records)
Dorati/Royal Philharmonic Orchestra	Deutsche Grammophon 2721 199 (8 records)
Jochum/London Symphony Orchestra	HMV SLS 5178 (8 records)
Maazel/Cleveland Orchestra	CBS 79800 (8 records)
Bernstein/Vienna Philharmonic Orchestra	Deutsche Grammophon 2740 216 (8 records)

Beethoven

The Nine Symphonies (single discs)

Looking back over recordings of the Beethoven symphonies made during the last few years I am struck by the extraordinary vitality and resilience of our musical traditions which have thrown up during a comparatively short space of time important revaluations of the symphonies by conductors like Jochum and Karajan, as well as fascinating new experiences: Giulini conducting the 'Eroica', Carlos Kleiber conducting the Fifth and Seventh Symphonies, and so on.

Paradoxically, one of the trickiest symphonies to conduct is the First; and here things have not changed a great deal, except, as it happens financially – with many fine and previously recommended performances now appearing on lower-priced labels. Cheapest of all is Eugen Jochum's wonderfully droll and characterful coupling of the First and Eighth Symphonies on Deutsche Grammophon Heliodor. That involves buying the Second Symphony by itself and there I would recommend, not Jochum, but Cluytens and the Berlin Philharmonic on Classics for Pleasure. I think the Cluytens cycle has been overrated, by and large; but this is a fresh and spontaneous performance.

Most collectors, though, will be looking for the First and Second Symphonies in harness. Here there are the famous, but to some ears rather fierce, Toscanini performances on RCA, Schmidt-Isserstedt now on Decca's mid-price Jubilee label, and Karajan, also at mid-price on DG's Accolade label. But that is Karajan's earlier, 1962 performance. Since then he has re-recorded all nine symphonies. In the difficult first movement of the First Symphony he is now much more rugged and relaxed, closer to Jochum or Klemperer than to Toscanini. The balancing of these latest Berlin recordings has not met with universal approval. As so often with Karajan, the woodwinds often seem backward in balance. Yet how exquisitely the Berlin woodwinds voice Beethoven's youthful imaginings, giving Karajan's new reading a relaxed yet visionary quality with which few versions can compete. I should warn you that there is no repeat of the first movement exposition, a strange omission. For the rest, Karajan's latest readings of the first two symphonies are fiery and graceful. They are on a full-price DG record.

I have discussed Karajan's new recording of the 'Eroica' Symphony, along with versions by Klemperer, Böhm, Solti, and Haitink in my comparison of complete cycles. (See pp. 16–17). Inevitably, there are at least half-a-dozen recommendable versions of the 'Eroica' in the catalogues. Though Klemperer's classic 1956 mono performance with the Philharmonia is currently deleted his equally memorable 1962 stereo recording has recently been reissued at mid-price on HMV Concert Classics. Awesome and uplifting, the reading gives us a sense, above all, of the enormous reach, harmonic and rhythmic, of Beethoven's symphonic thinking. Klemperer's broad tempos are controversial, of course; and dangerous to imitate. One conductor, though, has produced a remarkable account of the 'Eroica' which is very much in the Klemperer tradition, a reading which has, in addition, all the marks of radical and original musical thought. The conductor is Giulini, who builds Beethoven's great first movement rather as the Cistercians built their abbeys, as a series of interrelated statements in space and time: logical, pure, aesthetically rigorous. Nowhere are these qualities more in evidence than at the movement's much written-about moment of recapitulation.

Some may prefer the 'Eroica' faster and fiercer in the Toscanini style. Yet apart from Liszt's great piano transcription of the score, I know of no more lucid version of the symphony than Giulini's. The Deutsche Grammophon recording is superbly tailored to the reading, as is the playing of the Los Angeles Philharmonic Orchestra. Another outstanding version of the 'Eroica' comes from the Hallé Orchestra under James Loughran. This is a reading of tremendous character and integrity, taken at tempos which will, I imagine, find a large measure of assent among the work's many admirers. It is also a great delight to hear Beethoven's printed text respected by Loughran in ways which practically all the other conductors on record either modify or ignore. Stripped, for instance, of von Bülow's vulgar re-writing of the trumpet part, the coda of the first movement takes on new perspectives: the climaxes are re-distributed, whilst the musical argument retains its poise and dignity to the very end. Loughran's performance, like most recent performances on record, offers an exposition repeat in the first movement as well as an unbroken slow movement; this version comes from Enigma. Mid-price versions of the symphony are in much more abundant supply than they were five years ago. Here, in spite of excellent performances by Jochum, Wyn Morris, von Matačič, and Karajan, Bernstein probably leads the field with an electrifying performance on CBS Classics. This also has an exposition repeat and an unbroken slow movement. Then there is Karl Böhm's earlier Berlin Philharmonic performance for those who prefer something just a little mellower and more central European. There is no exposition repeat, but it is a fine performance, full of energy, but also relaxed and idiomatic. It comes from DG on the mid-price Privilege label.

Happily for those of us who love the work, conductors have played the Fourth Symphony with ardour and affection down the years. Most ardent of all are Toscanini in his 1939 BBC performance now available in a vivid transfer on the World Records label, and Karajan in a quite exceptionally brilliant and beautiful performance recorded with the Berlin Philharmonic in 1962; there is a Mediterranean fire and grace about this performance, available on Deutsche Grammophon. Given the continuing absence of Klemperer's recording, Schmidt-Isserstedt and Jochum offer plausible alternatives to Karajan. In its blend of energy and imagination Jochum's has always been a central reading. His performance with the Amsterdam Concertgebouw Orchestra on Philips has been deleted, but that still leaves an earlier Berlin Philharmonic performance, excellent value on DG's Heliodor label coupled with an Overture: Leonore No. 2. Even mellower though still beautifully articulated, is Schmidt-Isserstedt on Decca Jubilee.

In the Fifth Symphony Jochum is less successful, but then this remarkable and revolutionary work has been a graveyard of many a conducting talent. Starting the symphony is itself something of a nightmare. Even Karl Böhm gets it wrong. He miscounts the beats on the second *fermata* and introduces a *ritardando* at one of the most inappropriate places in the whole of symphonic literature. Some have argued that Carlos Kleiber begins the symphony in triplet rhythm, another famous solecism. If so, it is his only fault, for this is in all other respects a thrilling and literate performance, as well as being a brilliant vindication of Beethoven's demanding tempo markings. He conducts the Vienna Philharmonic Orchestra at full-price for DG; this is one of the great recordings of the last few years. No other full-price version can compete with this, though the curious may care to investigate James Loughran's performance on Enigma which gives us a rare chance of hearing the Scherzo in the extended form in which Beethoven originally conceived it. Karajan's most recent recording is very fine, but it is his 1962 performance which is of more immediate interest and on DG's Accolade label it is a clear recommendation in a mid-price and bargain field which is otherwise strewn with bad performances.

The 'Pastoral' Symphony rarely gets a bad performance on record, so it is difficult to know where to turn amid such an embarrassment of riches. There is, though, one problem. Put simply: different people respond to different pulses; one man's stroll is another man's jog. The collector who warms to the slow, earthy tread of a Furtwängler or a Jochum will not easily adapt to countrymen as mettlesome of tread as Pierre Monteux or Lorin Maazel. In Fritz Reiner's performance one thinks warm days will never cease, yet Sir Colin Davis conducts a performance as cool and clear as a May morning. However, to concentrate exclusively on the music's physical pulse is to miss its equally imaginative dimension. The perfect performance of the 'Pastoral' needs to marry body *and* mind. It needs to be meditative but not comatose, alert yet unhurrying: the poet-composer moving through nature with a profound sense of joy. Which probably explains why what are arguably the three finest performances in the catalogues – Klemperer's,

Böhm's, and Boult's – come from older conductors; from men who have mastered their perspectives, men whose music-making reveals a deep sense of *inner* joy.

If I prefer Klemperer to Sir Adrian Boult, it is because he has the finer orchestra, the Philharmonia at the height of its powers (HMV) and because the transition from the Storm is, to my ears at least, incomparably conducted. Some people do not like Klemperer's very slow Scherzo. This did not worry Klemperer; he merely observed that the dance was a *Ländler* and left it at that. Böhm's performance is not much quicker, but his performance has long been a top recommendation, and so it remains. A glorious reading, not least because of the memorable playing of the Vienna Philharmonic, who bring to this serene and measured interpretation a touch of earthy abandon. Böhm's, like the Klemperer performance, is at full price (DG). I think both are worth the outlay in spite of a long list of really quite good cheaper versions.

Like the 'Pastoral', the Seventh Symphony, equally lucky on record, needs fine sound if its blend of austerity and splendour is to come fully across. And so doffing my hat to the legendary 1936 Toscanini performance I must turn to the many-splendoured array of modern Sevenths, where there is a rich crop of bargain versions. For the genuinely hard-up there is a fine performance on RCA by Fritz Reiner and the Chicago Symphony Orchestra on Camden Classics. It is well recorded, there is an exposition repeat in the first movement and throughout the performance splendidly onward-moving tempos even in the notorious third movement Trio where the in many ways excellent Cluytens on Classics for Pleasure is so mind-bendingly slow. At medium price, Colin Davis's 1962 Royal Philharmonic Orchestra performance on HMV Concert Classics remains, technically and musically, fresh and vivid. Equally familiar is Schmidt-Isserstedt's assuringly central reading with the Vienna Philharmonic Orchestra on Decca Jubilee. But even more remarkable is Bernstein. What I like about Bernstein's reading is its blend of black-browed energy and simple exuberance. What is more, Bernstein, with the New York Philharmonic Orchestra on CBS Classics, gets the rhythms of the first movement right: his is a properly springing 6/8. All of which must leave you asking whether it is worth paying the extra money for such fine full-price versions as Solti on Decca, Muti on HMV, or Kleiber on DG. In the case of Kleiber, the answer is probably yes even though this is not in all respects the *tour de force* that his account of the Fifth Symphony is. The playing of the first movement has always struck me as being too literal in its rhythms and the recording is a shade monochromatic. Yet perhaps more than any other conductor in recent years Kleiber has brought to Beethoven's music a sense of rediscovery – though in rediscovering Beethoven he is old-fashioned enough to divide his violins left and right, to thrilling effect in the symphony's final pages.

I have already referred to one version of the Eighth, Jochum's coupled with Symphony No. 1. If you are looking for the Eighth coupled with the Fifth, then Schmidt-Isserstedt and the Vienna Philharmonic are splendidly trenchant in both works on the Decca Jubilee label. If you acquire that coupling you may well want a single-disc version of the Ninth, in which case Schmidt-Isserstedt again offers a sympathetic performance, well recorded and well sung, also on Decca Jubilee. But sound though Schmidt-Isserstedt is, his reading lacks something of the temperament and the electricity of a famous rival version which has recently been re-issued in single disc format: the 1962 Berlin Philharmonic performance conducted by Karajan, the third of four outstandingly successful sets of the Ninth Karajan has made over the last thirty years; it is available as a single record from DG. The same performance is available, without a side-break in the slow movement, coupled with an electrifying account of the Eighth Symphony, as a two-disc medium price set in the Accolade series. On two records, Klemperer, Böhm, Stokowski, and Karajan in his 1977 performance all conduct powerfully tragic accounts of the first movement. It is the Finale, though, which is so often the sticking point. Far from being an Ode to Joy, it all to often emerges, in G. B. Shaw's famous phrase, as an uphill effort of aspiration. I sense this uphill effort with several conductors: with Giulini, with Böhm, and perceptibly, though by no means entirely, with Klemperer. What is so striking about the approach of Toscanini, Stokowski, and Karajan is their awareness of an element of ecstacy as well as aspiration in the music. Unfortunately, the Toscanini is currently unavailable in the United Kingdom and the Stokowski, a gloriously liberating reading, is ruined by poor recorded balances in the Finale. Which leaves the newest Karajan, a reading full of blaze and beauty, with a choir that is less backwardly balanced than in the 1962 performance. He conducts the Ninth Symphony as part of a DG full-priced two-record boxed set which also includes a dazzling – at times over-dazzling – account of the Eighth Symphony. Collectors with a special interest in the Ninth should also note Furtwängler's famous HMV performance recorded at the re-opening of the Bayreuth Festival in 1951, a lofty, questing reading in every respect.

Recommended recordings
Symphony No. 1
Jochum/Bavarian Radio Orchestra

Deutsche Grammophon
2548 224

Symphony No. 2
Cluytens/Berlin Philharmonic Orchestra

CFP 193

Symphonies Nos. 1 and 2
Schmidt-Isserstedt/Vienna Philharmonic
    Orchestra

Decca JB3

Karajan/Berlin Philharmonic Orchestra

Deutsche Grammophon
2531 101

Symphony No. 3
Klemperer/Philharmonia Orchestra
Giulini/Los Angeles Philharmonic Orchestra

Loughran/Hallé Orchestra
Bernstein/New York Philharmonic Orchestra

HMV SXLP 30310
Deutsche Grammophon
2531 123
Enigma K 53543
CBS 61902

Symphony No. 4
Toscanini/BBC Symphony Orchestra
Karajan/Berlin Philharmonic Orchestra

Jochum/Berlin Philharmonic Orchestra

Schmidt-Isserstedt/Vienna Philharmonic
   Orchestra

World Records SH 134
Deutsche Grammophon
2542 104
Deutsche Grammophon
2548 225
Decca JB7

Symphony No. 5
Kleiber/Vienna Philharmonic Orchestra

Karajan/Berlin Philharmonic Orchestra

Deutsche Grammophon
2530 516
Deutsche Grammophon
2542 105

Symphony No. 6
Klemperer/Philharmonia Orchestra
Böhm/Vienna Philharmonic Orchestra

HMV ASD 2565
Deutsche Grammophon
2530 142

Symphony No. 7
Reiner/Chicago Symphony Orchestra
Bernstein/New York Philharmonic Orchestra
Kleiber/Vienna Philharmonic Orchestra

RCA CCV 5026
CBS 61906
Deutsche Grammophon
2530 706

Symphony No. 8
Schmidt-Isserstedt/Vienna Philharmonic
   Orchestra

Decca JB5

Symphony No. 9
Karajan/Berlin Philharmonic Orchestra (1962)

Karajan/Berlin Philharmonic Orchestra (1977)

Furtwängler/Bayreuth Festival

Deutsche Grammophon
2563 999 or 2725 101
Deutsche Grammophon
2707 109
HMV RLS 727

© Richard Osborne

Brahms   *The Four Symphonies*

RICHARD OSBORNE

Brahms is an ambiguous figure. His symphonies are tremendously vital yet, at the same time, they are really epilogues to a great tradition, a late flowering on that old musical root stock, the Viennese classical tradition. Some musicians have stressed Brahms's classicism; others have seen him as an essentially romantic composer. Charles Rosen, brilliantly arbitrating between these two seemingly irreconcilable views, in his book *The Classical Style*, observes that there is in Brahms's music a depth of romantic feeling which springs from a profound longing for an irrecoverable classical past. Brahms, he argues, can be said to have made music out of an openly expressed regret that he was born too late. Behind the First Symphony we recognize the twin presences of Beethoven, and Robert Schumann, whose life and musical method the symphony partially commemorates. Sir Adrian Boult's performance strikes me as being in every way exemplary, right down to the old-fashioned disposition of the fiddles, left and right. It is a performance which gives generous rein to the music's lyricism and power yet which never loses sight of the equanimity, that hard-won sense of proportion, which makes even this stormy masterpiece the characteristically Brahmsian thing it is.

In many ways, the Brahms symphonies require the touch of a mature musician. A composer of great rigour, severe in the disciplines of his art, he places much at issue just beneath the music's surface. In this respect, I think it is significant that two of our finest young interpreters of Brahms, James Loughran and James Levine, have clearly taken careful note of the Brahms of eminent predecessors such as Klemperer and Toscanini. It is also significant that Sir George Solti has waited nearly thirty years before making his first recording of a Brahms symphony. His Brahms will not be to everyone's taste, but there's no doubting the dark splendour of the playing of the Chicago Symphony Orchestra, nor of Solti's own extraordinary commitment to the music.

Brahms marks the slow movement of this First Symphony *andante sostenuto*. Solti, who treats the movement as expansively as Furtwängler used to do, clearly takes his cue from that word *sostenuto*. Yet some would argue for a quicker pulse at which the conductor can communicate the essentially confiding nature of Brahms's music. As Otto Klemperer demonstrates in the great oboe solo a quicker tempo – a proper *andante* – actually enhances the music's plaintive, grieving mood. There is, after all, much at issue just beneath the surface of Brahms's music, something which requires the very finest kind of musical judgement.

Karajan, in his 1964 Berlin cycle which is still available as a boxed set, makes great play of the dynamic shifts at the start of this slow movement: the sudden *pianissimo* in bar 3, the steep *crescendo* to the forte in bar 5. In spite of the typically *legato* phrasing, it is a closely observed reading, strikingly introspective. By contrast, Karajan's 1978 performance brushes swiftly over the first four bars which now act as preface to a long, nostalgic paragraph, marvellously phrased and projected, and sustained on the orchestra with a singer's art. In this later recording, I detect Karajan establishing his own *personal* dialogue with Brahms's music, but as he is a distinguished Brahms conductor it is a dialogue which is well worth hearing. The outer movements of this 1978 performance are played at white heat, though not without moments of exaggeration. Something which could equally well be said of James Levine's performance, though as this is self-evidently a young man's reading – the symphony gripping, in Weingartner's phrase, like the claw of a lion – the moments of frenzy are perhaps easier to take. By contrast, I am very disappointed by the erratic playing in the Munich Philharmonic Orchestra's performance conducted by Rudolf Kempe and by Kurt Masur's dispirited performance with the Leipzig Gewandhaus Orchestra: a double disappointment in the wake of Masur's splendidly characterful Beethoven cycle. Masur's approach to the First Symphony is comparatively gentle. It is an approach which is better handled by Eugen Jochum, though neither conductor seems to me to match Klemperer's stoic resolve, the trenchancy of Karl Böhm, or the mastery of Sir Adrian Boult. There is an old saying that no orchestra ever made its reputation playing Brahms. Be that as it may, the authentic Brahms sound is uncommonly satisfying. Here I am thinking not so much of the dark splendour which the Berlin Philharmonic or the Chicago Symphony bring to Brahms, fine as that is; but of a dark, rather grainy sound based on the very nicest balance of wind and strings.

It is a sound which is very much in evidence in Klemperer's set of the symphonies, and this is one of the distinctive features of James Loughran's Hallé cycle on Classics for Pleasure. As in Beethoven, Loughran has no truck with orchestral retouchings, something for which I am sure Brahms would have accorded him a friendly grunt of approval. Loughran is particularly successful in the first three symphonies and gives a thrilling performance of the Finale of the First where he sticks to the letter of Brahm's score in the brilliant wind fanfares at bar 267. Traditionally, conductors keep the horns playing throughout, thus all but obliterating the important jagged string descents. It is Brahms with a North Country accent, perhaps, and none the worse for that: a magnificent account of the First Symphony, textually authentic and orchestrally exciting.

Loughran's directness, his integrity and care for detail, make his account of the lyrical and dramatic Second Symphony equally satisfying, much as Klemperer's reading is satisfying, cogent, and alert – though neither enjoys a particularly sophisticated recording. Over the years a number of memorable recordings of the Second Symphony have been made with the Berlin Philharmonic Orchestra, going back to Max Fiedler's celebrated pre-war set and coming forward again to the profoundly lyrical Karajan recording of 1964. Not all orchestras play with the naturally luminous tone of the Berliners; nor do all conductors retain Karajan's, or for that matter Sir Adrian Boult's natural pulse and poise in the lyrical first movement or in the lyrical paragraphs of the second, where the phrasing can so easily become self-conscious. The slow tempos favoured by conductors like Böhm and Solti are something of a liability here, though I infinitely prefer either of these conductors to Lorin Maazel, who gives the impression of a very intelligent man passing the time of day with the Brahms symphonies, admiring what interests him, putting by what does not. A good deal of the music is skated over; other sections are rather strangely indulged.

Brahms marks the Finale of his Second Symphony *allegro con spirito* but adds such markings as *pianissimo, tranquilo, sotto voce*. All of which raises the question of what we should expect of a Brahmsian *pianissimo*. Karajan, in his 1978 Berlin recording, produces an elegant swirl of sound. Matched to a very swift tempo, it does not always make for the clearest articulation. Yet there is little doubt that Karajan gets his sweeping effect most beautifully: Solti's players, at a similar tempo, are a good deal less assured. Yet is the effect entirely the right one? To some extent, this depends on how you listen. If you are drawn to the broad sweep of Brahms's invention, you will probably be bowled over by the Karajan. On the other hand, more meticulous collectors will probably take exception to what is at times a brilliant blur of tone, like viewing an impressionist canvas from an insufficient distance. As Sir Adrian Boult is a shade disappointing in this finale, those who subscribe to the theory that the upper limit of a tempo is the point at which all the notes can still be heard should turn instead to Karl Böhm and the Vienna Philharmonic, a gutty, articulate performance, its roots very much in the Austrian soil; it is nice to hear all the notes for once. I think Karl Böhm's set has been rather underrated and I would commend to all those looking for idiosyncratic, slightly old-fashioned Brahms. Abetted by rather fierce string tone, the recordings are vivid, the playing characterful. It is comparatively easy to pick holes in Böhm's Brahms. There are some distractingly slow tempos in the inner movements and a total absence of exposition repeats. Yet at a time when many conductors' Brahms sounds just like everyone else's, it is marvellous to be reminded how satisfying in its rough-hewn way the Viennese Brahms tradition can be. Böhm never rounds off the edges of Brahms's invention as Istvan Kertesz sometimes did in his now deleted set with the Vienna Philharmonic.

James Levine conducts a distinctive account of the Second Symphony. I have already drawn attention to the fact that his Brahms is very much in the Toscanini tradition, a tradition which has been much revered, though perhaps with some reservations. 'Crystal clear but a shade cool' was how one long-serving member of the Vienna Philharmonic described Toscanini's Brahms; and Yehudi Menuhin, invoking the misty landscapes of Northern Germany and the sense they create of dreaminess and intro-spection, has written in his autobiography, 'It is no accident that the people of Hamburg and Bremen understand Brahms as no other public does; nor that Toscanini, formed in the clear hard light of Italy, could not fill the quiet spaces in Brahms's music'. If there is a fault in Levine's conducting of the composer, it is a tendency to understate, to miss the implications of the sub-text. Having said that, though, Levine's account of the difficult Third Symphony is in most respects masterly. It is one of the most compelling of all readings of the first movement, with rapt transitions, a beautifully poised coda and everywhere an electric tension in the tutti passages. Solti's performance with the same orchestra, the Chicago Symphony, is altogether more monumental, a less compellingly living thing, though the sound itself is superb. Böhm's performance is very fine, but it is weakened by the omission of the all-important exposition repeat, as are both Karajan's performances. Klemperer, Loughran, and Boult are all outstanding, and all take the repeat. The hauntingly melancholic slow movement is music which can easily be made lugubrious and bland. Boult, though, is wonderfully sensitive catching the free, speculative play of Brahms's mind, successfully exploring those 'quiet spaces' to which Menuhin so perceptively refers us. It is difficult to imagine the movement being more persuasively handled than by Sir Adrian Boult – though there is a case, perhaps, for an added degree of romantic intensity such as Jochum provides. Jochum belongs to that distinctive school of German Brahms interpreters of whom Furtwängler was the great presiding genius. It is a school marked out by generally glorious orchestral sonorities matched to very considerable freedom in matters of rhythm, phrasing, and emphasis. As such an approach weakens the structural coherence of the symphonies it is up to the conductor, by sheer force of personality, to restore to the music a sense of organic wholeness. This Furtwängler frequently did, working assiduously with his own Berlin Philharmonic. Jochum, less familiar with his orchestra, cannot always achieve this level of incandescence or, more important still, organic wholeness.

Fellow musicians attempting to describe Furtwängler's Brahms usually resorted to images of rivers in full flood. One sees their point if one listens to an imported EMI set; unfortunately it is expensive and may prove difficult to obtain, but Furtwängler's admirers will certainly want to investigate it. The alternative to Furtwängler, rarely as full-blooded as that and occasionally pulling his punches, is Jochum on a rather more accessible and cheaper HMV set. That is for those who prefer a distinctly romantic approach to Brahms, and do not mind the risk of such performances palling with repetition.

Finally, the Fourth Symphony and some general conclusions. Launching the Fourth Symphony and seeing it through to its tragic conclusion is probably the most formidable problem facing the conductor of a complete cycle. If he over-inflects the music, as Jochum does, he risks losing the great tragic line; on the other hand, if he concentrates on the line at the expense of Brahms's frequent expressive markings the performance will not seem lofty but merely cool and detached. Here I think of James Levine, possibly Solti as well. Many will, in any case, rule out Solti for his *molto adagio* treatment of the second movement. Loughran's version is also disappointing, with rusty string tone at the outset and a recording which stresses gaggling wind solos. Twenty bars into the first movement the strings are completely inaudible. Few of these problems, though, appear in Klemperer's performance; his Brahms is always full of character. Though the recordings are getting on for twenty years old, they come up surprisingly well, conveying something of Klemperer's fine ear for Brahms's strikingly individual blending of wind and string sonorities. The performances have great vitality, whilst Klemperer's own temperament unerringly picks out the laconic, ironic note in Brahms's music. It is an intellectually challenging set which has the advantage of being slightly less expensive than its immediate rivals.

Another classic set is Karajan's 1964 Berlin cycle. Musically I marginally prefer it to the later cycle, yet there is no denying the extra refinement and brilliance of the 1978 recordings. In both sets the Fourth Symphony is gloriously played. The earlier reading is more imperious, closer to Furtwängler, the later one quicker, more stoic, closer to Klemperer, though without Klemperer's unwanted *accelerando* in the first movement coda. I would recommend this later Karajan cycle to those who want to hear Brahms played with great brilliance and beauty – though the sweep of the readings does to my mind detract somewhat from the essentially intimate scale of much of Brahms's symphonic thinking. Still, as my first choice enjoys far less sophisticated sound in the cassette version of his cycle, there is a strong case for recommending the later Karajan set to those who want all the four symphonies on cassette rather than on disc.

For finely balanced sound, on disc at least, and for a manner which is less laconic than Klemperer's, less polished than Karajan's, Sir Adrian Boult is the obvious choice. Boult's performances always have the broad measure of Brahms's music. True, the finale of the Second Symphony is a shade heavy-handed and there is a switch of pace in the finale of the Third which is oddly untypical. For the rest, though, Boult paces Brahms's movements in a way which makes for great architectural cogency but never at the expense of the music's individual voice. The influences of Nikisch and Toscanini and Boult's own long association with the music of Elgar all help to give his readings a special authority. There is strength and passion here, but a measure of restraint, too, an instinctive awareness of the values of a vanished world. It is not the only way to play this marvellous music but as a basis for a Brahms collection Boult's cycle strikes me as being more or less indispensible.

Recordings discussed

Furtwängler/Berlin Philharmonic Orchestra	Harmonia Mundi HM 1C 149–53 422
Karajan/Berlin Philharmonic Orchestra (1964)	Deutsche Grammophon 2721 075
Klemperer/Philharmonia Orchestra	HMV SLS 804
*Boult/London Symphony Orchestra and London Philharmonic Orchestra	HMV SLS 5009
Böhm/Vienna Philharmonic Orchestra	Deutsche Grammophon 2740 154
Jochum/London Philharmonic Orchestra	HMV SLS 5093
Karajan/Berlin Philharmonic Orchestra (1978)	Deutsche Grammophon 2740 193
Loughran/Hallé Orchestra	CFP 78252
Levine/Chicago Symphony Orchestra	RCA RL 03425
Solti/Chicago Symphony Orchestra	Decca D151D4

In a subsequent programme Richard Osborne recommended what he considered to be the best single performances of the four symphonies. Wherever possible he suggested versions in different price-ranges. [Ed.]

Symphony No. 1

Furtwängler/Berlin Philharmonic Orchestra	Deutsche Grammophon 2535 162 (mono)
Loughran/Hallé Orchestra	CFP 40096
Boult/London Philharmonic Orchestra	HMV ASD 2871

Symphony No. 2

Abbado/Berlin Philharmonic Orchestra	Deutsche Grammophon 2542 101
Loughran/Hallé Orchestra	CFP 40219
Monteux/London Symphony Orchestra	Philips 6570 108

Symphony No. 3

Klemperer/Philharmonia Orchestra	HMV SXLP 30255

Symphony No. 4

Karajan/Berlin Philharmonic Orchestra	Deutsche Grammophon 2531 134
Boult/London Philharmonic Orchestra	HMV ASD 2901
Reiner/Royal Philharmonic Orchestra	RCA GL 11961

© Richard Osborne

Bruckner

ARNOLD WHITTALL

The twelve available recordings employ ten conductors, but only six
orchestras; Bruckner is still perhaps a relatively specialized undertaking, at
any rate compared with other late-Romantic symphonists – Dvořák,
Brahms, Tchaikovsky, or Mahler. No French, English, or American
orchestras appear at the moment in the current lists, though a version from
the Chicago Symphony Orchestra under Barenboim is apparently on the
way: and there is one notable East German absentee, the Dresden State
Orchestra. This absence is the more regrettable since the version of
Bruckner's Seventh by the other major East German orchestra, the Leipzig
Gewandhaus under Kurt Masur on RCA, is so disappointing. It is careful,
cautious, and well-disciplined, but tends to shy away from any hint of the
grand gesture, and from any real warmth of expression. Another single-disc
version, by the Danish Radio Symphony Orchestra under Kurt Sanderling
on Unicorn, is also lacking in authentic atmosphere. In Bruckner, the path
between under-characterization and over-exaggeration is a narrow one: the
music needs light as well as weight, and the balance between the two is not
easy to achieve, whether in individual phrases or across the span of whole
movements. Both Masur and Sanderling have problems at the very outset
in setting a suitably broad tempo which at the same time does not deprive
the music of all momentum: it is, after all, marked *allegro moderato.*

Other conductors are clearly more concerned with momentum than with
breadth: Eduard van Beinum, for instance, in the first movement with the
Amsterdam Concertgebouw Orchestra, on one of the oldest and cheapest
single-disc versions. This has much of the mobile feeling appropriate to an
allegro moderato, but most conductors manage a rather more spacious effect
without lapsing into mere lethargy. Eugen Jochum with the Berlin
Philharmonic Orchestra on DG is one of them. Van Beinum's performance
is well-integrated and convincing, if you like his generally brisk tempos;
and, although it was first issued as long ago as 1953, the sound is perfectly
tolerable for most of the time. Bernard Haitink was van Beinum's successor
with the Concertgebouw Orchestra, and his first recording of the symphony
was issued by Philips in 1967. A young man's performance, it now seems
more than a little brash and superficial, with plenty of freshness, but a lack
of Brucknerian profundity – a quality which must never be confused with
mere ponderousness, of course. Like van Beinum, Haitink prefers relatively
fast tempos, which can easily suggest impatience rather than excitement in
the work's more expansive episodes; and the recording, now available on a

single disc, lacks some vividness at the dynamic extremes, especially when it is compared with Haitink's new version. Of course, the main drawback of compressing the entire symphony on to one record is that the side break will occur during the Adagio, and any interruption in a movement of such intense concentration and finely balanced proportions is a major distraction. It would nevertheless be extremely self-denying to rule out all such versions when so much fine music-making can be found on them. Indeed, my two remaining single-disc versions, both available at low price, offer superb conductors who had the style and spirit of the music in their very bones – Hans Rosbaud and Wilhelm Furtwängler.

Rosbaud's orchestra is that of South-West German Radio, and the recording, on Turnabout, dates from 1959. The sound is forward, the balance and detail pretty good for its age, though fortissimos always seem a bit cut back, and the general perspective, especially in the Scherzo, is rather on the dry side. I particularly admire Rosbaud's way with the Finale, which he presents with a minimum of the kind of mannered fluctuations of tempo which afflict some other versions. He is at his most powerful and majestic in shaping the superb transition to the first movement's coda and there is all the immediacy of a live performance, though it is, in fact, a studio recording. Furtwängler's mono version is actually taken from a live broadcast given in Cairo in April 1951: it is not to be confused with his Berlin broadcast performance of 1949, which has been issued on disc, but is not now available. Considering the circumstances in which the recording was made, the sound is not at all bad. There is some fading at the big climaxes, but for the most part there is no lack of perspective, and, needless to say with Furtwängler, there is plenty of atmosphere. The Berlin Philharmonic are a little ragged and unsteady on occasion, it may well have been a rather warm night in Cairo, but the Furtwängler virtues are present in full. For me one of the major tests for any interpreter of this work is the launching and unfolding of the second theme of the Adagio, and with Furtwängler this is marvellously apt and uplifting. This record is now part of a five-record DG set including, in addition to No. 7, Nos 4, 8, and 9.

The same orchestra, the Berlin Philharmonic, though of a more recent vintage, dominates the field of mid- and full-price modern recordings which occupy three sides. It can be heard in two versions conducted by Karajan, and also under Jochum, a recording made in 1967 and currently available as part of a three-disc set with the Symphony No. 4. Jochum's version has had many admirers over the years, and as sheer sound it remains among the very best. I think your reactions to it will depend very much on how inevitable and necessary you find all the many deliberate touches of interpretation, and the concern with passing detail, which Jochum brings to the music. It is a grippingly personalized approach, and always very positive, save perhaps in a rather routine account of the Trio section of the third movement. At the very opening of the first movement the blend of spontaneity and concentration seems ideal; but at the start of the Adagio, for example, a more studied quality is evident, tending to underline what is already intensely expressive. Karajan's first version reveals an instinctive reponse to the music's inner propulsion and mode of utterance which ensures all the necessary richness and eloquence without ever lapsing into empty posturing. For example, Karajan prepares the great climax of the Adagio with a contained excitement which is breath-taking. Of my ten conductors, only Rosbaud and Masur exclude the percussion at this point in the movement. It is in the nature of Brucknerian studies that there is no absolute certainty as to whether the composer finally decided for or against cymbals, triangle, and timpani here. What is definite is that at one stage he did want them and most conductors, in my view rightly, choose not to deny themselves this extra means of emphasizing one of the great moments of harmonic revelation in all music.

My four remaining conductors – Böhm, Solti, and Haitink and Karajan in their second versions – are all notable for their concern to mould and manipulate the music in order to capture what they regard as its essence. All are remarkably well-integrated performances, and superbly played. Yet both Böhm and, to a lesser extent, Haitink, seem to me distinctly out of sympathy with that mystical element in Bruckner's style which can, admittedly, so easily become the excuse for interpretative self-indulgence. If it is side-stepped, however, the result can sound like an actual resistance to the full expressiveness and power of the music. Certainly, in the case of Karl Böhm's 1977 recording with the Vienna Philharmonic Orchestra, I am left with the feeling that for all his power and persuasiveness in moments of drama and animation, he is not completely at one with the work. I find the all-important second theme of the Adagio rather on the fast side, and distinctly lacking in tenderness, with heavy accentuation of the inner parts. Böhm is at his best when he can bring a Beethovenian thrust to the music. There is certainly nothing in the least negative in his performance; but it is a matter of more drama than magic, more passion than poetry. Haitink's second version is on rather similar lines. Like Böhm, he is far too fine a conductor ever to lapse into mere dullness or routine, and the Philips record-ing is first rate, with clear inner detail and particularly rich brass sound. Alongside this 1979 sound, Solti's 1966 recording on Decca with the Vienna Philharmonic Orchestra seems a bit clinical, dry, and close. As for the performance, it reflects a typical Solti tussle between self-consciousness and spontaneity. Like Jochum's, it can seem over-interpreted in places, though never at odds with the nature of the work itself. Solti may appear rather extrovert alongside Rosbaud or Karajan, but he is never superficial, and the Vienna Philharmonic produces playing as polished as their great rivals in Berlin. Yet what I feel to be Solti's tendency to over-phrase the music in the first two movements leads in the Finale to disturbingly extreme contrasts and fluctuations of speed. Many conductors have problems with the movement's subsidiary chorale-like theme, and Solti's deliberation, encouraging the momentum to slacken dangerously, is characteristic.

Karajan's later version also seems too solemn in the chorale theme, but in general the performance is so startlingly different from his first version as to suggest a deliberate lesson in contrasts of interpretation for the maestro's legions of admirers. . . If Karajan's first version evokes the cool spaces and rich colours of a great Catholic cathedral, this one seems to yearn for the rough and tumble of the opera house. It is undeniably exciting, but, to my taste, wildly overwrought and too rhetorical to be truly dramatic. Appropriately, the sound on this version is less spacious, more immediate – not to say importunate – in impact than the earlier recording. It is an extraordinarily exciting experience, but one which confirms my preference, as a clear first choice, for Karajan's earlier version. This may be less exhilarating, but it has all the noble and deeply-felt qualities of a classic interpretation, and a dimension of naturalness and inevitability which none of its often distinguished competitors quite match. One may detect occasional touches of that superfine blandness which, in so many of Karajan's recordings, lies on the far side of the eloquence which is their true essence: but it is difficult to imagine how anyone could resist the overall impact of this performance, as well as its countless affecting and subtle details. At the moment, it is available as part of a three-disc HMV box coupled with Bruckner's Symphony No. 4.

Recordings discussed

Furtwängler/Berlin Philharmonic Orchestra	Deutsche Grammophon 2740 201 (mono)
Van Beinum/Amsterdam Concertgebouw Orchestra	Decca ECS 571
Rosbaud/South West German Radio Orchestra	Turnabout TV 34083S
Solti/Vienna Philharmonic Orchestra	Decca SET 323–4
Haitink/Amsterdam Concertgebouw Orchestra (1968)	Philips 6833 253
Jochum/Berlin Philharmonic Orchestra	Deutsche Grammophon 2726 054
*Karajan/Berlin Philharmonic Orchestra (1972)	HMV SLS 811
Böhm/Vienna Philharmonic Orchestra	Deutsche Grammophon 2709 068
Karajan/Berlin Philharmonic Orchestra (1978)	Deutsche Grammophon 2707 102
Masur/Leipzig Gewandhaus Orchestra	RCA RL 31347
Sanderling/Danish Radio Orchestra	Unicorn RHS 356
Haitink/Amsterdam Concertgebouw Orchestra (1979)	Philips 9500 640

© Arnold Whittall

Elgar   *Falstaff*

MICHAEL KENNEDY

The first thing to remember about Falstaff is that he was fat. Elgar's work begins with the principal Falstaff theme depicting Sir John 'in a green old age, mellow, frank, gay, easy, corpulent, loose, unprincipled, and luxurious'. Rather a mixed lot for a musical theme to represent and Elgar, it seems to me, has concentrated on 'mellow, easy, corpulent, and luxurious'. Cellos, bassoons, and bass clarinet are just the instruments to depict mellowness and corpulence. Elgar himself recorded the work with the London Symphony Orchestra in the winter of 1931, but even allowing for the age of the composer's interpretation, and therefore the lack of a full rich sound, it seems like only about twelve stone. With the advantages of stereo and modern recording for the London Philharmonic Orchestra of today, conducted by Daniel Barenboim, it is not only the technical resources that produce a fatter sound but the conductor's weightier accents and tempo. This Falstaff tips the scale at nearer to eighteen stone, I would guess. Barenboim's interpretation is altogether more extreme in many ways than the composer's, and the five other conductors who have recorded the work come somewhere in between. As far as tempo goes, Elgar is the fastest, taking just over thirty-two-and-three-quarter minutes whereas Barenboim takes thirty-five-and-a-half. Between them come Andrew Davis, the next fastest to Elgar, followed by Anthony Collins, then Sir John Barbirolli and Sir Adrian Boult. The latest recording, is by Vernon Handley with the London Philharmonic Orchestra on the Classics for Pleasure label. He and Barenboim are both over a minute slower than Boult, Handley taking thirty-six minutes. This merely shows once again that there is always a good deal of interpretative licence in Elgar's scores, notwithstanding their extremely detailed instructions and metronome marks.

Falstaff was for a long time the least known of Elgar's major orchestral works, and it is still probably the least often performed. There are good reasons for this. For one thing it needs thorough and plentiful rehearsal (you cannot just run through this score and hope it will be all right on the night), and for another the audience has to do its homework. Like Strauss's *Don Quixote*, this is a very detailed symphonic poem, with each of the episodes Elgar selected from Falstaff's life translated into programme-music with extraordinary vividness and virtuosity. But, music being the equivocal art it is, the work exists on several other planes too. It is subtitled 'symphonic study' and its four sections or movements can be heard as the equivalent of a four-movement symphony, particularly as the themes are developed symphonically and the thematic cross-references and contrapuntal combinations are of the most masterly order, yielding new discoveries each time one hears the work. Then again, the programmatic element, though it cannot be denied, can also be regarded as an alibi by the composer so that he can produce a very concentrated and elaborate symphonic design, and also compose yet another piece of autobiography. There is as much of Elgar's personality in this work as of Falstaff's; his humour, his boisterousness, his love of military ceremonial, and his moody melancholy and self-torture, are all here. So any conductor who tackles this work has to understand it and to love it. It is not the sort of piece you record unless you really want to. Each of these recordings is distinguished in its own way and presents a fascinatingly different view of a fascinating and difficult piece. Ideally one would want to possess at least four of them, and there is not one I would not recommend in some way or another.

It is time now to meet the other leading character in the work, Prince Hal. His theme, Elgar said, shows him in his most courtly and genial mood. I have never thought it one of Elgar's best courtly themes and a composer once ingeniously suggested to me that that is precisely why it is such a great theme in its context, because its instability shows that eventually Hal is going to do the dirty on his disreputable companion – 'put not your trust in princes'. Anyway, Sir John Barbirolli and the Hallé, in their magnificent 1964 recording for His Master's Voice, now on Concert Classics, present him at face value as a courtly and genial Prince. The youngest of our Elgarian conductors, Andrew Davis, recorded *Falstaff* with the New Philharmonia Orchestra for Lyrita in 1975, and he emulates Elgar's own very animated approach in the first scene, where Falstaff and Prince Hal are shown testing their wits on each other. The score and the playing on this record brilliantly suggest the sparkle of the young prince and the boastfulness of the old knight.

Elgar himself said, two years before he died, that *Falstaff* was his greatest work and there is a large body of Elgarian opinion that agrees with him. I am not so sure. But then, when I first got to know it nearly forty years ago, real Elgarians were rather thinner on the ground than they are today, when they crop up in the unlikeliest places. *Falstaff* in those days (rather, I used to suspect, from snobbish reasons because of its literary basis and the scholarship of Elgar's famous analysis), tended to be used as a stick with which to beat the two symphonies, which were widely regarded as self-indulgent, undisciplined, rhapsodic, and all the rest of that claptrap. However, Elgar's estimate is not to be taken lightly but I wonder if he was thinking of it as his greatest work in the matter of scoring, because there I agree with him. Though I sometimes think his invention falters in *Falstaff*, the genius of his orchestration burns at its brightest and most intense and the whole work is a miracle of apt instrumentation: a little solo for the timpani, a trill on the cellos, grace-notes for woodwind – it is all most carefully etched. The second section is the most programmatically detailed and often, I think, the weakest in inspiration. So it presents the biggest challenge to interpreters. It contains the incident at Gadshill where Falstaff and his companions rob a coach at night and their booty is then stolen by the Prince and Poins in disguise, the idea being that the Prince wants to hear how Falstaff will wriggle out of it when he boasts about the episode next time they meet in the Boar's Head. The struggle for the stolen booty is described by fugal means and this section is conducted with a wonderful lightness of touch by the late Anthony Collins, a fine conductor not often mentioned these days, whose performance of *Falstaff* was recorded in 1954 and is now on Decca's Eclipse label. The recording is not as vivid as most of the others, but this is an interpretation, with the London Symphony Orchestra, which no student of Elgar should pass over. In this same section Sir Adrian Boult in his 1973 recording with the London Philharmonic Orchestra is much more heavy-handed, and though many will admire the symphonic breadth Sir Adrian gives to this score, on the whole I find it not one of his best Elgar interpretations, though it is coupled with the rare and beautiful *Sanguine Fan* ballet music.

Animation, as I said earlier, is a characteristic of *Falstaff* and Elgar's own generally fast tempos are probably a reflection of his determination that this quality should predominate, as it does in his 1931 recording where the customers of the Boar's Head are laughing at Falstaff's account of what went on at Gadshill. Barbirolli reaches this point with rather too much of a contrived gear-change at the *allargando*. It is marked *poco allargando*. Elgar hardly makes any change, whereas Barbirolli accentuates it. Even so his is a performance which might well have been my final choice were it not for an uncharacteristic lack of sensitivity in one of the most poetic and memorable parts of the score. *Falstaff* contains two interludes, both of which are the very essence of Elgar, especially the first one. Falstaff, after drinking too much, falls asleep, in a wonderfully orchestrated and imaginative passage, and Elgar seizes the chance to show us the old man's memories of his innocent youth when he was page to the Duke of Norfolk. It is one of Elgar's most poetic inspirations, for not only do we hear – in fact, we almost see – the fat knight drunk and snoring, but we hear, as if we can penetrate his fuddled mind, the conversation still going on round him and gradually the sweeter atmosphere of his dream creeps in. Barenboim and the London Philharmonic Orchestra are simply magical here, the muted horns and strings beautifully controlled, with a splendidly drunken bassoon solo and a fruity belch on bass clarinet.

The first interlude is of course not only Falstaff's nostalgic dream of youth, but Elgar's. This is the fifty-five-year-old composer, living in Hampstead, thinking of his boyhood days by the Severn. It is wistful and touching, and requires on the part of the conductor and the solo violinist a complete realization of the subtle *rubato* and little hesitations which mean so much in Elgar's music. In the composer's own recording the soloist was his great friend W. H. Reed, so there we have an historic memory. The playing is past its best, perhaps, and in the style of a bygone age, but the feeling is there. Curiously, Barbirolli and his Hallé soloist are much more prosaic in that passage and there is too little of that 'smiling with a sigh' quality which these intimate Elgar moments thrive on. The *tenuto* markings and the slight but crucial *ritardandos* provide the clue to what is needed, and Barbirolli somehow misses the heartbeat of Elgar. On Anthony Collins's record with the London Symphony Orchestra his violinist, at the climax of this interlude, lets us hear between the notes, as it were, the essence of their lovely performance. Also, the string playing by the orchestra has that fresh-air quality which is so necessary to Elgar's music.

The Scherzo which follows is the episode of Falstaff's part in putting down a rebellion against the king and his recruitment of what we should now call a 'Dad's Army' of recruits like Wart, Mouldy, and Feeble. Their military prowess was obviously enthusiastic rather than efficient.

This is a delightful piece of scoring by Elgar, for it is comic but also affectionate. Sir Adrian Boult takes a rather serious view of the matter and you may think, as I do, that he is a bit too straitlaced and prefer Barenboim and the London Philharmonic Orchestra. Their tempo is much the same as Boult's, even a bit slower at first, but the playing has more character and humour, bringing Falstaff's yokel-recruits to vivid life.

The finale begins with the accession of Henry V. We hear his procession to his coronation at the Abbey, his brutal banishment of Falstaff, and the old knight's death. This is the most brilliant and the most moving part of the work, and Elgar rises to his theme with some of his greatest music: it is the climax of Vernon Handley's superb interpretation. The LPO play for him with tremendous vitality and colour, and the church acoustic lends a resonance which suits the music. Particularly beautiful is the effect of the sudden *sostenuto* in cellos and basses just before sentence of banishment is pronounced: it is in the score, but not everyone observes it as accurately as Handley does. His performance is altogether big, expansive, and detailed.

Reluctantly I have to say that the Anthony Collins recording is variable in the quality of its sound, and Elgar's own, though amazing for its date, is obviously nearly fifty years old. Also, I do find that Elgar's fast tempos, though exhilarating, mean that some of the lovely detail cannot be relished as it should be, but, of course, as an historical record it is in a class of its own. For all the virtues combined, clarity and brilliance of orchestral playing with recording to match and an interpretation which seems to me to be filled with the spirit both of Shakespeare and of Elgar, and to give the fullest rein to the music's picturesque and imaginative detail while having a symphonic breadth and cohesion, then my choice is Daniel Barenboim and the London Philharmonic. Both he and Vernon Handley spread the work on to a second side and fill up with the *Cockaigne* overture. In the last pages of the work, the beautiful string playing is tenderly phrased, with every grace note delicately touched in, followed by remarkably expressive woodwind playing when Falstaff dies and the shadow of Prince Hal is thrown across the score for the last time. Barenboim, still a young man, shows astonishing insight into the elderly composer's elegiac musing in a performance that I feel sure will stand the test of time.

Note
Since completing this review, another coupling of *Falstaff* with the 'Enigma' Variations has come at full price from RCA Red Seal. The orchestra is the Scottish National, conducted by Sir Alexander Gibson. Until the first interlude of *Falstaff* is reached, this is a stolid, unimaginative performance, with the Gads Hill episode anything but exciting. After the Dream Interlude, however, Gibson becomes more poetic and also pays attention to some nice points of phrasing, notably in the cello solo in the coda. The recording is rather backward and favours woodwind and brass at the expense of strings but is spacious enough. This is a recommendable issue, but does not alter my final selection.

Recordings discussed

Elgar/London Symphony Orchestra	World Records SH 162
Collins/London Symphony Orchestra	Decca ECS 625
Barbirolli/Hallé Orchestra	HMV SXLP 30279
Boult/London Philharmonic Orchestra	HMV ASD 2970
A. Davis/New Philharmonia Orchestra	Lyrita SRCS 77
*Barenboim/London Philharmonic Orchestra	CBS Classics 61883
Handley/London Philharmonic Orchestra	CFP 40313
Gibson/Scottish National Orchestra	RCA RL 25206

©Michael Kennedy

Haydn *Symphony No. 101, 'The Clock'*

STEPHEN DODGSON

Now that prices are constantly rising it is perhaps a comfort to know that only three of the currently available records of the 'Clock' Symphony come into the top price category. And of those three, I suggest that only one – by the Academy of St Martin-in-the-Fields – need really concern the library builder. As a result, most of my survey concentrates on versions in what I suppose must now be regarded as the middling price range. There are several outstanding possibilities here, varied in style and all decently recorded. The question of whether or not you care for Sir Thomas Beecham's approach in Haydn should be faced at once, I think, since in terms of communicating the joyous spirit of this symphony, and the exuberance of its bounding rhythms, Beecham is indeed hard to beat.

The 'Clock' is one of the very few classical symphonies whose first movement is not a common-time *allegro* – but a *presto* in 6/8, virtually a tarantella; the sort of thing normally associated with Finales. Beecham's *presto* is, as you would expect, not so fast that he cannot relish the leaping motion of the music to the full. Haydn's 'Salomon' Symphonies were one of Beecham's last recording ventures, and there is nothing whatever faded or jaded about the sound of the orchestral tutti as it emerges in HMV's Concert Classics re-issue. The Royal Philharmonic strings play at full symphonic strength, yet the balance is very good at all dynamic levels, and twenty years later HMV apparently finds it hard to equal this quality. I judge by the fairly recent issue of Karajan and the Berlin Philharmonic where the tutti sound is very poorly defined. A 'Clock' Symphony without clear, bright colours is to me an oddity, but then I shall never understand Karajan's racing-car notion of Haydn's first movement, with its sleek phrasing. Karajan's style here actually creates an obstacle to believing in the Berlin Philharmonic as the great orchestra we know it to be; but the difficulty vanishes the moment you turn to Karl Richter conducting the same orchestra in the same symphony. Favouring an almost military swagger to the rhythms, Richter's *presto* is particularly steady, and the recording emphatically allows you to hear Haydn's trumpets and timpani in the bold way I am sure he meant. This version, made some fifteen years ago, is now on DG's mid-priced Privilege label. In its brightness of colour and firmness of rhythm, it has all the appeal I miss in Karajan's conducting of the same symphony with the same orchestra.

Furthermore, so long as DG has Richter's 'Clock' in the catalogue, I am unable to see their much newer full-priced version by the London Philharmonic Orchestra under Eugen Jochum making much headway. For one thing, the recording is much less good; and then Jochum seems rather bland in character. It is no bad thing to keep the 'Clock' movement itself moving along quite briskly, but the tune should surely have a little more sprightly pointing than Jochum brings to it. The London Philharmonic play nicely for him, especially the strings I think, but generally the performance disappoints in character, and the recording is rather poorly balanced in tutti. The London Philharmonic has also recorded the 'Clock' for Classics for Pleasure, under the Italian conductor, Gaetano Delogu – one of the cheapest versions available. This recording is definitely rather better, I think, but the performance is again somewhat lacking in character; and that is something you certainly could never say of the version conducted by Toscanini – which is still cheaper.

But perhaps the best comparison at this point would be with the Decca version played by the Philharmonia Hungarica conducted by Antal Dorati. For one thing, Dorati's notion of how the 'Clock' should tick is very similar to Jochum's, but how much more telling the shape he gives the music. The bold, minor-key tutti, too, has exceptionally good rhythm and clarity. This version is taken from Dorati's acclaimed series of all the Haydn symphonies, one of the grandest recording projects of modern times. No other performance reveals such close critical attention to Haydn's score as it is, and there is an impressive dignity and dedication about the Philharmonia Hungarica's response – always thoughtful, never spectacular.

Decca offers Dorati's 'Clock' in two couplings; with the 'Surprise' Symphony in the World of the Great Classics series; or with No. 102 in B flat, a choice which will cost you rather more, on Ace of Diamonds. This identical coupling is also found with Beecham, but musically they could hardly be less alike. In the slow movement especially, Beecham's very broad tempo makes a tremendous contrast. Nobody, I think, could possibly call his tempo *andante* (Haydn's markings). As always, Beecham shows himself to be a law unto himself and a bit high-handed, and this movement is played somewhat in the spirit of nineteenth-century ballet music. A little eccentric in taste as in tempo, yet it has his own infectious brand of life-giving vitality, and is beautifully played. It is the existence of Beecham's record, and of Dorati's – so different, yet both so good – that made me mention earlier that there was really only one full-priced version worthy of attention, Neville Marriner's with the Academy of St Martin-in-the-Fields. He takes the 'Clock' movement, as he does every movement in the symphony, at what you might call a central, indisputable sort of tempo. Everything is full of musical logic and lucidity, and the excellent playing shines out from what is probably the best of all the recordings in the technical sense. Yet, in terms of sheer character, I wonder if it is not surpassed by Karl Richter, whose virtually identical choice of tempo is animated by a brisk, almost military, rhythm. But Richter does have one substantial eccentricity; he is allergic to repeats. He omits the exposition repeat from the first movement – which one or two other conductors do. He also omits the longer of the two repeats from the 'Clock' movement, as does Beecham, but at his slow tempo he could hardly do otherwise. However in the Minuet, Richter cuts out the second half repeats from both Minuet and Trio. So by choosing his record, you get a performance which reaches the end almost five minutes before anyone else. For some tastes, too, I fancy Richter's ideas of rhythmic attack may seem a bit fierce, exhilarating though they are.

Out of the four low-priced versions there are two I have not yet mentioned; one on Helidor conducted by Rolf Kleinert, the other on Telefunken conducted by Joseph Keilberth and both, I think, are best forgotten. The recorded sound is foggy and confused, and the performances are nothing very special. The Decca Eclipse of Monteux and the Vienna Philharmonic Orchestra provides a superior picture of a vastly superior performance. But no match, any of them, for the cheapest record of the symphony of all: Arturo Toscanini conducting the NBC Orchestra; a roughish sound, but clear and bright. Predictably perhaps, Toscanini takes the *allegretto* Minuet rather fast, but significantly he has a steady hand in both first and last movements. Like Beecham, he employs a full string strength, and like Beecham too, he communicates a splendid refreshing vitality. That said, the difference in musical character could hardly be more striking. I do not think Toscanini's is the record to choose as sole representative of Haydn's 'Clock' in your library – the recording is a bit too gruff and primitive, and a trifle more relaxation in the Minuet does illuminate its charm rather more. Charm is, after all, one important factor here, and Neville Marriner, whilst quite without the assertion of a Toscanini, does have a keen nose for the music's charm. His coupling is the 'Farewell' Symphony, in the Academy's series of Haydn's 'named' symphonies for Philips. It is an excellent, musicianly performance, and never for one moment dull. And as a recording, it is certainly the only full-priced disc worth its cost. In fact, its admirable balance and instrumental colour is a strong recommendation. Everything it does is so good, that it is only as I start to think of the things it does *not* do that a little disappointment begins to creep up on me. Marriner does not touch me with the same sense of devotion to Haydn which is such a winning attribute of the Philharmonia Hungarica version under Dorati. Here, the thought underlying the music becomes steadily more apparent with repeated hearing. The beginning of the finale, for instance, where the strings present the musical material all alone, in two short repeating sections, all quiet. Then, suddenly the tutti arrives with every instrument placed for maximum brilliance. But the tempo mark is only *vivace*, compared with the first movement *presto*. Dorati resists searching for excitement in the string music, knowing that a carefully held speed actually gives a more robust brilliance to the tutti when you reach it. Decca's recording is rather more distant than all the others, but very clean in texture, and always appealing in instrumental colour whether loud or soft.

But Beecham's record of the 'Clock' is hardly less appealingly recorded and, as I must repeat, puts several of the newer ones to shame in this respect. It is generally a fuller, bolder sound: tutti and solo passages less decisively separated. This is partly Beecham's own doing of course. With his cunningly placed extra accents, for instance, the opening string music no longer gives the impression of an unbroken *piano*. Nor when he comes to the fugato later in the movement, and again allocated to the strings alone. In the 'Clock' Symphony, it seems to me, Beecham's special effects are always strictly related to conveying the joyous spirit of the music, and the last tutti of all is typical of him. If you call it irresistible, I should not blame you.

Recordings discussed

Toscanini/NBC Symphony Orchestra	RCA AT 120
*Beecham/Royal Philharmonic Orchestra	HMV SXLP 30265
Monteux/Vienna Philharmonic Orchestra	Decca ECS 574
Richter/Berlin Philharmonic Orchestra	Deutsche Grammophon 2535 289
Delogu/London Philharmonic Orchestra	CFP 40222
Jochum/London Philharmonic Orchestra	Deutsche Grammophon 2530 628
Karajan/Berlin Philharmonic Orchestra	HMV ASD 2817
Dorati/Philharmonia Hungarica	Decca SDD 504 (coupled with Haydn Symphony No. 102)
	Decca SPA 494 (coupled with Haydn Symphony No. 94)
Marriner/Academy of St Martin-in-the-Fields	Philips 9500 520

© Stephen Dodgson

Holst   *The Planets*

EDWARD GREENFIELD

Judging by the number of versions on record, getting on for twenty, Holst's suite *The Planets* easily outstrips all other works by British composers when it comes to international popularity. Admirers of Holst understandably tend to resent the discrepancy of appreciation between this brilliant and colourful suite of seven movements and everything else which the composer wrote. Its very approachability sometimes seems to be against it, but the moment you start looking at the score again, the consistent liveness of the inspiration, the sharpness of characterization between the movements, the memorability of each, explains everything. Holst may have cribbed some Debussy here and some Rimsky-Korsakov or early Stravinsky there, but it remains a masterpiece, an enormous achievement, particularly when one remembers the odds against its being a success, written as it was just before and during the First World War, when already orchestral economy was in the air.

It is the bigness, not just of the orchestration but of the musical gestures, always confident, which has attracted virtually all the most brilliant virtuoso conductors of the day to record it. Herbert von Karajan is threatening to record it for a second time. His first attempt – for Decca with the Vienna Philharmonic in 1962 – is still available on the mid-price Jubilee label, a marvellous example of Karajan's fine control.

Coming to the score fresh, his reading does not always sound idiomatic, as at the start of *Jupiter*, where he rushes on to the horn theme of the second section breathlessly without a pause, but what he does is riveting and the performance is a very fair recommendation at mid-price. But much as I admire the playing, any devotee of British music will know that the performance is not always quite idiomatic. Karajan is just a little too literal, and even with a British conductor there is sometimes the same problem when it is a non-British orchestra. I am not going back to the bad old attitude of refusing to see good in non-British performances of British music, but the performance by the Amsterdam Concertgebouw Orchestra under Neville Marriner on a fairly recent Philips version illustrates what I mean. This again, to my ear, is not always idiomatic though there is some fine precise playing, richly recorded on full-price Philips. What I mean by a performance being idiomatic is illustrated in the ninetieth birthday offering of Sir Adrian

Boult, who for HMV with the London Philharmonic Orchestra in super-lative sound, even finer than the Philips, recorded *The Planets* for the fourth time. It was Boult who in 1918 conducted the first ever performance, and as the composer wrote in his presentation score it was he who 'first caused *The Planets* to shine in public'. There is nothing stiff or evenly stressed about this performance with its hint of jazzing on the syncopations and its tremendous swagger. Two earlier versions by Sir Adrian are still available. A mono one, also with the London Philharmonic Orchestra, comes on two different labels, well worth hearing but not really a recommendation when this of all works needs brilliant recording. The twelve-year-old version which Sir Adrian recorded, also for HMV, with the New Philharmonia, is not quite so well played as the new one, though there are one or two points which I actually prefer on it, including the riper, more spacious view of the great melody of *Jupiter*.

That theme, the most obviously memorable sequence in the whole work, inspires some very different views. Eugene Ormandy, for example, with the Philadelphia Orchestra, treats it with an opulence very much in keeping with the Philadelphia string tradition. It is very impressive, but a little too sticky, not quite as noble as it might be. Boult has increasingly felt that the big tune from *Jupiter* should be treated flowingly three in a bar rather than run the risk of seeming square and heavy, and that is very much the view too of André Previn and the London Symphony Orchestra whose five-year-old version, also on full-price HMV, still sounds as rich as any, even Sir Adrian's latest. Previn is fine too, as you would expect, with the pointing of syncopations. But the account of this melody which to my mind excels all others is from a conductor you might not expect, Bernard Haitink, who with the London Philharmonic recorded the work for Philips in 1971. Again the recording is both superbly fresh and atmospheric, clearer on detail than the later Philips version with Marriner and the Concertgebouw. Haitink's version has come up very formidably in my affections as a result of my latest and intensive bout of comparisons. One obvious problem when trying to make a first recommendation on this work is that with seven contrasted movements as well as so many versions, the permutations are endless. If the great melody from *Jupiter* is a prime consideration with you, for example, then Haitink and the LPO make a splendid choice. For some there may be a snag in Haitink's account of the first movement, *Mars*. He takes it unusually slowly, but where others who adopt that view usually lose tension, Haitink sustains it marvellously, and makes the movement seem all the more ominous for not being at all hectic.

In a more recent version with that same orchestra, Haitink's successor as principal conductor, Sir George Solti, directs a performance of that move-ment at the opposite extreme, so fast and intense that even the London Philharmonic's brass find it hard to keep up. In *Mars*, at least, I find Solti's performance too fast and tense in the wrong way, and though there is much to admire in a bitingly brilliant account of the whole score, it would not for me be a first choice. Though Previn's tempo is very nearly as fast as Solti's, there is much more breathing space. The music has point and swagger, the brass is richer, not least the horns, and the six-year-old HMV recording is even richer than the newer Decca. Previn's way with syncopations matches that of Sir Adrian with the sort of freedom that sounds idiomatic.

In the scherzo movement, *Mercury*, Sir Adrian's new version with the London Philharmonic Orchestra has delectable point, the texture light and glowing. By comparison Zubin Mehta, who, with the Los Angeles Philharmonic Orchestra directs a very brilliant account of *The Planets* on full-price Decca, very immediately recorded, in *Mercury* lacks the point and lightness of that Boult version. I have to emphasize that though in this comparison I am passing Mehta's version over as a first choice, it still has much in its favour. In fact there are very few of these versions which I would actively dismiss. In various respects Holst's score never seems to fail to challenge any orchestra, and it is interesting that six of these eighteen versions have non-British orchestras, and six have the London Philharmonic Orchestra, with Boult twice over.

On the sleeve of Boult's ninetieth birthday version, Holst's daughter, Imogen, describes *Saturn*, the bringer of old age, as the composer's own favourite movement, and for many I know it is the key movement on which any performance has above all to be judged. It is apt that Boult at ninety should be more cunning than anyone in the mysterious balancing of sounds at the very start with the flute given more prominence than usual in the ominous ostinato.

At such a point Herbert von Karajan and the Vienna Philharmonic for example give a wonderfully measured and sustained performance, though they do not outshine Sir Adrian Boult in his latest version for HMV. Nor perhaps does André Previn with the London Symphony Orchestra, though his concept of *Saturn* is quite different, not so mysterious or atmospheric but very clear in every strand, and when it comes to the shattering climax of the movement, old age taking its toll, Previn is the most powerful of all, helped by magnificent recording. Where the HMV engineers for the latest Boult version divide the seven movements three and four, making the grooves closer together on the second side, they have done it four and three for Previn, so that with wider spacing in *Saturn*, the fifth movement of the suite on side 2, the dynamic range is even greater and the climax even more shattering, though Haitink and the London Philharmonic Orchestra on Philips have just as keen a bite with superb inner detail. One of the surprising things when you look at the long list of versions of *The Planets* is how relatively few there are at less than full price and the majority of those very old. But in my latest comparisons I have been much impressed with a bargain version on the Classics for Pleasure label, and only five years old, which until now I am afraid I have usually dismissed, from James Loughran and the Hallé Orchestra.

Loughran like Haitink takes a relatively measured view of *Mars,* and

Mercury is not quite as delicate as it might be, but, helped by clear and vivid recording, this is a performance with a most attractive bite to it. I have already mentioned that with such a work as this, it is false economy to go for a bargain version with old mono recording even if the conductors are as masterly as Sir Adrian Boult, or for that matter Sir Malcolm Sargent, who always excelled himself in this music, and despite some shortcomings, I would say that Loughran and the Hallé Orchestra on CFP make by far the best current bargain choice. The bite of the climax in *Saturn* is most impressive with Loughran, for example, and the fantastic sixth movement, *Uranus*, is sharp, spiky, and beautifully sprung.

Sir Georg Solti's full-price Decca version with the London Philharmonic Orchestra, also on the fast side, is not nearly so well-sprung in *Uranus*. The whole performance is brilliant but not one I would make a first choice.

Sorting things out, I would certainly place much higher two other versions from the six recorded by the London Philharmonic, those of Sir Adrian Boult on HMV and of Bernard Haitink on Philips. Quite simply, as the original interpreter, Boult is indispensable, and his latest version is his richest and most illuminating, not just because of the glorious recording quality, though being a Boult devotee I do hope that one day his 78 rpm version with the BBC Symphony Orchestra, made at the end of the Second World War, will one day be dubbed on to LP. It is a masterly rendering. Three-and-a-half decades later Boult is more relaxed, and that does not always mean tempos are slower. I have mentioned the great melody of *Jupiter*, and Boult is on the fast side for the final mysterious movement, too, *Neptune*. In that at least, as in *Jupiter*, I prefer Haitink. His performance is beautifully cool and poised. Anyone wanting a version which takes a fresh new view, not traditional, cannot do better than this full-price Philips issue, ten years old now but with finely focused recording. For a comparably refreshing view one might also suggest Karajan and the Vienna Philharmonic on Decca Jubilee, the only mid-price version currently available, but such points as the firebell clang of the chimes at the climax of *Saturn* are for me distracting in a way which nothing in the Haitink version is.

I have already mentioned Loughran and the Hallé Orchestra as an excellent bargain recommendation, bright and alert, on the CFP label, but my final recommendation must be that of André Previn and the London Symphony Orchestra on full-price HMV, rivalled in sound only by Boult's latest version on the same label and with a reading which in every single one of the seven movements takes a central view, intense and totally idiomatic with excellently chosen tempos. I must emphasize again that Previn, like Sir Adrian himself, has a way with syncopations. There are many fine versions of *The Planets*, as I hope I have made clear, but Previn's is the one I would settle for.

Recordings discussed

Karajan/Vienna Philharmonic Orchestra	Decca JB 30
Boult/New Philharmonia Orchestra	HMV ASD 2301
Boult/London Philharmonic Orchestra	Pye GH 503
Loughran/Hallé Orchestra	CFP 40243
Marriner/Amsterdam Concertgebouw Orchestra	Philips 9500 425
Haitink/London Philharmonic Orchestra	Philips 6833 327
*Previn/London Symphony Orchestra	HMV ASD 3002
Mehta/Los Angeles Philharmonic Orchestra	Decca SXL 6529
Ormandy/Philadelphia Orchestra	RCA RL 11797
Boult/London Philharmonic Orchestra	HMV ASD 3649

© Edward Greenfield

Mahler *Symphony No. 2, 'Resurrection'*

DAVID MURRAY

Mahler's 'Resurrection' Symphony sets out, naturally enough, to be an extraordinary experience, and its unprecedented length and orchestral scale should have ensured that it remained one. It presupposes a kind of festival performance, and an audience ready to be struck with collective awe. With this work there is something more than usually perverse about having it on tap at home. What are you going to *do* with it? Getting acquainted with it at leisure, bit by bit, as one might do with the *Art of Fugue*, would answer to a special analytical interest, but the symphony is intended as a cumulative dramatic whole. If, on the other hand, you want to play it once in a blue moon, as a special occasion, why not go to a concert hall instead?

I am not really proposing a boycott of recordings of Mahler's Second, but I am observing that the question 'Which version is best?' is peculiarly awkward here: best for what, exactly? If most of the available performances were simply mediocre, matters would be simplified, but at the moment there are nine two-disc albums on the market, and though they are all different none of them lacks distinction. One from CBS with the New York Philharmonic is conducted by Bruno Walter, who worked closely with Mahler from 1894, the very year in which the symphony was completed. Walter's basic tempo for the huge first movement is slightly but significantly slower than most other conductors'. This movement was first drafted in 1888, long before the others, and was entitled *Totenfeier* ('Funeral Rite') and marked *maestoso* ('with serious and solemn expression throughout'). *Maestoso* was later altered to *Allegro maestoso*. Mahler often changed his markings, not because he felt any uncertainty about how his music should go, but for fear of inviting misinterpretation. Obviously this movement needs enough tension to sustain its length, but the symphonic argument is enough to generate that. More important, it must have sufficient weight to counterbalance the vast, expansively varied Finale: the three intervening movements are much smaller, and the 'Resurrection' must have a well-founded rock of despair to spring from. A more urgent tempo is possible, but then it needs to be very grim. HMV's Klemperer is actually faster than anybody else. In abstract symphonic terms, his impersonal urgency loses nothing. He gives a brilliantly searching reading of this and every other movement, and he draws tautly committed, unsensuous playing from the Philharmonia, with more genuine and exciting *pianissimos* than the New York orchestra gives Walter. (A hostile critic remarked early that there is so much quiet music in the symphony that the extra forces Mahler demanded seem weirdly extravagant.)

Whether defiant vitality in the *Totenfeier* subserves the dramatic ground plan of the whole well enough is another matter. All the other performances strike off at a tempo between Walter's and Klemperer's, except Leonard Bernstein's (his 1973 television performance, not his old New York one). It begins slowest of all, but there is really no basic tempo: with his usual sympathetic intensity, Bernstein reacts violently to every nuance. At one point where Mahler asks for an imperceptible quickening, he takes off like a rocket, and cumulative argument is thus replaced by a series of shocks. This is not a performance to live with (and besides, there are rough patches in the playing); I shall set it aside, along with Kubelik's Deutsche Grammophon recording, which is at the other extreme, warm and musicianly, but exceedingly tame for the import of the work.

Mahler declared that 'the real art of conducting consists in transitions' – that is, in preserving continuity of sense through changes. In Mahler's giant scores, that requires virtuoso conducting. This is to be had from Solti, Claudio Abbado, and Zubin Mehta, each of whom is working with a virtuoso orchestra and benefits from virtuoso recording too (though Solti's Decca album is some fourteen years old). Each is fanatically faithful to Mahler's microscopically detailed markings, and that often throws their temperamental differences into relief. At the recapitulation of the *Totenfeier* Mehta with the Vienna Philharmonic Orchestra on Decca is prepared to melt; and his Vienna players rise by instinct to every *molto espressivo* passage. Mehta makes the coda that follows fully elegiac and resigned; Solti, also on Decca, finds fierce, black pomp in it, but it bristles almost to the dying bars.

Solti's relentless pressure is echoed in Abbado's Deutsche Grammophon performance with the Chicago Symphony Orchestra, though without Solti's continual sharp little jabs. Neither of them is quite happy with the first of the problematic middle movements, the slow *Ländler*. Neither was Mahler, who came to fear it was too lightweight to follow the *Totenfeier*. He asked that it should sound 'old-fashioned, comfortable, and measured' – a look back into the past, from a great distance; there are anxious undercurrents, but no irony. Walter plays it with simple gravity and, like Mehta, makes this Andante a real, if modest, slow movement, though one has to put up with the tape hiss on the recording. We know from Mahler's original metronome marks (eventually suppressed) that he expected its quaver beats to match the crotchet tread of the *Totenfeier*. The other conductors seem to worry that it may outstay its welcome: Klemperer and Solti keep it measured but tense, and Abbado takes it so briskly that its three-in-a-bar becomes one-in-a-bar, too much like the Scherzo which succeeds it. His Andante is at least elegant, if barely *andante*. The imposing breadth of Wyn

Morris's account of the whole symphony is marred by small untidinesses, as for example, in the Trio.

His performance with the Symphonica of London has great virtues, but in the Andante and Scherzo a sharply precise beat is sorely missed. Each of them has a fairly homogeneous musical texture, to be made vivid by nuances rather than by contrasts; and nuances do not survive woolly ensemble. Yet Haitink's Philips version with the Amsterdam Concertgebouw Orchestra, which has excellent ensemble, is hygienically nuance-free! Despite a fine choral blaze at the end, the whole performance is expressively under-committed; not only are key emotional transitions played blandly through, but characteristic Mahlerian details like his 'sentimental' string *glissandos* are politely expunged. It is a performance to convince one that the music is surely over-rated. Haitink has found a much closer rapport with Mahler in the eleven years since this recording.

The famous Scherzo, upon which Berio based his Sinfonia, is full of mischievous invention, and also of irony. Solti despatches it too quickly for either to be felt much. Bruno Walter rollicks irresistibly. Abbado and Mehta, like Klemperer, suggest that its wit has a razor edge. But Mehta and his Vienna trumpet play the sudden, tender vision in the middle to the hilt while Abbado gives this wistful passage only a non-committal nod.

Every version but Mehta's places the *Urlicht* song, the fourth movement, after the side-break. It is true the score directs that the last three movements should be played without pausing (not 'without pause', for both the Scherzo and *Urlicht* end with one); but Mahler himself came to feel that the humbly hopeful song belonged with the other shorter movements, and ought to be separated from the Finale. The effect of the contralto's first phrase entering after the teeming busyness of the Scherzo is far more telling than the gambit of having the orchestra crash in at the end of her 'chorale'; since the limits of side-lengths forbid us to have both, better far the former. Mehta's contralto is the splendid Christa Ludwig, but the other contraltos here are no less well attuned to the performances in which they figure: if only they were not all relegated to side 3!

The Finale should of course be overwhelming. Klemperer's opening is something less than the intended cataclysm, but after that everything is sternly sustained. His soprano, Elisabeth Schwarzkopf, does not rise magically from the chorus as specified, lovely though she sounds: like Walter's and Abbado's sopranos, she just appears suddenly in the foreground. Solti's Heather Harper is somewhere in between. Mehta and Morris, or their engineers, achieve the effect much more successfully.

But for the apparition of the soprano, Solti's musical stage-management is magisterial and immensely exciting. The long passages of nature-sounds, off-stage fanfares, and so forth are directed, and played by the London Symphony Orchestra, with amazing finesse. Walter makes the orchestral turmoils surprisingly powerful; his chorus, though, makes a less fervent noise than the others. In the main symphonic section, the *allegro energico*,

Mehta has to give points to Abbado; he weakens the drive of the music by a slightly nervous, over-hasty beat. Abbado keeps closer control of the passage, and finds more purposeful strength in it. With both Mehta and Abbado the choral perorations are solid and stirring, if not quite such as to raise the dead.

To sum up, guardedly, the Klemperer and Walter recordings, both old and modestly priced, are irreplaceable: the one for its penetration into the very bones of the score, and the other for its sturdy and loving recreation of the lyrical, human side of the symphony. But it is a masterpiece of orchestral composition too, and it deserves a sumptuous modern sound. Most of Solti's performance exercises a colossal grip, even to a fault; Abbado's often sounds the same implacable note, but it relaxes for welcome breaths too. If I prefer Mehta's to either of those, it is not only because of the details I have mentioned, but also because it displays the most generous range of responses, and very beautifully. Solti and Abbado, like Klemperer, extract from their orchestras exactly what they want; Mehta is plainly collaborating with the Vienna musicians, drawing upon their own tradition of Mahler playing. In a work of collective celebration, that is a great virtue.

A last word about the Wyn Morris performance. Its technical imperfections are obvious, and certainly they blunt some of the bite of the symphony. The real depth of Morris's reading opens up, with unhurried conviction, in the sustained development of the Finale, a musical vista which Morris holds in a magnificently long perspective. There is a breath of Furtwängler in this, even if the whole performance is only incompletely realized: I can imagine that some might treasure the recording for that.

Recordings discussed

Cundari/Forrester/New York Philharmonic Orchestra and Chorus/Walter	CBS 61282-3
Schwarzkopf/Rössl-Majdan/Philharmonic Orchestra and Chorus/Klemperer	HMV ASD 2691
Harper/Watts/London Symphony Orchestra and Choir/Solti	Decca SET 325-6
Ameling/Heynis/Netherlands Radio Chorus/ Concertgebouw Orchestra/Haitink	Philips 6700 024
Mathis/Procter/Bavarian Radio Orchestra and Chorus/Kubelik	Deutsche Grammophon 2726 062
Armstrong/Baker/London Symphony Orchestra and Choir/Bernstein	CBS 78249
*Cotrubas/Ludwig/Vienna State Opera Chorus/ Vienna Philharmonic Orchestra/Mehta	Decca SXL 6744-5
Neblett/Horne/Chicago Symphony Orchestra and Chorus/Abbado	Deutsche Grammophon 2530 775
Ander/Hodgson/Ambrosian Singers/ Symphonica of London/Morris	SYM 7-8

© David Murray

Prokofiev   *Symphony No. 5*

GEOFFREY NORRIS

When Prokofiev got down to work on his Fifth Symphony, fourteen years or so had elapsed since he had last embarked on a symphony, and it was considerably longer since he had actually written one from scratch, as it were. For both the Third and Fourth Symphonies are based on material from earlier works – the Third Symphony on the opera *The Fiery Angel*, the fourth on the ballet *The Prodigal Son*. It was Prokofiev's frequent habit to re-use material in this way, and it was also common for him to jot themes in a note book, sometimes over a great many years, and then to mould a work round them. The Third Piano Concerto is just one example of that; and the Fifth Symphony is another, some of the themes having been conceived during the 1930s: as Prokofiev himself has said, 'the music had matured within me'. He wrote the symphony in the summer of 1944, while staying in a country house run by the Soviet Composers' Union to the west of Moscow. It is, therefore, a 'war' symphony, Russia having entered the Second World War in 1941. But how very different the often serene, sometimes light-hearted mood of this symphony is compared, for example, with the sombre and bitter Seventh Symphony of Shostakovich, or even the 'war' symphonies of Myaskovsky. The reason lies in the date. When Shostakovich wrote his Seventh Symphony in 1941 Russia was in the thick of war; the outlook was grim. By the time Prokofiev wrote the Fifth Symphony, not only had Russia become more attuned to the horrors of this war, but also victory was clearly in sight. When Prokofiev conducted the first performance of the symphony in Moscow on 13 January 1945, the Russians were already driving the German armies back through the Ukraine, and were shortly to break through the two-and-a-half-year siege of Leningrad. It was a crucial time in Russian history; and it was a crucial time personally for Prokofiev as well: he regarded the Fifth Symphony as the 'culminating point' of his creative life, and shortly after conducting it he had a heart attack, fell down a flight of stairs, and was badly concussed. He never fully recovered.

The first movement of the symphony is a spacious *andante*; and there are some pretty wide divergencies of interpretation of that *andante* amongst the six conductors of the seven available performances: Ansermet, Karajan, Maazel, Martinon (twice), Rozhdestvensky, and Weller. In fact there is well over three minutes' difference in length between the fastest conductor in this movement (Ansermet) and the slowest (Maazel), which in a movement lasting on average only about thirteen minutes is quite a lot. For me, the music seems to unfold much more naturally at a tempo slightly on the slow side; and Weller, conducting the London Symphony Orchestra, paces the movement ideally. Within the general framework of *andante* there is a gentle flexibility, a slight urging on here, a little pulling back there. This approach seems to me to enhance the lyricism of the opening elegiac theme, so typical of the Prokofiev of this period, and adds to the grandeur of the later powerfully expressive music that so clearly reflects Prokofiev's aims to write a symphony about the 'greatness of the human spirit', a 'hymn to free and happy man'. Indeed, there is one passage in this movement (the climax to it in fact) where it seems to me the effect is lost if it is taken too fast. The almost lilting triple time adopted by Ansermet with the Suisse Romande Orchestra seems at odds with such dark music; Maazel, for example, with the Cleveland Orchestra, is much more menacing.

From the heroic heights of the first movement the mood changes abruptly for the second, a scherzo in Prokofiev's cheekiest vein, with an almost ragtime quality about it. There is little to choose between the performances here, save that Martinon, with the Paris Conservatoire Orchestra, is about the quickest. His performance, though, is curiously foursquare. Rozhdestvensky manages to instil much more life into the music. He takes it fractionally slower than Martinon, but he emphasizes much more strongly the irregular accents, makes the side-drum more prominent, and so on, investing the movement with a light, breezy, carefree tone. In the first of the two *meno mosso* sections in this movement, brief interludes of repose in this otherwise inexorable music, it is Maazel who coaxes just the right languorous atmosphere from the Cleveland Orchestra, notably in the wilting cello phrases. After the second of these short sections, there is a gradual *accelerando* to the rumbustious end of the movement; and Weller, even if the slow section is not done quite as meltingly as Maazel, gauges the progress of this *accelerando* to perfection.

As in the first movement, there are substantial differences of approach to the slow third movement. All the conductors opt for a tempo slightly slower than the marked crotchet = 60, but nobody takes it quite so slowly as Weller, whose crotchet beat is something in the region of 40. And he has a point. This is the most tragic of all four movements, and the slow tempo certainly enhances the tragic aura. Maazel opts for a slightly more forward-moving, less contemplative tempo, though it is nonetheless heartfelt. He is helped by sumptuous playing from the Cleveland Orchestra, though my own preference in this movement is for the heavy, grief-laden tread of Weller's interpretation.

By the time we reach the Finale, it is possible to do a little weeding out. The Ansermet recording with the Suisse Romande must be the first to go: to my mind the performance is too hurried throughout, though there are some gorgeous things in the slow movement. Martinon's performance with the Paris Conservatoire Orchestra is now twenty years old, and I am afraid it is showing its age by its very boxed-in acoustic and the thin, wiry orchestral sound. Although his performance is nowhere near as fast as Ansermet's, Martinon does have a tendency to rush, sometimes with near-catastrophic results. In the Finale, for example, he launches the main *allegro giocoso* with a much too optimistic speed, all very well while the slowish tune is on the clarinet, but not so good when the violins have to break into semiquavers: Martinon, quite noticeably, has to slow down. His later recording with the ORTF Orchestra is more controlled in tempo but the orchestral unanimity is not always what it might be; and in that respect there are certainly much more satisfactory records to choose from. Four, in fact: Karajan, Maazel, Rozhdestvensky, and Weller, and quite honestly there is very little to choose between any of them. The disadvantage of the Rozhdestvensky disc is that it is in a box of six records, containing all seven symphonies plus the suite from the ballet *Pas d'acier*, the Russian Overture, and a few other odds and ends. But this performance has a great deal to offer. As I have said, Rozhdestvensky's is the swingiest Scherzo; in the Finale, too, the music has lightness and bounce, though some may find the divided cello passage near the beginning too richly done for the *tranquillo* marking. This is a passage that Karajan and the Berlin Philharmonic do beautifully. Their record has a fairly spacious acoustic, and some may prefer here the rather sharper recorded sound of the Weller and Maazel performances, both on Decca.

With these two, the choice is well nigh impossible. If you have one or other of them I would be inclined to stay with it. But the Weller performance was new to me, and particularly in the slow movement said something – albeit an indefinable something – that I had not heard before. The London Symphony Orchestra is on fine form here; there is some exquisite playing in the more lyrical passages, and playing of the utmost clarity in the complex faster music.

Recordings discussed

Martinon/Paris Conservatoire Orchestra	Decca ECS 593
Ansermet/Suisse Romande Orchestra	Decca SDD 399
Karajan/Berlin Philharmonic Orchestra	Deutsche Grammophon 139040
Rozhdestvensky/Moscow Radio Orchestra	HMV SLS 844 (6-record set)
Martinon/Paris ORTF	Turnabout TV 37053S
*Weller/London Symphony Orchestra	Decca SXL 6787
Maazel/Cleveland Orchestra	Decca SXL 6875

© Geoffrey Norris

Stravinsky   *The Rite of Spring*

NOËL GOODWIN

'The idea of *Le Sacre du printemps* came to me while I was still composing *The Firebird*. I had dreamed a scene of pagan ritual, in which a chosen sacrificial virgin dances herself to death. This vision was not accompanied by concrete musical ideas, however, and I was soon impregnated with another and purely musical conception that began quickly to develop into, as I thought, a Konzertstück for piano and orchestra. This latter piece was the one I started to compose.

'I first became conscious of thematic ideas for the *Sacre* in the summer of 1911 in Ustilug, our summer home in Volhynia. (*Petrushka* had been performed in June 1911.) The themes were those of "Les Augures printaniers", the first dance I was to compose. I began with the "Augures printaniers", as I said, and composed from there to the end of the first part; the Prelude was written afterward. The dances of the second part were composed in the order in which they now appear, and composed very quickly, too, until the "Danse sacrale" which I could play but did not at first know how to write.'

Those remarks, spoken by Stravinsky himself, form part of a sixteen-minute talk which takes up half the first side of his own record of *The Rite of Spring*, one of the eighteen different versions now in circulation. Such a choice would have been unthinkable twenty years ago, when the work was still a rarity on the concert scene, and one to be approached with a certain amount of fear and trembling, certainly of awe. We all knew its reputation for having caused one of the most notorious scandals in theatre history, and, I beg you, do not for one moment forget that it was composed as theatre music, not for cosy armchair entertainment. Not until the '60s did it begin to be part of the repertory of most orchestras and conductors who fancied themselves virtuosos. At the same time, it began to attract a new generation of choreographers in the theatre, reaching the Royal Ballet in 1962, the Bolshoy Ballet in 1965, and then many other companies in Europe and America.

No other work of this century has been so much documented and discussed, and it remains one of the seminal works of our time. It can still sound as startling today as it did when one member of the first Paris audience nearly seventy years ago beat the head of the unfortunate person in front of him with his fists. Looking now at the range of records available, which themselves cover more than twenty years in the dates of original recording, two factors emerge. One is that exactly half of them have been issued within the last four years, from 1976 in fact. The other is that none of these, and few of the older ones, attempt to offer more than the one work on one disc, which means that one is paying whatever the current price is for around thirty-three minutes of music, which seems to me decidedly expensive time-value. If Stravinsky's own record could have sixteen minutes of him talking, and still get all of Part One on the first side, there really is no excuse for the others. Of Stravinsky's own performance on CBS, I have noticed one or two comments in reviews referring to the 'elderly sound', but it does not strike me as all that poor for a disc which first came out here in 1961. Furthermore, Stravinsky does keep the tempo up to just about his own marking for the 'Spring Rounds Dance', which is more than most of the others do, especially Zubin Mehta with the New York Philharmonic Orchestra, also on CBS. This is one of the most recent versions, and came out in 1978. His funereal plod in the 'Spring Rounds Dance' shows that he obviously has learned nothing more about *The Rite of Spring* since he conducted a previous record with the Los Angeles Philharmonic in 1970 for Decca, and set the same extraordinary tempo. Nor is he alone in this respect, others settling for it including Sir Colin Davis (Philips) and Lorin Maazel (Decca). Indeed, the only conductor to keep up with Stravinsky's own performance and even to push up his tempo still further is, as you might expect, Sir Georg Solti (Decca). His trouble is that, having set such a brisk tempo at the outset of 'Spring Rounds', by the time he has to push it up still more for the later part of it, marked *vivo*, the effect is something of a breathless gabble, for all the expertise of the Chicago Symphony players. Now, I do not for one moment want to suggest that conductors should always be slaves to the printed tempo marking at each section in the score. The composer himself takes his own liberties, and even at times contradicts his published opinions on interpretation in *The Rite*, which are set down in one of the conversation books with Robert Craft. In the 'Augurs of Spring' section, for instance, the only conductor to hold this back to the metronome mark in the score is Ansermet, in the second oldest of these records, with the Suisse Romande Orchestra (Decca). The record is now more than twenty years old, but is reissued at a cheaper price level. To be frank, I do not think the quality of it is sufficiently good by present standards to merit consideration as a possible choice, any more than the oldest of all versions, from 1957, which has the historic interest of being conducted by Pierre Monteux (Decca), who conducted the original première of *The Rite*, scandal and all, for Diaghilev in 1913, and who lived to conduct its jubilee performance fifty years later, to a very different reception in the Royal Albert Hall in London. But to get back to those 'Augurs of Spring' and the question of tempo, most conductors including Stravinsky feel the pulse a good deal faster than Ansermet. One of them is

Riccardo Muti, in the latest and plushiest-sounding recording with the Philadelphia Orchestra (HMV). It is perhaps worth remembering that the Philadelphia Orchestra in its heyday under Stokowski made one of the first-ever recordings of *The Rite* back in the late 1920s, taking four of the old 78 rpm discs, whereas Stravinsky needed five for a more lumbering version made at about the same time. The Philadelphia's new performance with Muti is in its own tradition of vigorous, assertive displays of texture and timbre which are undeniably exciting but which are more concerned with virtuosity than theatrical character. In theatre terms one of the great moments is when the noisy ritual of the 'Two Rival Tribes' is overtaken by the solemn procession bearing the Oldest and Wisest One. This, for me, is one of the crucial passages in *The Rite of Spring* which should instantly evoke your own visual pictures: first, a contest or competition between two rival groups, each trying to do down the other in some noisy way, then – before any result is achieved – falling back in a kind of reverence before the approach of the Elder, the slow, stately rhythm of his procession relentlessly overtaking the previous rhythm of the dance and becoming the totally dominant element on the scene. None of the performances evokes this quite so vividly, or with such clarity of instrumental texture, as Abbado's, with the London Symphony Orchestra (DG). I have no doubt that all the resources of studio technology have helped to achieve the instrumental balance on this record: this is something you could seldom expect in the theatre or concert-hall, but which I think gives such a work as this an acceptable immediacy of impact for armchair listening, in preference to the mushy swimming-bath acoustic of another DG disc conducted by Michael Tilson Thomas. The sharpness and clarity of Abbado with the London Symphony Orchestra has a lot in common with the famous Boulez version, the second recording he made of *The Rite*. This was in 1970 with the Cleveland Orchestra, but I was impressed to find how vivid and exciting it still sounded, not least in the clarity and colour which distinguish even the most congested passages, like the 'Dancing-out of the Earth' at the end of Part One.

Boulez and his recording team are no less successful in that quiet passage of impressionistic tone-painting which begins the second part of *The Rite of Spring*, evoking the sense of nocturnal shadow and the undercurrent of fear and mystery amid which the pagan ritual will achieve its climax. Although, as we all know, the great innovation of the work was, and is, the enthronement of rhythm as the dominant element above that of harmony or melody, these less assertive episodes have a subtle beauty of their own which is particularly apparent in armchair listening. As it is, there are four or five of the less competitive versions which I simply have no space to comment on, and there are still others which have something to reveal in relation to the dances of the second part: Karajan, for instance, on DG, whose hypnotic pulse in the 'Mystic Circle-dance' raises expectations that are not entirely fulfilled in its sequel. For all the expertise of the Berlin Philharmonic and

Karajan's controlled shaping of this performance, it emerges to me as rather two-dimensional in spirit, without a sense of the theatrical character behind it. The climaxes tend to be smoothly engineered and no more, the descriptive passages bland and even perfunctory at times. In short – as with some other conductors including Maazel, Mehta, and Tjeknavorian (RCA) – the work becomes a means to orchestral display for its own sake; and that, to me, is not enough. Eduardo Mata (RCA) would have us accept more character, but he labours it too much, with a recording balance that does little to help. This is a 1979 recording but the muffled texture and lack of clear balance tells against it in passages like the 'Naming and Honouring of the Chosen Sacrifice'. Incidentally, a word about titles. I never could see any good reason for persisting with a French title in an English context: the Russian *Vesna svyaschennaya* would be preferable if one wanted to be accurate. But quite apart from *The Rite of Spring* as an overall title, I find it incredible that even where the record companies use English they choose to ignore Stravinsky's own preferred translations from the Russian for the separate sections, as he published them some ten years ago, and keep instead the old, outdated adaptations from the French. It seems to me they could at least do Stravinsky the courtesy of following his wishes in this respect.

But to get back to the records, the performance by the Boston Symphony, conducted by Michael Tilson Thomas (DG), is the one I referred to earlier as having a 'swimming bath acoustic'. Yet this performance is one of the only two current records that dare to put some extra music on the same disc. In this case it is the intriguing male-voice cantata, *The King of the Stars*, an attractive choice, dating as it does from a year or two before *The Rite*. But the pleasure of such a bonus is unfortunately lost by the often pedestrian character and the over-resonant acoustic for the major work, even in its cheaper price range. Sir Colin Davis and Monteux share the distinction of being the only conductors on these records who have actually conducted *The Rite of Spring* as a ballet in the theatre, so far as I know. Davis did several performances with the Royal Ballet at Covent Garden in 1974, in the version by Kenneth MacMillan, but has not managed to do so since. Whether as a result of that or not, he has modified some of the tempos he adopted when I last heard him conduct it in the concert-hall, and his Philips record, in fact, has the slowest overall timing, by three seconds, of the eighteen I have listened to. Davis does, however, impart a dancing feel to the work even with the slow tempos, and although it is perhaps rather curious to find him partnered with the Amsterdam Concertgebouw Orchestra, he obtains a taut and crisp response, with bright instrumental colour in spite of a reverberant acoustic. Whether it is quite exciting enough to be worth repeated listening, I am not so sure. There is a cheap-price version featuring Igor Markevich and the Philharmonia (Classics for Pleasure) which dates from about twenty years ago and does sound its age, as well as being a very under-characterized performance, hurried rather than pointed. And there is still one more I have not mentioned, which is in a rather different category in being played by the National Youth Orchestra, all under eighteen years old. I cannot help but admire this performance under Simon Rattle (Enigma), a conductor not much older than the players. I have no doubt that it was worth putting on record for the sake of demonstrating what can be obtained in the way of technique, style, and sense of ensemble among gifted young players. In direct comparison with more experienced professionals, however, the sense of effort is occasionally apparent, as is the feeling of cautiousness here and there, so I have to leave it out of my final consideration. And in such a competitive field this brings me to one basic difficulty in making a recommendation: not knowing what you want, or think you want, from so powerful and historic a work.

If you want *The Rite of Spring* only for passive listening, and do not want to be too disturbed by it, there are three or four entirely acceptable, even virtuoso, performances which would be satisfactory: Muti with the Philadelphia Orchestra, for instance; Solti with Chicago; Haitink with the London Philharmonic Orchestra; possibly Sir Colin Davis and the Amsterdam Concertgebouw Orchestra. But there are three others which have very special qualities. There is Stravinsky's own performance from 1961, which obviously has documentary and historical interest, and is still, to my mind, stimulating, even exciting, listening; it is, incidentally, almost the fastest of all. Then, if you are a student and want to hear the maximum inner detail, or if you just like to hear every strand at its clearest, you should go directly for Boulez with the Cleveland Orchestra on their 1970 disc. If you want a performance that will demand all your attention, as I think the best performances should, that has theatrical dance character as well as stylistic and acoustic impact, then I shall recommend the 1976 record of the London Symphony Orchestra conducted by Claudio Abbado.

Recordings discussed

Monteux/Paris Conservatoire Orchestra	Decca ECS 750
Ansermet/Suisse Romande Orchestra	Decca ECS 818
Markevich/Philharmonia Orchestra	CFP 129
*Stravinsky/Columbia Symphony Orchestra	CBS 72054
*Boulez/Cleveland Orchestra	CBS 72807
Mehta/Los Angeles Philharmonic Orchestra	Decca SXL 6444
Tilson Thomas/Boston Symphony Orchestra	Deutsche Grammophon 2535 222
Haitink/London Philharmonic Orchestra	Philips 6500 482
Solti/Chicago Symphony Orchestra	Decca SXL 6691
*Abbado/London Symphony Orchestra	Deutsche Grammophon 2530 635

Maazel/Vienna Philharmonic Orchestra	Decca SXL 6735
C. Davis/Concertgebouw Orchestra	Philips 9500 323
Karajan/Berlin Philharmonic Orchestra	Deutsche Grammophon 2530 884
Mehta/New York Philharmonic Orchestra	CBS 76676
Rattle/National Youth Orchestra	Enigma K 23520
Tjeknavorian/London Philharmonic Orchestra	RCA RL 25130
Mata/London Symphony Orchestra	RCA RL 13060
Muti/Philadelphia Orchestra	HMV ASD 3807

© Noël Goodwin

Vaughan Williams   *Symphony No. 5*

MICHAEL KENNEDY

When it first appeared in 1943, everyone thought of Vaughan Williams's
Fifth Symphony as a summing-up of his life's work, a last will and testament
with the peaceful epilogue of the Finale as a codicil in the shape of a blessing.
Well, everyone was wrong. There were four more symphonies to come and
lots of other music including the opera, or morality, *The Pilgrim's
Progress*, from which several of the symphony's themes are taken. I shall
return to that in due course. The work made a profound impression at its
first performance, as I well remember, and its first recording was made on
plum-label HMV within a year. This was by the recently re-formed Hallé
Orchestra conducted by John Barbirolli. It was a beautiful performance and
it is doubly historic as one of the first recordings of the Hallé-Barbirolli era
and because the work was new at the time. So far as I can discover it has
never been reissued on LP., but I wish HMV would put it into their
Treasury series. Anyway, it is out of the running for consideration here.
Barbirolli recorded it again, with the Philharmonia, for HMV in 1962, Sir
Adrian Boult has recorded it twice, each time with the London
Philharmonic Orchestra, first for Decca in December 1953 and again for
HMV in 1970. The fourth, and most recent of the records we shall be
discussing, was made by the London Symphony Orchestra conducted by
André Previn in 1972 on RCA.

   At its start the symphony creates an air of tranquillity and of belonging to
some other world, but there is also – or there should be – a hint of mystery
and of tension. Boult's first recording, made with the composer present,
concentrates more on tranquillity than tension. It is very mellow, with the
distant horn call and the answering aspiring string motif suggesting a kind
of halo in sound. Nearly twenty years later, Boult seemed to take a different
view of the symphony's opening. The tempo is very slightly quicker but
sounds broader, the sound is more forward, partly due to the stereo
recording, of course, and the strings leaner and more wiry. It seems
stronger music, as if Boult had re-thought it in the context of later works.
André Previn, with a slower tempo, establishes at once the whole tenor of
his interpretation that this is a profound musical experience and a testing
spiritual journey. The London Symphony Orchestra plays wonderfully for
him, the horns absolutely pure and round-toned, and the violas' first entry

as a canonic counterpoint to the violins is beautifully clear and exactly balanced. There is a sense of space and distance.

A spiritual journey, yes, but is this merely a symphonic *Pilgrim's Progress*? You can take it that way if you wish, and you can point with authority to the fact that Vaughan Williams had been working for most of his life after 1906 on an operatic version of Bunyan's *Pilgrim's Progress*. In 1938 he decided he would never finish it and he used some of the themes in this symphony – not very many, as it happens, and none of the Scherzo has any thematic connection with the opera. Originally he put a quotation from Bunyan over the slow movement but crossed it out before publication, so he gives all the clues with one hand and takes them away with the other. The point is, of course, that he did not want this to be thought of in any way as a programme symphony and it clearly isn't one. What images it may suggest to the listener are the listener's affair, but it is basically a closely-knit symphonic argument, one of the most 'absolute' Vaughan Williams ever composed, the structure taut and strong and the tensions between the music's modality and the processes of classical tonality – especially in the first movement – are worked out in masterly fashion. The idea of Vaughan Williams as a clumsy, fumbling amateur in these matters – a pose he adopted himself, with tongue firmly in cheek – was never more clearly exposed as false than in this symphony. And the impression some writers give that this is a calm contemplative work is equally false. There is a great amount of discord in it, as much really as in the angry Fourth Symphony, but less violently expressed, and the music is swept by storms of passion and of disquiet. After the exposition, when an *allegro* section begins, the strings' pentatonic meandering is contrasted with an ominous falling semitone on wind and horns, perhaps tragic in its implications. Previn and the LSO are very fine here. The string playing does not degenerate into fuzziness: you can hear the cello line just as intended and the woodwind articulate with the utmost clarity and precision. Does this remind us, I wonder, of another composer, Sibelius perhaps? Vaughan Williams dedicated his Fifth Symphony 'to Jean Sibelius, without permission', though here too he changed his mind. The original dedication included the words 'sincerest flattery' and mentioned Sibelius's example as being 'worthy of imitation'. I suppose composers are wary of attaching the word 'imitation' to their scores. No one in their senses would think that Vaughan Williams was imitating Sibelius's themes in this work, but he is imitating his methods; and he also imitated Sibelius in presenting his music in this work by means of an orchestra shorn of any extraneous instruments. No percussion except timpani, for example, and no special trimmings – just good plain musical cooking. Like Sibelius, he can, with these ingredients, whip up a powerful climax, and Barbirolli, a notable interpreter of Sibelius as well as of Vaughan Williams, perhaps more than anyone else stresses the significance of the Sibelius dedication, though I do think that Sir John is a bit too hectic and impetuous in the climactic section of the first movement.

A little further on, I find Previn and the London Symphony Orchestra even more satisfying than Barbirolli and the Philharmonia. At the *tutta forza* Previn really does accent the notes, and his slightly more measured tempo gives him the edge over both Boult and Barbirolli in maintaining that elevated mood which is characteristic of his whole interpretation.

The Scherzo, as I have already mentioned, has no thematic connection with the *Pilgrim's Progress* opera, but in some ways it is the most Bunyanesque movement of all. Like so many Vaughan Williams scherzos, it is ambivalent music. It sounds in parts like some etherealized folk dance, but there is something sinister about it too, with disruptive brass and jeering woodwind, hobgoblins and foul fiends, if you like. Sir Adrian Boult's two London Philharmonic Orchestra recordings differ considerably in their approach to the start of this movement. In 1954, he is very much on tiptoe with the oboe's grace-notes very lightly tripped off the tongue. In the 1970 recording, the tempo is slower, the oboe's trills have a hint of menace, yet somehow this performance is not quite as convincing, not quite as much a scherzo as in the earlier version, despite the extreme clarity of recording.

The heart of the symphony is the slow movement, which Vaughan Williams called Romanza. Of course it was the deeply spiritual content of this movement which led listeners in 1943 to regard the work as a summing-up of Vaughan Williams's whole life. Now we can see that it is a summing-up of one aspect of his musical personality, that lyrical side which produced works like the *Tallis Fantasia*, the *Pastoral Symphony, Flos Campi*, and the *Serenade to Music*. The movement has something of the same romantic mystery as its counterpart in the *London Symphony*. This is exemplified by the passage near the start for strings alone, but first there are the hushed chords and the cor anglais solo giving the main theme of the movement. The slow tempo – a true *lento* – and sustained intensity of Previn's conducting of this passage are slightly marred by the London Symphony Orchestra's tendency to play too loudly – everything is marked either *p*, *pp*, or *ppp*, except the cellos' *mp*, and here the cor anglais just is not *pp*.

In Boult's later recording the London Philharmonic Orchestra's attention to dynamics is closer but after the cor anglais, where Vaughan Williams has marked *un pochino più movimento* – a little more movement – I feel that Boult has interpreted *movimento* as *mosso*, giving the music a very slight restlessness which is not yet required, though I do admit that this is to be hypercritical. I want to repeat that this is in no way a pallid or ascetic symphony – and the central section of the slow movement has a passionate climax which again pays tribute to Sibelius in its power and richness and in the way it suddenly blows up into a storm, beginning with a swirling wind on oboe and cor anglais which soon foments the rest of the orchestra. This is Barbirolli territory. His is by far the most spacious and dramatic account of this movement and the Philharmonia's solo horn and trumpet really achieve that exaltation which the composer must have intended when he gave the cor anglais theme to them.

Despite what is sometimes said, Vaughan Williams was a master of orchestration. He is so often called clumsy by people who do not really listen, and he was inclined, in this as in other respects, to denigrate himself. To hear some people, you would think he composed in hobnailed boots. Yet if there is one thing obvious about this symphony, it is that it is written with exceptional finesse. The contrasts of wind and strings, learned from Ravel, are outstanding, and the writing for strings throughout the work is magnificent. This should not surprise us, if we remember that he wrote the *Tallis Fantasia*, that masterpiece of string sonorities, as early as 1910. He always knew how to get the effect he wanted – and if he sometimes wanted to sound like hobnailed boots, he knew how to do that, too. In many ways the Passacaglia last movement of the Fifth Symphony is the most superbly scored.

Every strand in the texture is most carefully picked out and in the first tempo change, achieved by syncopation and the cellos' urgency against the rest of the orchestra, Boult keeps a light rein on the music in his 1970 recording and allows us to hear the oboe's *cantabile* as the composer intended. In fact, in both his recordings Boult excels in touches of this kind, with which the score abounds. The climax of the Finale, and of the symphony, is the return, as inevitable as the sunrise each day, to the horn-call which opened the work – but it returns on the full orchestra. This is a moment which must seem entirely natural and yet it must also have its rightful dramatic effect. This is where Previn is in his element, carefully preparing for the tempo-change and then letting his strings rise and fall like a groundswell, as the brass and woodwind sail triumphantly into the promised land.

In the passage which follows no one else matches Barbirolli and the Philharmonia, for Sir John's genius in obtaining maximum colour from his string players and his skill in both blending and separating the strands of the texture are here paramount. Solo cello and viola must be heard here as the symphony's *Nunc Dimittis* begins and this is where Barbirolli's art is incomparable. It is just a pity he cannot resist putting in an unauthorized comma, thereby spoiling the music's smooth flow, yet his string playing is of luminous beauty.

This is not a work in which you are likely to find marked differences of interpretation. In the recordings I have been considering I have only noted very minor points of detail. Boult and Barbirolli are experienced interpreters of Vaughan Williams, and they both enjoyed the composer's admiration and confidence. To choose between them is largely a matter of personal taste. The first Boult version shows its age a little, but it is coupled attractively on Decca Eclipse with Vaughan Williams's *Pastoral Symphony*. His second recording has the *Serenade to Music* as fill-up. Barbirolli's recording, now on HMV Concert Classics, has the *Tallis Fantasia* as an equally attractive filler. You cannot go wrong with any of these – Boult is statelier, Barbirolli more incandescent. But my first choice is André Previn, because his interpretation combines the stateliness and the incandescence and because throughout the London Symphony Orchestra plays so consistently well.

Recordings discussed

Boult/London Philharmonic Orchestra (1953)	Decca ECS 607
Boult/London Philharmonic Orchestra (1970)	HMV ASD 2538
Barbirolli/Philharmonia Orchestra	HMV ASD 2698
*Previn/London Symphony Orchestra	RCA SB 6856

© Michael Kennedy

Wagner   *Siegfried Idyll*

JOHN WARRACK

On Christmas Day 1870 Cosima Wagner described in her diary how she had awakened that morning. 'I heard a sound, it grew louder, I could no longer imagine myself in a dream, music was sounding, and what music! After it had died away, Richard came in to me with the five children and put into my hands the score of his "Symphonic Birthday Greeting". I was in tears, but so too was the whole household. Richard had set up his orchestra on the stairs and thus consecrated our Triebschen forever! The Triebschen Idyll – thus the work is called.' Cosima treasured the music with special affection, and not least since it had begun life as a string quartet movement written for her six years previously when she and Wagner were in love but not yet living together; and it was only financial necessity that led Wagner to publish what we now know as the *Siegfried Idyll*, as it was re-named, from the dedicatory poem to her and their son Siegfried and from the hero of the opera in which some of the themes are to be found.

The first subject of the string quartet later became the theme of Brünnhilde's love song, 'Ewig war ich'. What we hear on most records, of course, was not the exact sound that Cosima wakened to, for though the stairs at Triebschen are broad, they could not accommodate an entire symphony orchestra. Wagner had gathered together a few players, showing incidentally that he was as great a master of the chamber orchestra as of a huge orchestra; and there is good reason for playing the music with only a string quintet to balance its eight wind and brass instruments, as Georg Solti (on Decca) does. The players are drawn from the Vienna Philharmonic, and the performance was, suitably, recorded as an appendix to Solti's complete *Ring*. There is a delightful intimacy, even a sense of privacy in the playing, though one should not insist that because the original intention was for chamber music we should therefore ban the symphony orchestra; there are passages that are difficult with string quintet. Herbert von Karajan, for example, on DG, draws succulent sounds from the Berlin Philharmonic at the start, though he seems impatient with any tender lingerings and presses quickly on from phrase to phrase. He is, as ever, very high on orchestral efficiency but seems not to let much emotional warmth or commitment join the tonal warmth. Two other conductors try a half-way course between using single instruments and a full orchestra. Neville

Marriner, with the Academy of St Martin-in-the-Fields (Argo) begins with solo quartet, adding to it from time to time when the textures seem to need the greater richness of full strings, making a kind of change in registration. Here we have nice warm playing and a clear, well-balanced recording. Marriner attempts to get the best of both worlds by using both string quartet and a full ensemble. Edward Downes, with the London Philharmonic (Classics for Pleasure), opts for a small group so as to provide a softer bed of tone than is possible with a quartet, but also so as not to swamp the more intimate moments of the score with too much orchestral richness. Downes is a fine Wagner conductor with an obvious affection for the work, which makes it hard to understand why some of the wind entries are not always very clear.

Sir Adrian Boult with the London Symphony Orchestra (HMV) has larger forces, but a better balanced recording. Sir Adrian has said that one of his few regrets in a long and contented life is that he has not spent more time in the opera house; and listening to his beautiful performance of the *Siegfried Idyll* one can share this regret, for he could surely have been a great Wagner conductor, of more than the excerpts that fill up this particular record and others in his Wagner series. Herbert von Karajan has, of course, conducted much Wagner, and made one of the complete *Ring* cycles. Yet when he conducts the Berlin Philharmonic (DG) in the little lullaby which the oboe plays, about two sheep in the garden, the oboe sounds distant and constrained, and greater attention seems to be given to the luscious string answer. Boult holds matters in better balance, allowing the oboe to play his solo freely and simply, and replying with free, expressive, relaxed playing that suits this episode beautifully. Downes and Marriner are also good in this passage, but Kubelik (DG) is a little dull; he comes more into his own at the work's climax, a very difficult passage to judge right.

This music was the second subject of the original string quartet, then became the theme, suitably enough, associated with Siegfried as the world's treasure; here it is put into triple time and built up into a climax with the first, Brünnhilde theme sailing in over it on oboe. The climax that follows is the most powerful of the work. With Kubelik and the Berlin Philharmonic Orchestra, not everything is clear, but there is, as with most other conductors, a good, powerful burst of orchestral tone to make the climax tell. At the other extreme is Solti, who uses single instruments and achieves a nice clarity but at the expense of some strain among the string quintet in providing the wind with a rich bed of sound. The greatest difficulty is for the viola, who has double and even treble stopping at the centre of the quintet texture, while his colleagues are almost entirely in single notes. Neville Marriner, as at the start of the work, uses both solo quintet and full, or fairly full, strings. He takes a middle course and adds more strings when he feels it necessary to give stronger support in a fully scored passage.

In 1951 Guido Cantelli made a record of the *Siegfried Idyll* with the

Philharmonia Orchestra (now available on World Records). Old though this is, much of the quality of Cantelli's compelling musicianship comes through; and in the passage that in *The Ring* is associated with love's resolution as the woodbird warbles away, the unmistakable artistry of Dennis Brain is heard.

It was the trumpet music at the end of this passage that in 1870 became one of the memorable moments for the young Hans Richter. Cosima Wagner had been surprised and somewhat put out to find the young musician endlessly practising the trumpet in the bushes in the garden of Triebschen, but all was revealed when the man who was later to be the first conductor of *The Ring*, and one of the great Wagner conductors of history, turned out to have been learning the instrument specially for this moment. In the recording by Boult, the horn cracks one note; in Downes's version, it is well played, and the ensuing climax is strongly handled, but one of the best of all is by Marriner – fine horn playing, a firm climax, and a ringing piece of trumpet playing at the end, even if there is rather an aggressive woodbird clarinet. His is one of the liveliest available perform-ances, yet a straight selection is hardly possible, partly for musical reasons and partly simply because, being a short work, the *Siegfried Idyll* presents such coupling problems. The cheapest of all is a good version by Edward Downes, on a bargain Music for Pleasure record that includes the usual *Meistersinger* excerpts, and the *Flying Dutchman* and *Rienzi* overtures. In the middle price range is Kubelik on DG, less successful than some others; he also includes Wagner excerpts, from *Lohengrin, Meistersinger,* and *Tristan*.

The three finest versions, however, are all in the top price range. Boult, with full orchestra, the London Symphony, gives a beautifully judged performance on HMV, cooler than some but lucid and fresh; this is part of a Wagner series, and the volume includes some finely played *Parsifal* excerpts. Neville Marriner's performance with the Academy of St Martin-in-the-Fields on Argo loses by trying to compromise between solo quintet and full strings, but the performance is very sensitive and both well played and well recorded; the coupling is Strauss's *Metamorphosen*, plus the Adagio for Clarinet once thought to be by Wagner but actually by Bärmann. The performance that seems to come closest to the spirit of this most touching of works, the most moving present a great artist ever gave to the woman he loved, is that by Solti; and perhaps it is not only the chamber group used but the fact that it came as the afterthought to the whole great project of recording *The Ring* that gives this version such a quality of affection and almost private conversation. Once part of Deryck Cooke's *Ring* lecture, it is now issued coupled with *Ring* excerpts; but it is surely for the *Siegfried Idyll* that the record will be valued.

72   *Orchestral*

Recordings discussed

Cantelli/Philharmonia Orchestra	World Records SH 287
Kubelik/Berlin Philharmonic Orchestra	Deutsche Grammophon 2535 212
*Solti/Vienna Philharmonic Orchestra	Decca SXL 6421
Marriner/Academy of St Martin-in-the-Fields	Argo ZRG 604
Boult/London Symphony Orchestra	HMV ASD 3000
Downes/London Philharmonic Orchestra	CFP 40287
Karajan/Berlin Philharmonic Orchestra	Deutsche Grammophon 2530 919

© John Warrack

Bach   *Concerto for Two Violins*

JEREMY SIEPMANN

If I have one regret about having become a professional musician it is that my necessary concern with performance tends to interfere with my direct experience of music as a listener. There are some pieces, however, whose spiritual abundance and whose straightforwardness of expression disarm me from the start. And one of them is the Bach Double Violin Concerto. It is a work, or so it seems to me, which is very nearly performer-proof. There is plenty of scope, as in all pieces, for highly contrasting tastes and views, but only a very bad performance could distract me from the sheer sublimity of this music.

The slow movement, I think most people would agree, is the real heart of this concerto and it is likely to be the performance of this movement in particular which will decide the listener. But of course there are other, more general considerations. The most sensitive, the most personal perhaps, concerns the size and type of instrumental forces, and here the range is fairly wide. The most authentic approach, from a historical point of view, comes from Nikolaus Harnoncourt and the Vienna Concentus Musicus. With Alice Harnoncourt and Walter Pfeiffer as the soloists, and an orchestra of only eight players – all using original instruments – this performance demonstrates very nicely that 'authentic' baroque string-playing need not sound, as to me it all too often does, like a band of harmonica players. This performance from Telefunken is very much a chamber-music conception, not only in the modest forces used but also in the concerto grosso-type integration of the soloists and the orchestra. While I would never describe it as ascetic, it is certainly the most under-stated of all the currently available performances. In allowing the music to speak for itself, through the absence of any highly coloured individual stamp, it also offers the listener a chance to participate in the recreation of the music – a chance not afforded by some more vividly characterized performances. In those cases, the extent, or lack, of agreement between your own personal preferences and those of the performers will radically affect your responses. If, for instance, you feel strongly drawn to the restrained, historical approach of, say, Harnoncourt, then a performance which pleases me, by Henryk Szeryng, Maurice Hasson, and the Academy of St Martin-in-the-Fields, directed by Neville Marriner (Philips), may very well not please you.

It is a very much more 'public' approach than Harnoncourt's, a version in which the whole piece emerges as a fairly brilliant, almost virtuoso affair – full of spiky drive, polished, even shiny orchestral playing, and a wide range of dynamic and tonal contrasts which in some quarters, I realize, will be stylistically unacceptable. I personally find nothing in it which prevents the music grabbing hold of me and carrying me off, unprotesting, but if you do then obviously we must explore further. In the same very slightly nineteenth-century vein – or perhaps mid-twentieth would be fairer – is the performance given on an HMV disc by Pinchas Zukerman, Itzhak Perlman, and the English Chamber Orchestra under Daniel Barenboim. Here the impression is of a large and rich orchestral body, long lines, and a generally creamy texture. Though the soloists are both renowned virtuosos their relation to the orchestra is perhaps a little less forward, less redolent of the limelight, than Szeryng and Hasson's in the Philips version, and still perhaps, for some tastes, a little on the romantic side; yet nothing in it distracts me from the music.

To turn to something 'purer', Eduard Melkus and the Vienna Capella Academica, like Nikolaus Harnoncourt, take a historical approach to the piece and also use original instruments. As far as the historical approach goes, there are some moments of what sounds like psychological confusion. Under his academic dress I suspect Melkus is really a romantic – and I think this is no bad thing. But it does lead to some very fervent *crescendos* which ultra-purists may find as unacceptable stylistically as those in the lusher performances, by Szeryng, Hasson, and Marriner. Consequently I can well imagine that a number of collectors may be inclined to confine the field of choice to the two ostensibly authentic versions.

If you like the sound of baroque-style string-playing but find Harnon-court's approach a little too restrained, then the Melkus performance may strike an acceptable balance for you. The orchestra is slightly larger, the tempos are on the brisk side, and the soloists, Melkus himself and Spiros Rantos, are perhaps a little more prominent, more overtly soloistic, than those in the Harnoncourt version. If, on the other hand, you like your Bach romantic, in tone as well as sentiment, you might want to sample a recently released Bulgarian performance, on the Harmonia Mundi label. The soloists are Stoika Milanova and Georgi Badev, and they bring to their playing enough vibrato to send purists howling from the room.

The question I have to try and answer now is what you do if you like your Bach neither rich and glossy nor pure, small-scaled and, for want of a better word, 'authentic'. Fortunately there is still quite a lot of choice. The middle ground, with varying degrees of bias toward one pole or another, is well represented by Menuhin and Ferras on HMV, the two Oistrakhs on DG (both of which versions have held their place in the catalogue for nearly twenty years now) and (more recent additions) Suk and Jásek with the Prague Symphony Orchestra and Kenneth Sillito and Hugh Bean with the Virtuosi of London on Classics for Pleasure. This last, by the way, is far and away the cheapest of the available versions, and I think it is good value. Not maybe the most polished performance in the world, but full of vitality and altogether without distracting mannerisms. The playing is a little helter-skelter, perhaps, but if you want something more sober you can always turn to Menuhin and Ferras on HMV or to the Supraphon release which features Josef Suk and Ladislav Jásek. Suk is a violinist whom I have often admired very much, but I must confess I find this recording very disappointing. I can take all kinds of excesses in Bach; I can love it romantic, I can love it authentic and simple, I can love it on the synthesizer – but the one kind of performance which I do find hard to like is the kind which lends even the smallest authority to Colette's mischievous description of Bach as a 'divine sewing-machine'. The fatal mistake of all too many Bach-players, and the one which puts this performance out of court as far as I am concerned, is the confusion of rhythm with metre. Bach's rhythms are, for me, perhaps more vital, more varied, and more subtle than any other composer's. But their source is more often in the melody, in harmony, in texture, than it is in the sometimes quite illusory stresses of the barline. Having singled out Suk – if only because I admire him and because he is the best known performer involved here – I should add that the principal fault here lies, to my ears, not with either soloist but with the leaden, relentlessly four-in-a-bar performance by the Prague Symphony Orchestra under Václav Smetáček.

It is not by mere chance that Yehudi Menuhin and Christian Ferras, with the Robert Masters Chamber Orchestra, have held their place in the catalogue for two full decades. The playing quite simply stands up to repeated scrutiny and to changing fashions. Instrumentally, neither soloist strikes me as being quite at his peak but with some artists that seems not to matter so much. This performance is free of the stage make-up which some people may detect in the more conspicuously brilliant readings, but it is very far from being ascetic. Where most of the other performances, in the outer movements anyway, emphasize the sheer vitality of the music, this one, it seems to me, captures a good deal of its intrinsic nobility as well. There is a sense of balance, without compromise – and of wholeness, without its ever being fulsome. Almost equally venerable is the version recorded by the Oistrakhs, father and son, with Sir Eugene Goossens and members of the Royal Philharmonic on DG's Privilege label. Though I put them earlier among what I described as the middle-grounders – and though their playing of the outer movements justifies that placement I think – the slow movement is romantic enough to put some people off.

The time has now come for a short list which, theoretically at least, will make a final selection easier. I have listened several times to all the versions and more than several to some of them. The ones to which I find myself returning are the Harnoncourt performance on original instruments, the much glossier Szeryng-Hasson-Marriner version, Perlman-Zukerman-Barenboim with the English Chamber Orchestra, and the Menuhin-

Ferras performance. I like them all in their various ways but oddly enough the two which put me most directly in touch with the music itself are from opposite ends of the spectrum. One is Harnoncourt on Telefunken, the other is the Szeryng-Hasson-Marriner version on Philips. I find myself caught on the horns of an authentic, perplexing, and rather intriguing dilemma. Neither version represents my ideal – none of the versions does – yet each, in its way, says more to me about the music than any of the others. It raises an interesting question. Or rather it prompts an interesting answer to a very obvious question. The natural conclusion to draw from my dilemma is that my ideal either lies somewhere between the two performances or would combine somehow their respective virtues in a way which would eliminate their flaws. Yet the more I think about it the more I find myself wondering whether their virtues are not perhaps antithetical – that they are two sides of a coin, as it were. Obviously I would like the whole coin: I would like to choose both performances. But forced to a choice, I have to follow my instinct (one cannot be rational about this sort of thing!) and opt for the Szeryng-Hasson-Marriner version, for the simple and essentially unarguable reason that it provides me with a richer experience.

There is, of course, one important factor in making your own decision which has nothing to do with performance as such. This is the question of couplings. All but two of the available versions give you the E major and A minor solo violin concertos, though Philips throws in the Air on a G string for good measure. The DG recording, on the other hand, offers the sublime Violin and Oboe Concerto, as well as two Vivaldi concertos and an extremely reasonable price. Good value all around. And with the full-price Barenboim-Perlman-Zukerman version you get Perlman playing the E major concerto and Zukerman playing the little-heard G minor concerto. So if coupling is important to you there is an abundance of choice.

Recordings discussed

Menuhin/Ferras/Orchestra/Menuhin	HMV ASD 346
D. and I. Oistrakh/Royal Philharmonic Orchestra/Goossens	Deutsche Grammophon 135 082
Suk/Jásek/Prague Symphony Orchestra/Smetáček	Supraphon SUAST 50672
A. Harnoncourt/Pfeiffer/Vienna Concentus Musicus/N. Harnoncourt	Telefunken AW6 41227
Melkus/Rantos/Vienna Capella Academica/ Melkus	Deutsche Grammophon 2722 011
Perlman/Zukerman/English Chamber Orchestra/Barenboim	HMV ASD 2783
Bean/Sillito/Virtuosi of England/Davison	CFP 40244
*Szeryng/Hasson/Academy of St Martin-in-the-Fields/Marriner	Philips 9500 226
Milanova/Badev/Sofia Chamber Orchestra	Harmonia Mundi HM 113

© Jeremy Siepmann

Berlioz   *Harold in Italy*

STEPHEN DODGSON

The story is that Paganini took one look at Berlioz's score and instantly complained that the solo viola part contained far too many rests. If he had looked closer, which of course he did not need to, he would undoubtedly have had a second cause for complaint: that the composer wilfully intrudes upon the soloist with excessive doubling in the orchestra. The composer's Byronic soulmate is indeed often half lost in the crowd; but, as every devotee of the work knows, herein lies some of the fascination of its very special colouring. Balancing a soloist in a recording of a conventional concerto poses a problem often enough, but it is nothing beside the subtlety of balance the recording producer is up against here.

The long introduction to the first movement divides itself in two. The impressive brooding minor key *fugato* suddenly dissolves to reveal Harold with his slow reflective song, the only true solo of any real length in the whole work. It peters out in hesitations with the harp. Then, on a *sforzando*, two horns launch the soloist upward into the throng. A *tutti* version of the Harold theme now follows, the prominent cornet leading a fairly strict canon. The canon is taken by the viola, but much doubled, so that his sound is almost entirely absorbed into a blended tonal quality. There are harp chords, a triangle, and an upward whirling figure for the strings by way of accompaniment. The pace, the balance, and the fascinating interest of the whole tonal spectrum all seem to me specially appealing under Colin Davis conducting the London Symphony Orchestra on Philips, with Nobuko Imai, solo viola. She is probably best known as viola player of the Vermeer String Quartet, and her performance generally has the polished refinement of that renowned group. When I first heard this record when it was new a few years ago, I thought she was too detached, too cool, for so impressionable a hero as Berlioz's Harold. The important recent reissue of the first version (1963) conducted by Colin Davis (HMV Concert Classics) raises the question of expressive character in an acute form, and from exactly the opposite viewpoint. Yehudi Menuhin projects Harold as a soft, somewhat hesitant and always soulful singer, hardly able to brush away the tears of his opening *Scène de mélancolie* (very convincing) when Berlioz confronts him with increasingly infectious merriment in the ensuing *allegro* (taken very deliberately, and not at all convincing). Conductor and orchestra

(Philharmonia) seem occasionally held in check by so soft-grained a hero, though they listen with consummate transparency to his beautifully disembodied arpeggios in the *Canto religioso* section of the *Pilgrims' March* – the highlight of the performance. The recording lacks the lustre of the later Davis version. But, at a lower price level, it is a reflective alternative to the extrovert Bernstein CBS version.

It comes to me forcibly, now, how much more I respond to Imai's and Menuhin's restraint alongside the opulent expressiveness brought to the part by Pinchas Zukerman with the Orchestre de Paris under Daniel Barenboim. This is on CBS, and the balance is wrong in several respects; the soloist is just too close, so that he does not get sufficiently absorbed into the crowd during the canon. The harp is ridiculously close up. In fact, the more one listens to the overall balance the less convincing it seems: the ministrations of the mixer are so very evident. Furthermore, Barenboim drags the pace, and what I can only call the sunlit quality is dimmed; and this rather generally characterizes his view of the work.

The introduction fades away in horn-like ruminations, which are very sweetly done by Zukerman in the Barenboim recording. Harold stands on the brink of the main Allegro of the first movement, whose opening paragraph provides a brisk introductory flourish. At last the stage is set for the soloist to announce *his* theme for the Allegro, and after a few preliminary stutters, he succeeds. At once the orchestra leaps in loudly, hardly allowing the viola another chance to utter in the enthusiasm of its welcome.

Enthusiasm is the word, I think, and this is the salient quality of one of the oldest of the available recordings, now on mid-priced CBS, by the New York Philharmonic Orchestra under Leonard Bernstein. The soloist, William Lincer, makes the traditional opening hesitations, but labours neither them nor his delivery of the tune. The whole atmosphere is bright with anticipation and excitement. The orchestral detail is very clear and good in its balance of timbres. It is a version full of an open and appealing vitality.

Zubin Mehta and the Israel Philharmonic Orchestra on Decca have an admirably warm-toned soloist in Daniel Benyamini. This, too, has a brisk speed for the Allegro in mind, but reaches it gradually after a more tentative beginning: a more self-conscious interpretative idea, I would say, and underneath its lively surface with less instinctive affinity with the work's peculiar genius. I feel sure this version is surpassed in vividness as to the notes, as well as an insight into their poetic intention, by versions conducted by Davis, Bernstein, to say nothing of Toscanini. Between them, these four versions (there are two with Bernstein) have so much to offer, that I am omitting altogether the Supraphon version with Joseph Suk and the Czech Philharmonic conducted by Fischer-Dieskau, which, no matter what one's artistic response, is so badly balanced as to make a mockery of Berlioz's marvellous judgement in these matters. My other omission is also a recent issue. It is by the Cleveland Orchestra under Lorin Maazel on Decca, is thoroughly dependable, but hardly ever rises above a fairly routine dullness. The Pilgrim's March, so difficult to get to move at just the right pace, shows this clearly enough. The other miniature movement is the Serenade of the Abruzzi Mountaineer to his Mistress. A rustic piping over a heavy drone introduces the movement. Soon afterwards the serenade itself is heard, with the tune on the cor anglais, and is instructed to move at exactly half the speed, for the reason, so typical of Berlioz, that the two are destined to combine in the coda.

Toscanini's recording of the work dates from very late in his long career and was made at a public concert. There is no mistaking his view of this movement as real outdoor music, and all in broad daylight. The serenader here, one feels, has never taken elocution lessons or fussed about his etiquette, and Toscanini keeps his wooing strictly at the half speed asked for and no less. Colin Davis, who sets his piper going hardly less briskly, gradually allows himself to make a more sentimental fellow of the mountaineer. Mood and motion become increasingly nocturnal after the point where Harold himself wanders on to the scene, gradually inspiring the orchestral strings to join his slow tune as counterpoint to the serenade. Leonard Bernstein is close to Davis, I feel, in Romantic ideal, yet has a quite different concept of the motion. I refer now to the newer of Bernstein's discs, which is with the French National Orchestra, in a particularly warm and sonorous recording by HMV. It is interesting to me how Bernstein has developed as an interpreter of Berlioz, a composer for whom he has long had a strong attachment. This second *Harold*, recorded in Paris, is more sensitive to tempo relationships and their place in the overall design, and more thoughtful somehow as a whole. And it is specially in this little Abruzzi episode that Bernstein seems to me to score not only over his own more obviously excitable New York performance, but also over Colin Davis whose serenader gets distinctly comatose. To clinch matters, the Paris Bernstein is unsurpassed in the coda of this movement, achieving a rare magic in the simultaneous combination of the three musical germs; Harold, the serenader, and the distant drone of the piper.

Then, with crash of cymbals, the Brigands are impatient for their Orgy. Yet Berlioz causes them to go through a Beethovenian process of dismissing quotations from previous movements before the party is in full swing. And once the party *is* in full swing, the viola is firmly dismissed from the scene. Toscanini's averts all danger of the movement falling apart before it has properly begun, by keeping a tightish rein. Each quotation makes its point simply, but is brushed aside without ado. Once again, an outdoor view, fresh and full of sunlight. He has a firm upstanding soloist in Carlton Cooley. This version, dating from 1953 and recorded live in Carnegie Hall, is in the invaluable Arturo Toscanini edition, separately available, at bargain price in mono only from RCA. It is like a tonic in its immediacy, gusto, and sanity.

Of the more modern performances currently available, the one which, in the Finale at least, perhaps comes closest to the Toscanini ideal is the mid-priced CBS issue of Bernstein with the New York Philharmonic Orchestra. The recorded sound is full, heard after Toscanini, though a little thin alongside several others, including Bernstein's own later recording. That too is vital in the Finale, but does not actually quite match the vivid exuberance felt in this older version. It has one very un-Toscanini-like feature, by the way. After the eventual climax arrives in syncopated chords rocketing across the orchestra, there comes a brief passage of incomparable magnificence, for which Bernstein holds back. Slowing up for this passage, whilst very effective, is of course arbitrary, and Bernstein significantly no longer does it. The older version, finely played though it is, is just a little given to histrionics, though it is true that even these are strongly imaginative in trying to serve the composer. On CBS Classics label this is, I suggest, a better choice than all the full-price versions except two; and those two are hard to choose between.

First, there is Colin Davis and the London Symphony Orchestra on Philips. The Brigands are, as I said, altogether too noisy for Harold. So the viola simply stands aside and lets them get on with it, until, in the coda, there is a sudden hush, and a ghostly vision of the Pilgrims marching ever onward rouses Harold to a few softly parting sighs. This brief poetic moment is as beautifully done by Nobuko Imai as everything she does – a little cool, but none the worse for that. Yet, in the Bernstein version, with the French National Orchestra on HMV, the viola soloist, Donald McInnes, speaks through the music just a little more I think, though with an equally dignified restraint. There are aspects – specially the Pilgrims' March movement itself – in which I believe Sir Colin Davis surpasses Bernstein's Paris version, but it is largely the greater sensation of musical personality that I find in Bernstein's soloist that would finally tip me in favour of his recording as my final choice.

Recordings discussed

Cooley/NBC Symphony Orchestra/Toscanini	RCA AT 112
Lincer/New York Philharmonic Orchestra/ Bernstein	CBS 61091
Benyamini/Israel Philharmonic Orchestra/ Mehta	Decca SXL 6732
Imai/London Symphony Orchestra/C. Davis	Philips 9500 026
*McInnes/French National Orchestra/Bernstein	HMV ASD 3389
Zukerman/Paris Orchestra/Barenboim	CBS 76593
Suk/Czech Philharmonic Orchestra/Fischer-Dieskau	Supraphon 410 2005
Vernon/Cleveland Orchestra/Maazel	Decca SXL 6873
Menuhin/Philharmonia Orchestra/C. Davis	HMV SXLP 30314

© Stephen Dodgson

Handel *Twelve Concerti Grossi Op. 6*

I think anyone who tries to make value judgements ought to declare his criteria. The philosopher George in Tom Stoppard's *Jumpers* remarks that not all value judgements are the proper study of the moral philosopher and instances the absurdity of analyzing the statement 'This is a good bacon sandwich'. If I am going to say 'This is a good performance of a Handel concerto', I must try to account for my claim. Attitudes towards what the German scholars have made us call baroque music have changed so much in the past thirty years that the first thing in many peoples' minds is the question of 'authenticity'. If you belong to the Exclusive Brethren of old music you will reject any performance that does not use historically correct instruments, which means, in the case of these twelve concertos, nearly all the string orchestras that play them. That is only the beginning; one sees now a concert describing itself as 'played in authentic style on original instruments'. You do not have to be an analytical philosopher to realize that two different kinds of statement are being made here, mixing fact with opinion. I think they are also separate categories and I will try to treat them as such.

I do not mean that style is not a matter of facts, but rather that the most important criterion, though it includes to some degree both types of authenticity, is not guaranteed by their presence. What I have looked for in the available versions of Handel's Op. 6 is a pervasive sense of the stature of these compositions, matched only by Bach's Brandenburg set as standing high above all the rest of the baroque repertory. With a total of more than sixty movements the only thing to do is to select as far as possible a limited number covering the various types to be found in these concertos. This is not really possible, because of Handel's Shakespearean wealth of inventiveness, but one can take, say, a fugal piece, a concerto grosso movement with its Corellian concertino of two violins and cello, a dramatic overture opening, a dance or two, a broad singing slow movement, and so on.

The modern string sound of Neville Marriner's Academy of St Martin-in-the-Fields at the opening of the third concerto, for example, should satisfy all but the most severe puritan, but where is the dialogue of *tutti* and *concertino*, an exchange made three times, followed by the complete statement? And why should this last be soft instead of loud? The Collegium Aureum play on 'original instruments', but they make such a nice sound that I have heard their authenticity called in question by some of the more extreme brethren. They take more or less the same tempo as the Academy but like other authentic ensembles they play at low pitch. I do find their playing more convincingly shaped and phrased. The strings of the Berlin Philharmonic, directed from the harpsichord by none other than Herbert von Karajan, on the other hand, are undeniably grand, perhaps a shade self-consciously so, and experts will have to put up with the wrong trills. All the same, an essentially Handelian quality is expressed in their majestic, broadly phrased opening of the Third Concerto. Of course Karajan knows his long drawn *legato* is unauthentic, but he makes more sense of the *tutti-soli* relation and of the harmonic rhythm of the whole piece. The fourth movement of this E minor concerto is a Polonaise, marked *andante* in most editions. Like so many things in these works it uses the chosen medium with the imaginative resourcefulness of a master unsurpassed in writing for strings. Both in the tonic of the piece, G major, and its dominant, the open strings provide drone basses and these give the music the much-liked *musette* quality. Karajan gives us the drone if not much else of any pastoral atmosphere but in this delightful piece his liking for the smooth undulating line of rich tone produces, for me, an over-sophisticated effect very far from pleasing. The rustic waggon seems to have been replaced by a Mercedes.

The Academy play this movement, as everywhere, with incisiveness and exemplary ensemble. These qualities are apt to be won at the expense of significant phrasing, and although it is perfectly true that Handel's *andante* is not a slow tempo in the nineteenth-century manner, it is not *allegro* either, which is what we find in the Polonaise. It sounds a bit smart-society, and I do not care for the busy little tinkling of the harpsichord, a too recurrent feature in the Academy's performance of these concertos. The perhaps slightly factitious brilliance of effect comes largely from the short quavers, made almost staccato in the modern way. This is not what is meant by Handel's notation; he puts four notes under a slur with a dot to each note, meaning a carrying of the sound, as it were, from note to note, with virtually no silence between. The Collegium Aureum do this and, as it happens, the observing of the bowing makes for a proper tempo.

If we consider the second movement of the Sixth Concerto, this is a straightforward fugue in four parts for *tutti* throughout, with no *concerto grosso* episodes. Its subject is derived from a chorus in the tenth Chandos Anthem, where it has the words 'They are brought down and fall'n but we are risen'. The tempo here is *a tempo ordinario*. The concerto fugue – both are in 4/4 time – is *a tempo giusto*. There are no dynamics and this is the kind of piece that would be played *organo pleno* if it were written for keyboard. It is a movement that shows the best qualities of Karajan's Handel, strong and phrased according to the harmonic sense of the music, free from any trace of affectation. Marriner takes a not very different view, but the phrasing is rather metrical and I do not care for the arbitrary dynamics, put in for no structural purpose but for effect. Both he and Karajan read *a tempo giusto* as *allegro con brio*. In contrast to the Franzjosef Maier and the Collegium Aureum are nearer to the sense of Handel's tempo indication, which means *allegro* only if you add *moderato*. In fact he first put *allegro ma non troppo*. It is surprising what a difference a slight reduction of speed makes especially when the phrasing is as musical as it is in the Collegium Aureum performance.

From time to time both Mariner and Maier, but not Karajan, include oboes and bassoon besides the strings. In four of the Op. 6 concertos – Nos. 1, 2, 5, and 6 – Handel added these extra parts to his score, but left them out of the published material. Probably he used them when performing the concertos in his oratorios, when the wind would have been available. I think we can ignore this aspect in trying to assess the merits of the available recordings. For my part, I could well do without the extra instruments, but both methods of performance are 'authentic'.

If the tempo is wrong, nothing else will come right and I am afraid in this respect there are things in all these recordings that go beyond the range of reasonable possibility. The fact that Bach and Handel often left a piece with no indication of tempo does not mean, as used to be thought in circles where people ought to have known better, that you can choose any speed you like. It means, on the contrary, that there is little room for error if you are properly familiar with the conventions and, of course, are prepared to observe them. The Minuet of the Fifth Concerto compels me to eliminate Karajan from my comparisons. Since it is so far from any conceivable baroque minuet, it spoils what otherwise is an impressive performance; and although Handel sometimes left out movements, I cannot very well say Karajan is fine in these Op. 6 concertos, but do not play the following ... What I will say is that a collector who knows his Handel and wants to broaden his selection will find some valuable things in Karajan's DG set but there are limits.

We are left then with a choice between Marriner's Academy and the Collegium Aureum and I must try to justify my clear preference for the Collegium, in which, incidentally, their use of authentic instruments, though pleasing to me, is not a deciding factor. I have already stated that what I look for is a sense of the stature of the music. Vague enough you may think, but supposing you compare Beethoven with Hummel, Mozart with Dittersdorf, Haydn with Boccherini, Bach with Telemann, or Handel with Arne. My complaint about the admirably executed performances of the Op. 6 concertos by the Academy of St Martin is that they convey charm, gentle pathos, sophisticated wit, a slightly dandyish animation, faintly languid tranquillity (a bit like the Yeats of Innisfree) – all estimable qualities but none of them Handelian. Some of the playing is undoubtedly beautiful and I am not deliberately looking for faults. Sometimes in the Collegium Aureum's performances the more austere sound of the old instruments is an advantage, as in the *largo* of the Fourth Concerto. The kind of thing I do grumble about in the Academy's playing is apparent in the second movement of Concerto No. 11 where there is a featureless detached string sound, no phrasing of the scale theme, elegance in the place of strength. The Collegium offer an improvement though the harpsichord is also hyperactive but less audible. The fourth movement of the Eleventh Concerto has one of those rough-hewn themes so characteristic of Handel, with splendid dissonances between tune and bass. The Academy make it a rather limp-wristed affair. The Collegium are on the slow side but what a contrast in general vitality; if, as seems to be agreed by experts, the organ version of the work is the original, this fact favours a broad tempo. It should also be noted that Marriner makes a large cut in the Finale of this concerto.

When, in summing up, I show preference to the Collegium Aureum (Harmonia Mundi) this does not mean I think them beyond reproach. Some of their tempos are too deliberate; they perpetrate a few solecisms in ornamentation, the baroque oboes occasionally sound a trifle duck-like. However, they do, on the whole, come nearer to the true Handelian grandeur, depth, and sheer energy of invention; and this is the heart of the matter, the only real authenticity, of which the other kinds must be the servants if they are to be worth bothering about.

Anyone who records for the gramophone gives hostages to fortune; the Marriner interpretations of Op. 6 (Decca Ace of Diamonds) were first issued in 1968 and the attractive Op. 3 concertos that now go with them in a set were recorded four years before that. So I am not, in fact, giving a critique of the Academy of St Martin-in-the-Fields of today. Perhaps it is time they gave us a new version. What I miss in the present one is, in a phrase of Pope's, 'the long majestic march and energy divine'. Such things as the fifth movement of Op. 6 No.5 will show why I recommend the Collegium Aureum in these works. Sparing us the miseries of 'period' style, they play this magnificent Scherzo with irresistible verve and enthusiasm.

Recordings discussed

Marriner/Academy of St Martin-in-the-Fields	Decca SDD B 294–7
Karajan/Berlin Philharmonic Orchestra	Deutsche Grammophon
	2726 068
*Collegium Aureum/Meier	Harmonia Mundi
	HM 1C 153–99645–7

BRYCE MORRISON

'I am half Franciscan, half gypsy,' exclaimed Franz Liszt. In this brief declaration he suggested an essential, ultra-romantic duality, a worldliness and remoteness, and the way the poet and exhibitionist in him so often vie for attention. Today, thanks largely to recordings, we can range over the vast landscape of Liszt's output and become increasingly aware of the sheer scope of his work, which extends from an extravagant, wholly nineteenth-century glitter to a strange, dark-hued austerity that already foreshadows Debussy, Bartók, and even Schoenberg. Again, Liszt wrote compositions which are a product of his life-long vacillation between the secular and erotic, between an equal love of monastic seclusion and scandalous publicity. It is both amusing and, perhaps, reassuring to realize that the worlds of compositions such as the *Bénédiction de Dieu dans la solitude* and the *Liebesträume* are not so very far apart after all, and are, indeed, opposite sides of the same romantic coin.

Where, then, does the E flat Piano Concerto, composed in 1849, come in all this? The answer is, firmly in the virtuoso category, because for all its variety of mood and pace it is the *brio*, inventiveness, and sheer style that strikes one most, a scintillating proof that, in the words of William Blake, 'exuberance is beauty'. At the same time, the finest performers of this concerto are as quick to capture its inner repose as they are to relish its drama and rhetoric and also to provide that special touch of magical eloquence without which such rhetoric can quickly seem sham and empty.

It is here that the truly great performances of the Liszt E flat Concerto, and what might unfairly be called the 'also-rans', divide. How many pianists (to say nothing of conductors who also have a vital role to play in this work) can recreate such an inclusive form of virtuosity, or ring the expressive changes so rapidly or effortlessly? Martha Argerich, superbly partnered by the London Symphony Orchestra under Claudio Abbado on DG provides a characteristically volatile answer. Her blood is up as she launches the opening octave roulades with the greatest possible panache. Yet it is no less characteristic of this extraordinary artist that having pushed ahead so fiercely she can also calm her fiery temperament and achieve, when required, a fine, improvisatory poise. Alfred Brendel, in his Philips recording with the London Philharmonic Orchestra under Bernard Haitink, is perhaps more responsive to the opulence and drama of Liszt's opening. Less inflammatory than Miss Argerich, his conception is imposingly grand and spacious, a different yet no less convincing way of answering the orchestra's opening challenge as it defiantly flings down the gauntlet. Ivan Davis, on Decca's Phase 4, may add the odd bass reinforcement here or an extra ornament there for good measure and Horacio Guiterrez's trill, just before the second subject, may go off like a steam whistle, yet neither pianist, in my opinion, creates quite the same sense of true grandeur or occasion. The young Hungarian pianist, Gyla Kiss, on Hungaraton, although hardly of the same calibre as Brendel or Argerich, is a good deal more convincing than many of his more celebrated colleagues. He is partnered by the Hungarian State Orchestra under János Ferencsik and can be both grand and nimble even if he is apt to run out of steam towards the end of the concerto. And at the beginning of the second subject one is reminded that a young pianist can seem cruelly exposed when compared to so richly experienced an artist as Alfred Brendel. Brendel, for example, brusquely introduces the clarinet theme (Bar 45) and then magically calms the music's progress, His way with the short cadenza or flourish, too, tells us that he never flicks aside such passages as so much musical dust, but potently suggests how they are invariably an organic part of Liszt's overall argument. Brendel produces a wonderfully rich variety of responses at that crucial point and, as the first section moves via brilliant passage work and octaves to its conclusion, he closes with a confident yet flexible and expressive glitter that is virtually ideal.

The opening of the second movement or section is a no less testing moment than the start of the first. Blazing virtuosity is now calmed into a long, sustained *cantabile* and Leonard Pennario on RCA is not the only pianist to miss rather too much of the music's contemplative ardour and vision. Tamás Vásáry, too, in his generally light-weight account, sounds curiously tentative about such poetry. Ivan Davis and Julius Katchen, on the other hand, hardly need a second invitation when they see the direction *con espressione*, and Davis's old-fashioned glamour will doubtless sound endearing to some though fulsome and self-conscious to others .Turning to Brendel's veiled and gentle expression, with its natural improvisatory sense of the music's long, arching paragraphs, is to enter an altogether different imaginative world; something far removed from other less instinctively poetic players. Martha Argerich, too, brings a rare delicacy to her performance and she launches into the ensuing dramatic recitative in a style that will, I believe, make even the most *blasé* listeners jump out of their skins. This pianist is a prima donna indeed though once more Miss Argerich finds just the right degree of calm before the start of the last movement, music which caused a minor furore when first performed. Liszt's use of the triangle to announce and underline the music's rhythm was greeted with astonishment and led to a temporary and ironic title for the work *The Triangle Concerto*. Arthur de Greef on Pearl serves to remind us that though it is valuable to hear a Liszt pupil play one of his master's compositions, poor sound quality can be a serious set-back. The record was made in 1922 and Hi-Fi enthusiasts will steer clear. In any case De Greef is rather too frequently swamped not only by the music's more savage technical demands but also by its finer, poetic qualities.

Lazar Berman on DG, whilst of course hardly inadequate to the technical occasion, also sounds oddly lethargic in music which is headed *capriccioso scherzando*. He is accompanied by the Vienna Symphony Orchestra under Giulini and although his performance has many beautiful qualities I feel that he sacrifices too much of the music's sparkle and aplomb in his evident anxiety to avoid superficiality, or the barn-storming image once associated with his pianism. Julius Katchen, on the other hand, has all of the music's athletic grace and lilt at his finger tips and although the recording (a mid-price reissue on Decca's Ace of Diamonds label) begins to show its age, what you *will* hear is a remarkably faithful reproduction of that problematic triangle. Katchen's, though, is a brilliant and sensitive reading. Martha Argerich, too, provides a memorable example of how display need not necessarily be empty, and later in the *allegretto vivace* her sky-rocketing bravura is breathtakingly and gloriously assured. Brendel's performance also has an enviable ease at this point and later plunges downwards to a truly menacing reminder of the work's opening subject.

Horacio Gutierrez on HMV is much less characterful and provides a revealing instance of an enviable professionalism that often fails to extend to very much personal magic. Exceptionally powerful, his performance is insufficiently subtle, though he is finely accompanied by the London Symphony Orchestra conducted by André Previn. From such ominous rumblings, in the cadenza and bridge passage leading to the last section, the music boils up to assert the opening challenge twice, and here Brendel is once more supreme, playing with all the imposing grandeur and breadth at his command. Wonderfully sensitive to detail, his performance also shows an overall grasp of Liszt's very characteristic method, his novel way of endlessly varying his material whilst at the same time securing one's sense of his total structure.

For the final *allegro marziale animato*, Liszt transforms his dreamy opening proposition from the second movement into a full blooded martial display, complete with sounding brass and cymbals, and the music's concluding pages are taken up with an increasingly flamboyant and ingenious restatement of all that has gone before. Not surprisingly Martha Argerich seizes every opportunity for high-wire virtuosity. Few other pianists could match her exhilarating fleetness as she reels off Liszt's figurations and accelerates towards the finishing post in the grandest of grand manners.

In conclusion, it is Martha Argerich and Alfred Brendel who provide the richest experience in this concerto. Choice is a hard matter, yet if pressed I would opt for Alfred Brendel on Philips. His performance is such a *total* experience and he is finely accompanied and recorded. Unlike many of his colleagues (or rivals, if you like) his disc includes the *Totentanz* as well as the Second Piano Concerto, and so it would seem fitting to add that rarely can quality and quantity have been united so successfully. Taken as a whole, his performance represents great Liszt playing as remarkable for its distinctive poetic profile as for the total command of the virtuoso idiom.

Recordings discussed

De Greef/Royal Albert Hall Orchestra/ Ronald	Pearl GEM 139
Katchen/London Philharmonic Orchestra/ Argenta	Decca SPA 318
Vásáry/Bamberg Symphony Orchestra/ Prohaska	Deutsche Grammophon 2548 235
Pennario/London Symphony Orchestra/ Leibowitz	RCA CCV 5047
Argerich/London Symphony Orchestra/ Abbado	Deutsche Grammophon 139 383
Kiss/Hungarian State Orchestra/Ferencsik	Hungaraton SLPX 11792
Davis/Royal Philharmonic Orchestra/ Downes	Decca PFS 4252
*Brendel/London Philharmonic Orchestra/ Haitink	Philips 6500 374
Berman/Vienna Symphony Orchestra/Giulini	Deutsche Grammophon 2530 770
Guiterrez/London Symphony Orchestra/ Previn	HMV ASD 3262

© Bryce Morrison

Mendelssohn *Violin Concerto in E minor*

JOHN WARRACK

With so many versions of Mendelssohn's E minor violin concerto available in the domestic lists, ruthless selection is necessary in choosing records for close consideration – and I mean ruthless, since every prominent violinist has the work in his repertory, and many have recorded it more than once. There are versions by Menuhin, Zukerman, Perlman, Milstein, Stern, Campoli, Szeryng, plenty more besides, and choice is not made easier by the fact that we are dealing with a work that, though a masterpiece, is not one that offers the depth of experience of Beethoven's or Brahms's concertos. A good many violinists play Mendelssohn's concerto in very much the same way. However, any suggestion that there is only one approach is dispelled by the finest of the violinists who have recorded the work, even in the opening bars. Here, Isaac Stern, for example, is simple, direct, and lyrical. His orchestra is the Philadelphia under Ormandy on CBS; the playing is easy and fresh, if, perhaps, a little too easy and uncommitted. It is, in fact, the kind of approach adopted by most players, though four other versions show that the options are more open than might be supposed. Nathan Milstein, in the second of his two recordings with the Vienna Philharmonic Orchestra under Claudio Abbado on DG, takes it very fast, though he is in complete technical control and uses the fast tempo to suggest nervous energy and even a slight note of frailty. Milstein, emphasizes the *allegro* in the marking *allegro molto appassionato*, where Itzhak Perlman, with the LSO and Previn on HMV, chooses to emphasize the *molto appassionato*. The effect is much grander, with Previn stressing the drum taps as something solemn rather than as merely rhythmic impetus, and the orchestra in general supporting Perlman's view that this is an opening statement of considerable grandeur. Compared to Perlman, Yehudi Menuhin, on HMV with the London Symphony Orchestra conducted by Frühbeck de Burgos, is more relaxed and lyrical. His gift for expressive emphases on phrases within a long melodic line is beautifully apt throughout his whole performance: he balances very expertly the easy melodic flow with graphic short phrases, and his tone is rich and attractive. One curious feature of Menuhin's playing in the opening section is that he changes the music at two points, playing four quavers where Mendelssohn wrote a crotchet and two quavers – perhaps he has some authority for this which is unknown to me. Pinchas Zukerman, in the opening melody, avoids the pace of Milstein or the grandeur of Perlman and seems to prefer a less detailed treatment than Menuhin; though in some ways similar in manner to Stern, he manages to charge the melody with greater meaning. He also plays with the London Symphony Orchestra but this time the conductor is Antal Dorati. A sixth violinist who gives a nice, unaffected, musicianly performance is Josef Suk, with the Czech Philharmonic Orchestra under Karel Ančerl on Supraphon. The orchestra is not all that well recorded, and the ensemble is not always ideal, but there is nonetheless an engaging quality about his performance, as in his sympathetic handling of the first movement's second subject.

In this most consistently lyrical and melodious of concertos, the way in which the principal themes are introduced or reintroduced is even more than usual of expressive importance. Another artist, Ion Voicu, on Decca Ace of Diamonds, particularly appreciates this point, and after a good, sympathetic start to the whole concerto leads into the second subject very expressively, though then, having prepared it very well, he sounds a trifle restless. His orchestra is the London Symphony again with Frühbeck de Burgos. Itzhak Perlman prepares the second subject well, with plenty of spacious phrasing and, as when he opened the concerto, a sense of grandeur. He treats the violin's arpeggios and passagework as melodic and phrases them very well into the held open-string low G over which the woodwind give out the melody. Yet splendidly as Perlman plays the second subject, I have a feeling that it is a manner really better suited to Brahms than to Mendelssohn's lighter lyricism. Where Perlman comes down the introductory appeggios as if introducing something grand, and indeed then plays the music grandly, Menuhin treats the descending arpeggios as a relaxation into the second subject. He then plays it very simply, though still with sensitive inflexions to the phrasing within the whole melody, and he moves back into the first subject as if the entire violin line, from those connecting arpeggios through the held low G and then the tune and finally the return of the first subject, were a seamless melody.

One other violinist who gives an agreeable performance of the concerto is Ruggiero Ricci, with, for the fifth time, the London Symphony Orchestra, now conducted by Pierino Gamba on Decca. For the most part he shares Milstein's view of the work, without pressing the opening tempo so keenly, but playing it lightly and attractively; he sustains this easy-going approach in the Andante, which he keeps moving well so that there is a pleasantly lilting feeling of the tune moving along with two beats in a bar, almost like a barcarolle. Ricci seems to me to have a more sympathetic approach to the Andante than Itzhak Perlman, who brings much warmth and intensity to bear upon the melody but in so doing weighs down something that should be light, even perhaps rather understated, to make its best effect. This is a more imposing performance, well in keeping with Perlman's whole approach, but almost too magnificent. He is more intense than any other violinist with the Andante, and beautiful though the playing is, it does seem to demand more of the music than is appropriate. Zukerman keeps matters easier, and allows the tune to flow more naturally, but better still is Menuhin, whose phrasing is shapely, pointed with subtle contrasts of tone and intensity, yet as ever fresh and related to a long, arched melodic line. It is his command of a long line that most distinguishes Menuhin's performance, and it is indeed one of the most important single characteristics for the successful performance of a work that is essentially melodic.

The middle section of the movement brings some rich double stopping, with the violin sometimes bearing the real weight of the textural richness while the orchestra either falls silent or is confined to the slenderest *pizzicato* on a few strings; but as ever, there is a very clear melodic thread running through the passage, which the soloist must sustain seamlessly back into the main theme. Milstein handles it simply and easily, if perhaps a little lightly. Stern in this passage is rather casual, and there is a touch of mannered phrasing that can intrude into his performance. Menuhin is excellent; so are Zukerman and Perlman. Zukerman produces especially strong, warm playing and resonant tone, well recorded, to help give the passage its effective contrast of richness dissolving into the original simple line; however, he does make slightly heavy weather of the closing phrases, for all the warmth and charm with which he plays the passage. His tremendous technical assurance is used but never flaunted; neither is it in the flying fingerwork of the Finale. It is there, it must be faced, that Menuhin sometimes sounds at a disadvantage. In the opening theme, he frankly misses notes and smudges some others, though you may think that this is a small price to pay for the elegance and musicianship of his playing.

Technically more secure than Menuhin is Itzhak Perlman, who launches into the Finale with splendid brio. His performance of the work is somewhat grander, more expansive than any of the other players; it does not, however, prevent him from letting it all dissolve into a brilliantly energetic Finale, indeed he makes the Finale seem the necessary resolution of his powerful phrasing into something lighter and more carefree. Even better than Perlman is Pinchas Zukerman, and this is partly because of the clarity and point of the orchestral playing. Though five of the versions discussed are with the London Symphony Orchestra, it is this one which makes the most of the detail without labouring it.

How, then, to choose a final version? Couplings may be some guide: much the most popular are the concertos by Tchaikovsky and Max Bruch, with Tchaikovsky being chosen by Stern, Milstein, and Zukerman and Bruch by Perlman, Voicu, Suk, and Ricci; only Menuhin, of those we have been considering, goes for the other, early Mendelssohn concerto in D minor. So if you want a good performance of Tchaikovsky's concerto to go with Mendelssohn's, then I think the obvious choice is Pinchas Zukerman on CBS — a fine, sensitive, lyrical performance with excellent orchestral playing by the London Symphony Orchestra under Antal Dorati. If you prefer Max Bruch as a companion work, then the field is led by Itzhak Perlman, a touch on the powerful side for so fresh and lyrical a work, but very impressive: this is with the same orchestra, the London Symphony Orchestra, under Previn on HMV. Among mid-price versions, probably the best is Ricci's, with the same orchestra under Pierino Gamba, though I would not commend it above the others, and certainly not above the version by Yehudi Menuhin which I feel comes closest to a complete performance of the concerto. His playing comes in for much criticism, and undeniably in the Finale of this concerto there are places where he is technically less secure than any of the others. But for a performance that responds most fully to the work, to its lyrical elegance, its touching, sometimes rather wistful character, its contrasting high spirits and good nature, Menuhin's is by a good way the subtlest and most satisfying. It is filled with perceptive detail, with delicate strokes, yet it has a lyrical freshness and ease that Menuhin seems to have preserved untainted through all his long association with the work. It is pleasant to be able to suggest that this great if uneven artist is here giving the performance to prize above all others.

Recordings discussed

Ricci/London Symphony Orchestra/Gamba	Decca SPA 88
Stern/Philadelphia Orchestra/Ormandy	CBS 61029
Voicu/London Symphony Orchestra/Frühbeck	Decca SDD 443
Suk/Czech Philharmonic Orchestra/Ančerl	Supraphon SUAST 50546
Zukerman/London Symphony Orchestra/Dorati	CBS 72768
*Menuhin/London Symphony Orchestra/Frühbeck	HMV ASD 2809
Milstein/Vienna Philharmonic Orchestra/Abbado	Deutsche Grammophon 2540 359
Perlman/London Symphony Orchestra/Previn	HMV ASD 2926

© John Warrack

Mozart   *Flute Concerto No. 1, K313*

FRITZ SPIEGL

The story about Mozart's alleged aversion to the flute and his apparent unwillingness to write for it is of course well known; but has, I think, been rather exaggerated, if not misunderstood. It is based on a single passage in a letter to his father: 'I immediately get fed up when I have to write for an instrument I can't abide.' But by the 1790s the old baroque flute of Quantz was beginning to give way to a slightly more sophisticated instrument. It is possible that what Mozart could not abide was the simple, six-holed flute with one key at the bottom for playing the D sharp. But some players already had at their disposal more sophisticated flutes with several keys, including one that extended the range down to the bottom C, a note which Mozart duly uses in the flute and harp concerto, K299. In any case, unwilling or not, Mozart composing music with a pistol held to his head still has the advantage over any mere mortal writing in the white-heat of inspiration.

His works for the instrument date from the late 1780s, that is, round about the three-hundred mark in the Köchel catalogue. Of the three concertos, one, as mentioned, has a harp as fellow-soloist, another is a transposition into D of an earlier oboe concerto in C, and then there is No. 1 in G major. This has an extra slow movement, an Andante in C, which can be used as an alternative to the original middle movement in D major. Herein possibly lies another clue. If Monsieur de Jean did use the simpler baroque flute, which Mozart 'could not abide', he would have found the original, and extremely florid, Adagio rather more difficult to play on it than the far less chromatic substitution Mozart supplied for him. It was a common practice of the time: a kind of after-sales-service, for composers then were treated like plumbers or any other kind of tradesman. If the work they had been commissioned to undertake did not completely satisfy the customer, a free alteration was expected. Nowadays, the C major Andante is always played separately; although Mozart would certainly not have objected to the substitution being made today. However, as the two solo concertos do not quite fill two sides of an LP, most recordings do include the C major Andante as a fill-up anyway.

At present, there are ten versions available, with English, French, Austrian, American, German, Irish, and Dutch, soloists, respectively with various conductors to match. I turned first to the greatest Mozartian among the conductors: the veteran Karl Böhm, conducting the Vienna Philharmonic Orchestra. And sure enough, the opening has a lovely relaxed poise, with nice gentle phrasing and is above all not too fast: a real Allegro *Maestoso* just as Mozart specified. Unfortunately the soloist, Werner Tripp, does not quite measure up to Böhm's backdrop. As soon as he comes in, his slightly flat, curiously lifeless, sound breaks the spell. I know exactly what the soloist is trying to do – and that is, adapt his style to the straight, almost vibrato-free, baroque sound which is all the rage nowadays. It would come off well with a baroque orchestra, for Tripp is a fine player, but against the polish of the Vienna Philharmonic it sounds incongruous. A pity, because he and Böhm between them chose tempos that are ideal and natural.

So I turned to the diametric opposite of straight, classical purity – the throbbing, sexy French flute sound, with its constant, unvarying vibrato. The two available Frenchmen are Michel Debost, with the Orchestre de Paris under Barenboim; and Jean-Pierre Rampal with the Vienna Symphony Orchestra under Theodor Guschlbauer. Debost can play very fast indeed: he gets round the awkward corners at a rare speed. But exciting as it is it did not seem to be characteristic of the piece; so I disqualified him for a start – for speeding in a built-up aria, you might say. Rampal is even more characteristically French. It seems to me that compared with Tripp his style is a little self-conscious, with a lot of *rubato* and a curious leaning on some notes – more in keeping with nineteenth- than eighteenth-century practice. Yet Rampal plays a lovely slow movement, in which the super-expressive French style comes into its own: after all, M. de Jean, or Dechamps (as Mozart called him), was probably a Frenchman – although Mozart also calls him a Dutchman as well as an 'Indian': maybe he was a Frenchman from the Dutch East Indies!

Of the other foreign flautists, one was eliminated by the amazing feat of playing each of the four repeated notes that open the main theme of the last movement with different intonation: a micro-tonal feat which could be of use in Stockhausen but has limited application in Mozart. Of the two English players, Richard Adeney, with the English Chamber Orchestra conducted by Raymond Leppard, was unfortunately not very well served by the recording quality which (on my copy at any rate) fails to do justice to his beautiful tone and sensitive phrasing. The other one, William Bennett, also with the English Chamber Orchestra, but conducted by George Malcolm (on Argo) would have been my first choice had I not been captivated by an unknown, of whom more later. However in the slow movement, Bennett's playing is intense, yet perfectly relaxed and limpid. His *rubato* is always beautifully judged and the little hesitation in the last bar perfectly ravishing in its subtlely. James Galway, whose style could hardly be more different from Bennett's, has quite another idea of *rubato* and rather perversely gives emphasis to what in the context is merely a connecting link – a throwaway

– between more important notes. To me it sounds just like the modern speech fad of ever stressing *the* most unimportant word *of* a sentence so as to give more interest *to* it. Yet, the beautifully-forward, throbbing, vibrant (for Mozart perhaps over-vibrant) unmistakable Galway style is there all right. But he seems almost reluctant to move on to the next note: rather like a speaker who relishes the sound of his own voice so much that he forgets what he is saying. I find it interesting to compare this RCA record of Galway, accompanied by the Lucerne Festival Strings under Baumgartner, with the only slightly earlier 1973 recording on which he is accompanied by the New Irish Chamber Orchestra under Prieur. Here Galway heeds Mozart's express instructions that the *adagio* should be *non troppo* – not too slow; and the effect is most beguiling, instead of sounding rather like a slow bicycle race as it does on the RCA record. But I understand that at the later recording he did not see eye to eye with the conductor on certain matters.

So far I have not commented on the various interpretations by the different artists of those troublesome small notes, the *appoggiaturas* – grace-notes seemingly invented by eighteenth-century composers in order to cause modern players to have fierce arguments, and to keep musicologists and editors in gainful employment. The other movements in Galway's Irish recording are equally delightful. In the last movement, which is a Rondo Minuet of the type Mozart learnt from J. C. Bach, André Prieur and Galway between them hit on a tempo which is sheer perfection, and allows full play to the soloist's effortless articulation and those amazingly nutty low notes of his; and by 'nutty' I mean that they have a nice centre – a kernel – to them, not nutty in the Irish sense. And special compliments to Monsieur Prieur who displays a true Mozart style and should surely be heard more often.

In Galway's RCA recording, poise gives way to speed, virtuosity, and eccentricity, so much that in the first movement the metronome reading between bars varies by as much as twenty per cent. And if you wonder how I determined that, the answer is that I used a 'Tempo-Check', which is a cunning gadget a friend of mine invented: you press a button in time to the music, slowing down or speeding up with the performance, and a digital display gives you an instant read-out of the prevailing metronome speed. So, if you are a Galway-fancier, the earlier version is far superior to the second recording – at any rate, if you prefer Mozart to acrobatics and showmanship. Unfortunately you can only get this record, from Pickwick, through certain chain stores, not from record shops.

For the true Mozartian, my choice would be a record by a flautist whose name was new to me: Wolfgang Schulz, who recorded it for Telefunken in 1977, with Leopold Hager conducting the Orchestra of the Salzburg Mozarteum. This is a performance which has everything. Technique and intonation can nowadays be taken almost for granted but Herr Schulz has more. His vibrato is a variable commodity, which changes as required by the phrasing and is not just a continuous throbbing bleat; and this is well illustrated in the Adagio. The cadenza, not by the soloist but Helmut Deutsch, though perhaps a little long, is in keeping not only with the period but also with the reflective mood of the movement. This recording was made in the great hall of the Mozarteum in Salzburg, so perhaps the spirit of Mozart was not very far away. There is another charming effect in the Adagio when the solo flute is echoed by two more flutes in the orchestra. Two flutes are specified in the score for this movement, but are often substituted by oboes. This is sometimes done for the sake of economy – say if the first flute of the orchestra is playing the solo part and they cannot afford to engage a third player – and is no great crime against Mozart. But it is also done because Alfred Einstein claims in the third edition of the Köchel catalogue that the 'flutes must quite certainly be substituted by oboes' and in effect accuses Mozart of having made a mistake in the score. What Einstein did not know in 1947, but we know now, is that eighteenth-century oboists would as a matter of course be expected to double on flutes, not as soloists but in the orchestra. If you compare Schulz with Galway in his Irish recording, he does not sound quite so effortless, but the phrasing is more Mozartian: there is less tendency to end phrases with a bump on the last note (Mozart loved his shaded-off feminine endings); the tonguing is lighter and dances more and the high notes are more mellow. Schulz reveals what I believe is true Mozart style, elegant but strong and masculine, virtuoso without any suggestion of virtuosity for its own sake.

Note

Since the review was broadcast, Philips (Festivo Series) have made a welcome reissue of a version by another Dutchman, Hubert Barwahser, with Colin Davis 'driving' the London Symphony Orchestra. I use this orchestral players' colloquialism advisedly; for this is early Davis (1963) and he gives the impression of pushing both orchestra and soloist quite relentlessly. Barwahser, a marvellous player, is seldom able to relax, constantly having to scramble semiquaver passages through probably no fault of his own. His excellent taste (apart from a tendency towards pear-shaped bulges in some longer notes) is confirmed also by the stylish cadenzas, which are his own. Unfortunately for collectors of the G major concerto Barwahser is much better in his coupling (the Andante and the D major concerto).

Recordings discussed

Bahwahser/London Symphony Orchestra/ C. Davis	Philips 6570 091
Adeney/English Chamber Orchestra/ Leppard	CFP 40072
Tripp/Vienna Philharmonic Orchestra/Böhm	Deutsche Grammophon 2530 527
Galway/New Irish Chamber Orchestra/ Prieur	SHM 3010
Galway/Lucerne Festival Strings/ Baumgartner	RCA LRL1 5109
Rampal/Vienna Symphony Orchestra/ Guschlbauer	Erato STU 70330
*Schulz/Salzburg Mozarteum Orchestra Hayer	Telefunken 6 42185
Bennett/English Chamber Orchestra/Malcolm	Argo ZRG 910
Debost/Paris Orchestra/Barenboim	HMV ASD 3320

© Fritz Spiegl

Rakhmaninov   *Piano Concerto No. 4*

GEOFFREY NORRIS

My first ever contribution to 'Building a Library' was a review of all the available records of Rakhmaninov's Second Concerto. There were then something like twenty-six versions to choose from. Since then I have covered the Third Concerto, of which I think there were nine versions, and the Paganini Rhapsody, of which there were thirteen. But now that I look at the Fourth Concerto, I find there are only six, and this, I think, is symptomatic of that lack of popular appeal that has always dogged this particular work. One critic at the first performance in 1927 described it as 'long-winded, tiresome, unimportant, in places tawdry . . . an interminable, loosely knit hotchpotch of this and that, all the way from Liszt to Puccini, from Chopin to Tchaikovsky'. 'Cécile Chaminade', the review concluded, 'might safely have perpetrated it on her third glass of vodka.' 'Thinness', 'monotony', 'bombast', 'fluent orotundity' – these tags were all applied to the concerto in those early American reviews. Even Rakhmaninov's close friend Alfred Swan remarked that 'the opening movement . . . is only able to revive some of the images of the past and hold them together by a tried technique'. And indeed the opening theme does have those characteristics that are familiar from Rakhmaninov's earlier concertos – what one commentator called 'the vaulted architecture of phrase, the undercurrent of Romantic sadness, the harmonic solidity'.

But there is far more to the Fourth Concerto than simply an unsuccessful re-hash of old ideas and techniques; for, with the benefit of hindsight, we can see that the concerto is in many respects a transitional work: a link between the rich Romanticism of the works of his mature Russian years – like the Second or Third Concertos – and the sparser textures, the spicy harmonies, the rhythmic incisiveness, the frequent changes of metre that characterize his later works – like the Paganini Rhapsody, the Third Symphony, or the Symphonic Dances. When the Fourth Concerto was new in the 1920s however, a public accustomed to Rakhmaninov's perform-ances of his Second and Third Concertos seemed reluctant to become attuned to these new traits that are seen in embryo in the Fourth; and the caustic reception given to it encouraged Rakhmaninov to withdraw it from his repertory.

He had already had considerable difficulty with the piece. There is some evidence to show that he had contemplated the concerto as early as 1914, while he was still in Russia, but he did not get down to serious work on it until 1926, when a lengthy gap in his by now exhausting annual concert schedule gave him time to concentrate once more on composition. He composed it quite quickly; but when he received the fair copy back from the copyist he was amazed by its length: he joked to Medtner, the dedicatee, that it would have to be performed on consecutive nights, like *The Ring*. He made a number of cuts; but these failed to appease the critics, though Rakhmaninov did have the score published in 1928.

In 1941 he took a further look at the score, made more cuts, altered the piano figuration in many places, rewrote and redistributed the orchestral parts, and so on. He himself recorded it in December 1941 with Eugene Ormandy and the Philadelphia Orchestra. All the recordings considered here use this later version. (That is a slight over-simplification, but I am not going to complicate matters by bothering about minor textural differences between recordings that result from the fact that, even after he had recorded the concerto, Rakhmaninov made further alterations to the score before it was published. Such changes do not affect the substance of the piece.) The six pianists are Rakhmaninov himself, Ashkenazy, Michelangeli, Orozco, Vásáry, and Ivan Drenikov. If, in comparing them, we take the passage leading to the second subject, Drenikov, on Harmonia Mundi, crashes headlong into what should be a magical modulation, marked *p* in the score. In fact, his entire interpretation, with the Bulgarian Radio and Television Orchestra, conducted by Vasily Stefanov, leaves me absolutely cold. The piano playing is almost always heavy and laboured, the orchestra dull and lifeless, rarely responding to the score's many *espressivo* markings. Raphael Orozco, on the other hand, on Philips, with the Royal Philharmonic Orchestra and Edo de Waart gives true *leggiero* playing at the beginning of the same passage, a nice *cantabile* sound for the second subject, and a gloriously hushed key-change, but Tamás Vásáry with the London Symphony Orchestra and Ahronovitch on DG take a rather too languid view of the music.

One of the critics at the first performance of this concerto complained of the number of different musical ideas in it; or, as he put it rather more laboriously, 'new material appeared without the sanction of necessity'. Rakhmaninov eliminated much of this material when he tightened up the concerto for its second version; but there is still quite a diversity of ideas in the two outer movements, and I imagine one of the secrets of bringing off the piece is to gauge finely the tempo changes that these involve. Whereas in the Drenikov performance one can so often see the joins, as it were, things seem to flow more naturally in other recordings, as, for example, when the music has to increase gradually in speed and excitement from a dark and lugubrious passage towards the exhilarating first movement climax. Ashkenazy, with the London Symphony Orchestra and Previn (Decca), do this superbly, but for sheer electricity at the climax

Michelangeli's performance, with sumptuous support from the Philharmonia strings under Ettore Gracis, is hard to beat: his playing is marvellously invigorating and tempestuous.

The second movement is marked *largo*, though Rakhmaninov sets a nearer-to-*andante* tempo in his recording, which is available in volume 5 of RCA's *The Complete Rachmaninoff* (he plays with the Philadelphia Orchestra under Eugene Ormandy, and their 1941 recording is, of course, in mono). Much of this short movement comprises repetitions of the opening theme and all but one of the other five pianists takes it at much the same pace as Rakhmaninov does. The exception is Vásáry. To my mind his reading is so slow that it is on the verge of coming to a halt altogether; and this, as is also the case in the first movement, is a dominating characteristic of the whole performance (which, incidentally, lasts a good four minutes longer than any of the others). I feel there is sometimes tension too, where Vásáry seems (understandably enough) to want to press on, but Ahronovitch and the orchestra seem to hold him back; and his exquisite playing and Deutsche Grammophon's rich recorded sound notwithstanding, I really do not think the music can bear such a relaxed approach. Although Orozco and de Waart by no means rush in this movement, the music has far more momentum; and towards the surging theme at the end of the movement, de Waart sensibly keeps his orchestral forces in reserve, only deploying them all at the climax. This passage, with its prominent string theme which seems to evolve so naturally from the rest of the music, was in fact lifted wholesale from a solo piano *étude-tableau* that Rakhmaninov had written fifteen years earlier but had withdrawn before publication; it comes therefore from his rich, ripe Russian years, and for my taste needs slightly more emotional warmth than Orozco's rather restrained performance gives it.

It is Michelangeli's interpretation – or rather the Philharmonia's, for it is their cellos and first violins that actually have the tune – that I find the most consistently affecting, with its perfectly rounded arch shape of *crescendo* and *diminuendo*, and the subtle *cantabile* reinforcement from the horn at the peak. Michelangeli virtually retires into the background with his supporting piano chords, gently emphasizing the first of each group, and then dying away. Moreover, when we enter the Finale Michelangeli's is the only recording in which the marked *attaca subito* really is a startling *subito*.

I have dwelt at some length on the first two movements, primarily because there is little to choose in the Finale between my three favourite versions: those by Michelangeli, Ashkenazy, and Orozco. All three strike an ideal balance between the robust rhythmic passages and the more relaxed moments of lyricism. I would willingly own (in fact do own) all three; yet my recommended version is Michelangeli's. The recorded sound of his HMV Concert Classics disc may not be as brilliant as Orozco's on Philips or as full-blooded as Ashkenazy's on Decca. But on the other hand I confess I am not too keen on the – to me – over-clever recording technique of the

Philips disc. Although the scoring is often sparse and soloistic, the instruments can emerge from the texture quite naturally and effectively without the help of individually turned-up microphones. I am quite sure, for example, that Rakhmaninov intended the woodwind triplets at the opening of the concerto to provide a rich background of sound for the majestic piano theme, not that they should come at you from the speakers like machine-gun bullets. If you already possess Ashkenazy's masterly record – as you may well do, if you bought my recommended version of the Paganini Rhapsody which is on the back – you probably will not want to, nor do you in any way need to, invest in another. But if you are looking for your first recording of the Fourth Concerto, Michelangeli's is decidedly the most exciting of the lot. In some respects it is idiosyncratic; some, for example, may not like the way he spreads some chords. But it is a performance full of delicate expressive nuance and one of unparalleled verve.

Recordings discussed

Rakhmaninov/Philadelphia Orchestra/ Ormandy	RCA AVM3 0296 (3-record set)
*Michelangeli/Philharmonia Orchestra/ Gracis	HMV SXLP 30169
Ashkenazy/London Symphony Orchestra/ Previn	Decca SXL 6556
Orozco/Royal Philharmonic Orchestra/de Waart	Philips 6598 483 (3 record set)
Vásáry/London Symphony Orchestra/Ahrono-vitch	Deutsche Grammophon 2530 905
Drenikov/Orchestra of Bulgarian Radio and Television/Stefanov	Harmonia Mundi HM 119

© Geoffrey Norris

Ravel   *Concerto for Piano, Left Hand*

CHRISTOPHER PALMER

The Concerto for the Left Hand, one of Ravel's greatest works, came into being as the result of a commission from the Austrian pianist Paul Wittgenstein. Wittgenstein came of a distinguished Viennese musical family who had been on familiar terms with Joachim, Clara Schumann, and Brahms. A pupil of Leschetitzky, he was all set for a career as a concert pianist when the Great War broke out and he lost his right arm in action on the Eastern Front. Undeterred, he set about creating a repertory for himself and commissioned new concertos from a number of distinguished contemporary composers including Strauss, Korngold, Hindemith, Prokofiev, and in later years Britten. However, few of these new productions seem to have met with Wittgenstein's unqualified approval, and Ravel's was no exception. When Ravel first played the new piece through to Wittgenstein (incidentally using two hands) his initial reaction was not encouraging, and, although Wittgenstein claimed that in the course of a few months he came fully to appreciate the concerto's great stature, a dispute between composer and performer over some of the modifications the latter insisted on making meant that, although Wittgenstein played in the world première, Ravel did not conduct. They did however appear together for the Paris première, but in a recording he made around the age of seventy – unfortunately, or perhaps fortunately, not available today – Wittgenstein departs quite substantially from Ravel's printed text. But what Wittgenstein cannot be expected to have recognized in 1931 was that the Concerto for the Left Hand was a personal document of deep and tragic significance. There was an almost Jekyll and Hyde-type schism in Ravel's creative personality which is perfectly reflected, as it happens, in the opposing characters of his two piano concertos. What is more, and significant, they were both written, as it were, hand in glove with one another. But whereas the G major two-hand concerto is a *divertissement*, the Concerto for the Left Hand peers over the abyss. Ravel was an unassuming, dapper little man with a bland air of seigneurial correctitude. All the more may we wonder at the psychic disturbances to which he must have fallen prey in order to be assailed by the kind of traumatic visions he transmits to us in *La Valse*, the *Bolero*, and the Concerto for the Left Hand. For Ravel's mind was one of the most brilliant and most complex in the history of music; and it was the cruellest irony that one who depended as much as he did on the superbly controlled functioning of his brain should have been afflicted by a process of slow but steady mental disintegration of which he himself was a horrified but helpless spectator. I think we may see the Concerto for the Left Hand as a premonition of his horror. Moreover, it is often given to creative artists to see farther into the future than ordinary mortals. The central section of the concerto is a kind of terrifying jackbooted nocturnal march, nominally a scherzo but about as much a scherzo in the conventional sense as the scherzo in Vaughan Williams's Sixth Symphony. Is it I wonder too fanciful to read into this music a prophecy of the coming Nazi scourge?

Be this as it may the fact remains that the concerto is a work of extraordinary power and dark dramatic intensity, and one which makes great demands on the soloist's technical and emotional stamina. But for me the success or failure of a recording of this work depends not only on the soloist but on the extent to which the composer's orchestral intentions have been faithfully realized. The role of the orchestra is exceptionally important here and in a way which places a burden not so much on the players and conductor as upon the recording producer and engineers. It is surely true that when a composer goes to the trouble of writing special effects or subtleties of detail into his scores we have a much greater right to expect to hear them on a recording than in a concert hall where acoustic conditions may vary *ad infinitum*. From the point of view of orchestral balance and integration the Concerto for the Left Hand is fraught with problem areas, and these should be examined first because they are by no means satisfactorily dealt with in all cases.

First the opening. Martin Cooper once related it to the E-flat primordial darkness of the *Rheingold* prelude, but I think of it more in terms of another work of Ravel's which as it happens also has links with Wagner, *Daphnis et Chloë*, more precisely the famous dawn scene which is clearly a descendant of the Rainbow Bridge music. The opening of the Left Hand Concerto is arguably a kind of diabolic inversion of the *Daphnis et Chloë* dawn scene. If there the day breaks in heaven, here it breaks in hell; we are back to my Jekyll-and-Hyde analogy. Instead of that wonderful cello sentence which seems to enfold all the space and peace of the universe, here the black contrabassoon oozes up from the depths like a reptile out of the slime. The opalescent shimmer of the flutes and clarinets is transferred to the opposite end of the spectrum and becomes a murky agitation in the double-basses. Now, if Ravel had wanted a mere amorphous noise here he would have written simply trills or tremolos for the basses, as he did in the opening of *La Valse*. Instead he wrote arpeggiated figures across the strings, and we should hear them as such. If, on the other hand, they are too well-defined, the *misterioso* effect is negated, as at the outset of Ciccolini's recording with the Orchestre de Paris under Jean Martinon (HMV). Conversely, Andrey Gavrilov and the London Symphony conducted by Simon Rattle (HMV) begin with merely a featureless blur of sound. Another point is that when the contrabassoon enters he drags the work's main theme in with him; it may be at the nethermost limit of his compass but it must still be articulated with all reasonable clarity otherwise we cannot recognize it for what it is. And, again, artificial favouring merely distorts our view of the sound picture as a whole.

Only two of the available recorded versions really solve these problems. Julius Katchen's, on Decca, and Alicia de Larrocha with Lawrence Foster and the London Philharmonic Orchestra also on Decca. Good in the Larrocha performance is the *misterioso* effect of the distant horns, like lamps coming ever more clearly into focus as the fog begins to disperse; in some other recordings they sound calamitously too close too early. This entire passage is virtually one enormous dominant pedal-point awaiting the entry of the soloist; and Larrocha, after she has entered magisterially, protracts it still further for a number of bars, before finally settling in the home key of D in preparation for delivering the contrabassoon theme in its fully-fledged form. This main theme causes more recording trouble at the latter end of the concerto, at the point where the orchestra returns after the cadenza. This time the theme is taken up by the bass clarinet as opposed to the contrabassoon, but again in its very lowest register; then it is picked up imitatively by B flat clarinet, cor anglais, oboe, and flute. How difficult it is for any of the lower wind to make themselves heard, for they are marked only *p* and the soloist is already playing quite loudly and in much the same register. On a recording there is no reason not to give them a little artificial help since the 'atmosphere' of the contrabassoon passage is missing here; yet much too infrequently that help is denied them. In Gavrilov's recording, for example, the orchestra is almost totally inaudible after the cadenza. In Anne Quéffelec's (Erato) the bass clarinet cannot be heard: in Larrocha's it can but not the other woodwind entries it sets in motion. With Ciccolini, Martinon, and the Orchestre de Paris everything is as it should be, including the powerful piano entry in the penultimate bar of the score, a point missed by some of the alternative versions.

The central so-called 'scherzo' presents yet another problem of balance. Here, in what Edward Lockspeiser described as a nightmare version of the *Daphnis et Chloë* bacchanale, we find two themes locked in devilish combat in opposing keys – one the bouncy 6/8 theme of the scherzo itself, the other the descending horn motif heard in the introduction, here decked out with sadistically dissonant diminished octaves. At the climax the first is given to muted trumpets, the second to *divisi* strings. Obviously the one must be heard as clearly as the other or else the whole contrapuntal point of the passage is lost. Yet as often as not the muted trumpets *are* lost in the general hurly-burly. In the Alicia de Larrocha recording, however, everything strikes through with exemplary clarity.

Those are three of the most important of a number of similar matters of orchestral texture; no single one of the available records deals with them *all* satisfactorily. And when we come to consider the five respective soloists we are reminded of the old adage that there may be any number of ways of playing Debussy, but only one of playing Ravel. This may be an over-simplification, but the relative uniformity of approach I have noted in listening to these five performances suggests a tangible element of truth in it. The Left Hand Concerto is not, in fact, a work which allows for any great flexibility of interpretation. Tempos are set sure: for instance Ravel slows down the sarabande-like main theme and as a result it sounds laboured instead of majestic. This is where Martinon and the Orchestre de Paris give an exemplary reading. Similarly, were the tempo of the 'scherzo' to be speeded up it would turn into a kind of goose-stepping parody. The character of each episode is, in fact, so inbuilt in the music as to allow for the barest minimum of 'personal' intervention; you play the notes and the music takes care of itself. There are no radical discrepancies between any of these solo performances, and I must confess I have looked in vain for one to knock me sideways. Far more variable, I must emphasize, is the orchestral element. If I take each record in turn, I do not think I can make any one clear-cut recommendation, but I can indicate some personal preference.

I rule the Gavrilov/Rattle version on HMV out of court because the orchestra is so inadequately provided for both at the beginning, end, and elsewhere. Another point is that the saxophone-like bassoon solo in the scherzo is much too prim and proper: this is one of Ravel's strange urban night-club stylizations and should be played as such, just like the trombone solo which follows it. The piano is sometimes spotlit when only playing an accompanying or decorative role, and Gavrilov's is a generally rather rough-and-ready approach: the main theme is a sarabande, a stately Spanish dance, but in this record it sounds distinctly flat-footed. The gain is naturally the scherzo with a much-increased spikiness and venom. The coupling is Prokofiev's likeable First Concerto, and incidentally I am surprised that no-one has thought of coupling the Ravel with another left-hand concerto concerto – Prokofiev's, for example, or Britten's *Diversions* which certainly deserve a modern recording. The generally-favoured pairing is Ravel's other concerto, the G-major, a work as feminine as the Left Hand Concerto is masculine. Nonetheless, Anne Quéffelec plays both, likewise Alicia de Larrocha. At the risk of being considered a male chauvinist pig, I must point out that this piece is a very tricky proposition for a woman's small hands. This was the reason that Marguérite Long never played it, much as she wanted to. The opening solo is particularly difficult in this respect; there are some gigantic stretches, and Quéffelec breaks some of the chords in a way that distorts the melodic line. There are moreover too many imperfections of orchestral balance to make for entirely happy listening. But Quéffelec is a refined artist, and I note many lovely things in her reading: for instance to the pearly delicacy of her playing of the rather Grieg-like figurations which shimmer and glitter around the melody of the second subject when recapitulated in the cadenza. Her orchestra is the Strasbourg Philharmonic conducted by Alain Lombard.

Alicia de Larrocha's orchestral support is a good deal more alert and responsive, but I have to fault Lawrence Foster on his approach to the sarabande. He seems to forget it is a dance which combines elegance with grandeur, and a *marcato e pesante* treatment in this case rules out either. Miss de Larrocha is a more robust player than Anne Quéffelec, but I find the rather lean and stringy piano tone worrying. Yet on the whole it is a satisfying performance very vividly recorded, with some marvellously idiomatic 'dirty' solo trombone playing in the scherzo. The coupling is the G major Concerto with a bonus in the form of the Fauré *Fantaisie* for piano and orchestra.

The Ciccolini version with Martinon conducting the Orchestre de Paris is one of the best. Among its assets are a conductor with a lifetime's experience of French music, and a soloist who understands the peculiarly personal way in which emotion is articulated in Ravel. In the second subject, for instance, Ciccolini brings out all the innate wistfulness and pathos precisely by not indulging in the kind of rubato which the character of the passage might seem to invite. Innocence is no longer innocence when it becomes self-conscious, and there are few moments in Ravel more revealing of the little-boy-lost which in a sense he always was. The effect, too, is exquisite as the cor anglais steals in with the sarabande and the piano laps around it in ripples of soft arpeggios. The main drawback here is that this record is one of a box of ten containing the complete orchestral works of Ravel and cannot be bought on its own.

Perhaps the most consistently satisfying account is also the cheapest – Katchen with the LSO under Kertesz on Decca Ace of Diamonds. Sound-wise it is not quite the peer of its competitors: a lack of depth to the bass means that the dimension of richness and resonance which the bass drum frequently adds is missing. The internal orchestral balance is excellent, and there is one particularly felicitous touch, barely perceptible in any of the other versions, when the viola and cello *glissandos* in harmonics encircle the scherzo theme in the piano like catherine wheels in the sky. Katchen's playing is superb: controlled, aristocratic, by turns poetic and searching, virile and intense. In his first solo his supple and expressive shaping or sculpting of the sarabande is a joy to experience, and so is his virtuoso handling of the brilliant downward cascades which lead into the orchestral *tutti*. No-one should miss this wonderful medium-priced opportunity of acquainting themselves with one of the great masterpieces of twentieth-century music.

Recordings discussed

Ciccolini/Paris Orchestra/Martinon	HMV SLS 5016
*Katchen/London Symphony Orchestra/ Kertesz	Decca SDD 486
Larrocha/London Philharmonic Orchestra/ Foster	Decca SXL 6680
Quéffelec/Strasbourg Philharmonic Orchestra/ Lombard	Erato STU 70928
Gavrilov/London Symphony Orchestra/Rattle	HMV ASD 3571

© Christopher Palmer

Bach   *St John Passion*

PETER DODD

For anyone who, understandably, insists on Bach in English, there are only
two versions of the St John Passion to be considered. The choice between
them is not made any easier by the fact that in each case the crucial role of
Evangelist is taken by Peter Pears, which means that the gospel narration is
sung in both versions with faultless clarity, and with sensitive regard for the
text. There may be many who, like me, prefer the simple and unaffected
delivery of his 1960 version, even though he sounds distanced from us in
King's College Chapel. In the 1972 version recorded in the Maltings,
Snape, his voice has greater immediacy, but he tends to dwell on
momentary effect at the expense of the forward momentum of the story.

In spite of the clear and expressive way in which Peter Pears performs the
Evangelist's part, there are serious reservations to be expressed about the
presentation of the recitatives in both his recordings. In the first place the
speed of the delivery is generally very slow. On occasions this may seem a
virtue, but during the dialogues between Jesus and Pilate, or the long
unbroken stretches of narrative towards the end of the work, such deliberate
declamation can become tedious. Secondly, there is no evidence to support
the use of the harpsichord, still less the use of the organ to isolate the words
of Jesus; Jesus should not be differentiated instrumentally at all. Bach
clearly did not intend this, wishing to stress the humanity, and human
suffering of Christ – 'Behold the *man*', as Pilate says to the crowd.

In choosing between the two English versions, one must look beyond
the Evangelist, as Peter Pears is so good in both. A defect in the earlier one
is the acoustic in King's College Chapel, which unfortunately plays havoc
with the involved textures of Bach's choruses. Parts of the opening chorus,
for instance, sound distressingly confused, and in the crowd, or *turba*
choruses as they are called, the necessarily harsh edges are blurred by the
resonance of the building. No such acoustical problems exist at Snape
Maltings, and the crowd choruses are much more effective, with the
instruments standing out better in their important independent accompani-
ments. Also, in this recording, conducted by Benjamin Britten, the prominent character parts of Jesus and Pilate are authoritatively sung by Gwynne
Howell and John Shirley-Quirk. The other soloists are impressive too, particularly Robert Tear. Another reason for choosing the later of the two

English recordings, is the very slow tempo of many of the chorales in the earlier version conducted by David Willcocks. The chorales were, after all, the parts of the Passion music with which the congregation would most closely identify, even if they did not actually join in the singing of them during the Passion performance. So one cannot imagine that the choir would have sung them at speeds very much slower than the congregation usually did, or have applied as much variety of expression as Willcocks does. All the other versions, particularly the German-language ones, are generally free from such eccentricities in their performances of the chorales.

Except for the employment of all-male choirs in both, the English versions cannot be said to offer many concessions to authenticity, either in style or the use of period instruments. With the first of the versions sung in German, the one directed by Karl Münchinger, we move at least one step nearer what we know to have been Bach's intentions: in this case, the use of the organ as the sole keyboard continuo instrument, not just in the recitatives, but also in the arias. Take, for example, the episode in which the High Priest questions Jesus about his teaching. Dieter Ellenbeck, the Evangelist, fails to command the attention that a story-teller should, as he does not vary his expression very much, and the overall pace of the recitative is still slow. He is not helped by the fact that throughout this particular passage of recitative the cello notes and the organ chords are sustained almost continuously, which makes for monotony and lifelessness. Elsewhere in the Münchinger set, the quality of the singing in the arias is high, as one would expect with Elly Ameling, Julia Hamari, Werner Hollweg, and Hermann Prey as soloists. If the soprano arias are indeed to be sung by a woman, then it would be hard to find a more attractive performance than this of 'I follow you likewise, with joyful steps'. Elly Ameling is in fresh and buoyant form, using vibrato sparingly for expressive purposes on long notes, but on quicker ones leaving her tone pure and limpid. Another noticeable feature of this set is the vital singing of the Stuttgart Hymnus Boys' Choir. In the *turba* choruses, the crowd is well characterized, as is the insistence of the people outside the house of Annas as they question Peter: 'Art thou not one of his disciples?'

The next step in the process of removing the effects of relatively recent tradition, and getting back to the performing practice Bach knew, is taken in the recording directed by Michel Corboz. Perhaps the most important difference between this and the other recordings I have referred to is the way the recitatives are sung. The dialogue in which Pilate asks Jesus if he is really a king includes Pilate's jest 'Was ist Warheit' – 'What is truth?', and ends with his asking the crowd whom he should release, Jesus or Barabbas. The pace at which this scene is played is very much nearer the speed of normal speech than what we mostly hear today in the singing of *secco* recitative in oratorio, though not, it is interesting to note, in comic opera – *The Marriage of Figaro*, for example, or *The Barber of Seville*, where it has always been much faster. The quicker delivery makes for greater clarity, realism, and dramatic interest, without loss of dignity, musical or textual. The crowd's reply, 'Not this man, but Barabbas', is a measure of the precision and vigour of the choral singing in Corboz's recording.

The recitatives have now achieved a pace at which they more easily come to life, although the organ chords are still sustained, and a stringed instrument supports the organ only when a character in the Gospel story is singing – an arbitrary whim quite at variance with eighteenth-century practice. The Evangelist in the Corboz version is Kurt Equiluz, to my mind the most accomplished singer of this part, who also sings it with more appropriate accompaniment in the 1965 recording directed by Hans Gillesberger. If the arias are not as well sung as in the Münchinger version, the chorus in the Corboz recording is generally the equal of Münchinger's, and sometimes has the edge over it. For example, the singing of the 'Let us not rend it' chorus, where the soldiers cast lots for Christ's coat, is very well defined and full of life. This is the only choir in the recorded versions to use women, incidentally.

An aspect of the striving after authenticity which may not be to everyone's taste is the use of boy sopranos and altos for the arias. Even though you may now accept counter-tenors instead of altos, and may indeed prefer them for earlier music, the sound in the alto arias may well strike you as unnecessarily austere. Yet it is undoubtedly what Bach intended, a boy from the St Thomas's School choir (not a counter-tenor, but an unbroken voice) singing the alto arias. In the version directed by Hans-Martin Schneidt, the boy alto is Roman Hankeln. The sound may not be beautiful, in the sense that many international contraltos or mezzos of today can be said to have beautiful voices, but I think it fair to ask whether it is right that Bach's treble and alto arias should be subjected to the interpretive approach of singers who are more at home in nineteenth-century lieder or opera. It was, after all, not until 1839, when Mendelssohn revived the St Matthew Passion, that women started to take part in performances of Bach's choral music. Perhaps only boys' voices can let these arias speak for themselves, without the varnish of applied expression. The style of singing in the aria 'Es is vollbracht' – 'It is finished' – in the Corboz recording might be appropriate to the performance of one of Brahms's *Serious Songs*, but its over-expressive emphasis, however well-intentioned and deeply-felt, only does a disservice to Bach.

In the Gillesberger version, the alto soloist is from the Vienna Boys' Choir (I take it to be the same boy who sings both arias, although no names are given): he is, if anything, rather more austere than Roman Hankeln, although personally I prefer the Vienna boy's relatively sparing use of vibrato. In the case of the treble solos, my preference is for the Vienna boy's unaffected but very musical phrasing. Besides using only men and boys as soloists and in the chorus, Schneidt and Gillesberger have both made similar efforts to use only the resources available to Bach, by using instruments of the period or replicas of them, and a small number of performers. If the chorus and strings of the orchestra are kept down to the numbers we know Bach had, and if the right instruments are used, then the balance problems so often experienced with present day performances go a long way towards solving themselves. It should be possible, for example, in the first chorus, to hear the woodwind as well as the strings and voices, and in both Schneidt's and Gillesberger's versions the textures are very clear, though Gillesberger takes it at a more deliberate tempo, one which is more successful in conveying the heavy feeling of apprehension at the tragic events which are to follow, as well as the sense of glorification which is uppermost in the text. I find both Gillesberger and Schneidt admirable but, whereas the Schneidt chorus has an excellent sense of style – nearly all the varnish has been removed – Gillesberger offers us more. The orchestral playing is superb, with Nikolaus Harnoncourt's Concentus Musicus playing their baroque instruments with great artistry, and the recording balance ensures that they are properly heard. Also, Gillesberger has obviously considered the text very carefully and how best its significance can be conveyed without going outside the musical conventions of Bach's time. If one considers a *turba* chorus, for instance, the one where the crowd call for Christ's crucifixion with the one word 'Kreuzige', the Regensburg choir under Schneidt sing with accuracy and clarity, but the effect is a little tame for a crowd bordering on hysteria. Bach did not intend realism in such choruses to the degree that, say, Britten did in the crowd choruses in *Peter Grimes*. Nevertheless, it is possible, without distorting the music stylistically, to give it a malign edge and savage momentum more appropriate to the context, as the Vienna chorus under Gillesberger manage to do.

When it comes to the bass and tenor arias, the soloists in the Schneidt version have, perhaps, the more distinguished voices, but the performances in the Gillesberger recording are generally more satisfying. For me, a critical factor in deciding between these two versions conducted by Gillesberger and Schneidt is the Evangelist, and here I have no hesitation in preferring Kurt Equiluz. If you prefer a more deliberate declamation than I have been advocating, you may well prefer Heiner Hopfner who sings in the Schneidt version; personally, I find his voice rather colourless, lacking the ardent and vibrant communicativeness of Equiluz.

A firm recommendation to a first-time purchaser of St John Passion is not easy; everything depends on the language and authenticity questions. If you have to have the work sung in English, then the Benjamin Britten recording must be your choice on Decca. If you want it in German, and want women soloists in the arias, then I think, in spite of my preference for Kurt Equiluz as Evangelist in the Corboz version, that the best overall performance is Münchinger's, also on Decca.

Of the two sets that have boy soloists, the recording on Telefunken, directed by Hans Gillesberger, was really a remarkable achievement in 1965, and set a new standard for authentic Bach recordings; to my mind it remains unsurpassed. It occupies two-and-a-half discs. The recording directed by Hans-Martin Schneidt comes from DG Archiv. This version, like the Gillesberger one, takes up only five sides, but the sixth side of the Schneidt set is enterprisingly filled with four pieces which Bach composed for the second performance of the St John Passion: two arias and two choruses.

Recordings discussed

In English:

Pears/Choir of King's College, Cambridge/ Philomusica/Willcocks	Decca GOS 628–30
*Pears/Wandsworth School Choir/English Chamber Orchestra/Britten	Decca SET 531–3

In German:

*Equiluz/t'Hoff Choir/Vienna Concentus Musicus/Gillesberger	Telefunken FK6 35018
*Ellenbeck/Hollweg Prey Choir/Stuttgart Chamber Orchestra/Münchinger	Decca SET 590–2
Equiluz/Lausanne Vocal Ensemble/Lausanne Chamber Orchestra/Corboz	Erato STU 71151
Hopfner/Regensburg Cathedral Choir/Colle- gium St Emmeram/Schneidt	Deutsche Grammophon Archiv 2565 108–10

© Peter Dodd

Haydn   *The Creation*

TREVOR HARVEY

Having only six versions to deal with is very agreeable, not because it makes
the final recommendation any easier but because I do not have to discard
ruthlessly the less recommendable candidates. First, one or two general
observations. Five of the half-dozen versions of *The Creation* are sung in
German. Fair enough; but since the work is so loved by English choruses
and their audiences, I think it a pity that there is not a good, representative
version in English. The one that *is* in English, whatever its merits, is
scarcely representative of the general run of English choral singing, since it
is from King's College, Cambridge.

A second point is that three recordings employ five soloists, a different
pair singing Adam and Eve in the last part from those who sing Gabriel and
Raphael in the rest of the work. This does not affect my choice in the least.
Haydn himself never expected more than three; nor would any choral
society engage two extra soloists for Adam and Eve – the Treasurer would
see to that! And on a gramophone record there is no point in it unless the
voices are different enough to be easily and recognizably different. I should
add that one set, Karajan's on DG, names *six* soloists; but that is because
the tenor, Fritz Wunderlich, died before the recording was completed.
Luckily, he had recorded all the arias, and Werner Krenn stepped in for the
recitatives, very successfully.

The oldest recording – it first came out in 1960 – is that by Horenstein
on the Turnabout label and, not surprisingly, it does not compete in sound
with later issues; nor is the performance very distinguished. But two things
do surprise me. One is that the bass, in his very first recitative, not only
sings flat but sings a G flat on the word 'void' – 'and the earth was without
form, and void'. I think it is well established that the correct note, despite
the G flat that soon follows in the accompaniment, should be G natural; and
certainly it is on every other record. The other thing that depressed me was
the stolid, four-in-a-bar, tempo for 'The Heavens are telling', another thing
I thought had disappeared years ago.

In the newest recording, with the Philharmonia Orchestra and Chorus
under Frühbeck de Burgos, the chorus sings with a light gait; and how
much more delightful it sounds than Horenstein's stodgy tempo; and it is
typical of most of the other conductors. The soloists in the HMV version

under Frühbeck de Burgos are Helen Donath, Robert Tear, and José van Dam.

Robert Tear is also the tenor in the only English version, from King's College, Cambridge; but good as he is, I thought him slightly less impressive than in the later HMV version. John Shirley-Quirk, on the other hand, is in outstanding form, especially in the aria 'Rolling in foaming billows' with a particularly beautifully sung G major arpeggio at the end. Nobody else makes such poetry of it and indeed most basses make it stick out like a sore thumb. However, the orchestral detail is not very clear, certainly not when compared with the best of the other versions, but that, I am afraid, is King's College Chapel. Heather Harper is the excellent soprano soloist. The choir sings with its usual spirit and Sir David Willcocks conducts admirably. If you particularly want the work in English, then you have no other choice. My only warning is that you must accept the acoustic of the Chapel.

One would expect Dorati to give a good account of the work, since he has become such a Haydn expert, but it has too many small defects to come top of the list. He is one who has different soloists for Adam and Eve. Benjamin Luxon as Adam certainly sounds very different from Kurt Moll, who sings in the rest of the work; but Moll's voice is very heavy and he cannot sing quietly, so that I prefer most of the other basses on these records. To prove this you only have to listen to John Shirley-Quirk in 'Rolling in foaming billows'. Yet if I would prefer Luxon to sing the whole bass role throughout, the opposite is true of the sopranos. Lucia Popp in the main part sings really beautifully, whereas Helena Döse is most unhappy as Eve. Her intonation is all too often suspect; she is not plain flat – it is just this note and that that is below pitch. The whole performance is much less than my favourite.

Karajan also has a quintet of soloists; and here the sopranos and basses are clearly differentiated. You could hardly confuse the cool, almost detached, singing of Gundula Janowitz with the far more womanly Eve of Christa Ludwig: likewise the voices of Walter Berry and Fischer-Dieskau. Karajan starts with a slightly romantic approach to the opening prelude, the 'Representation of Chaos', taking it rather out of its period, though I need hardly say that the playing of the Berlin Philharmonic Orchestra is superb throughout. However, one need not fear; any tendency towards over-expressiveness on Karajan's part disappears once the singing begins.

One thing I looked for in vain in all the recordings is what I regard as the right tempo for that fine soprano aria 'On mighty pens' which should, I submit, go swiftly at two-in-the-bar, not four. I am supported in this view by no less an authority than Donald Francis Tovey. What is more I have tried it in performance and it comes off marvellously. Karajan's tempo is about typical of all the others. Gundula Janowitz produces a very beautiful sound: but I think that if the mighty eagle soared aloft on wings as slowly beating as that, it would fall to earth like a wing-clipped hen. But in the end I rule Karajan's version out because it is the only one that is cut. There are two cuts in the third part, one of only twelve bars which is so short as to be pointless; the other, often made in concert performances I admit, is the whole of the last four pages in the vocal score of the duet between Adam and Eve – 'Graceful consort'. There is plenty of room for it, as all the other recordings show; and if I buy a record of a work I do want it complete.

My two remaining conductors make me happiest of all – Münchinger on Decca and Frühbeck de Burgos on HMV. Frühbeck's is the most recent issue and Münchinger's dates from 1968, though you would never guess it, and his orchestra is the one which perhaps most of all has Haydn's music in its very blood, the Vienna Philharmonic. They are totally in style in the 'Representation of Chaos' but, of course, one of the first great moments one looks forward to is the choral outburst on the word 'Light' at 'Let there be light, and there was light'. I thought this very impressive on the Frühbeck/HMV set. The preceding recitative is sung by José van Dam with the Philharmonia Chorus and Orchestra, and is followed by a very dramatic outburst where the much older Münchinger/Decca set, with Tom Krause and the Vienna State Opera Chorus is rather less telling. Elsewhere, too, the other recording of my chosen two, the Frühbeck on HMV, sounds perhaps just a little cleaner in texture for it is hardly fair, after all, to judge a work of this length and variety by one loud chord!

I think the answer is, if you already have the Münchinger, stay with it; if you have no recording at all then consider Frühbeck de Burgos. These are the casts. Münchinger on Decca has five soloists, all good, but with voices a little lighter. Gabriel is beautifully sung by Elly Ameling, Uriel by Werner Krenn, and Raphael by Tom Krause, who is very fine indeed. Adam and Eve are Robin Fairhurst and Erna Spoorenberg. The Vienna State Opera Chorus, at that time trained by the famous Wilhelm Pitz, and the Vienna Philharmonic Orchestra are both superb.

The Frühbeck de Burgos/HMV version contents itself with three soloists, all of them first class – Helen Donath, Robert Tear, and José van Dam – with the Philharmonia Orchestra and Chorus, the latter trained by Norbert Balatsch. I must also especially mention the inventive continuo playing by Leslie Pearson.

Recordings discussed

In English:
*Harper, Tear, Shirley-Quirk/Choir of King's   Decca SLS 971
College, Cambridge/Academy of St Martin-
in-the-Fields/Willcocks

In German:
Coertse, Patzak, Ernster/Singverein der Gesell-   Turnabout TV 34184–5S
schaft der Musikfrende/Vienna Symphony
Orchestra/Horenstein

*Ameling, Krenn, Krause/choir/Vienna Phil-
harmonic Orchestra/Münchinger

Decca SET 362–3

Janowitz, Ludwig, Wunderlich, Krenn, Fischer-
Dieskau, Barry/Singverein der Gesellschaft
der Musikfreunde/Berlin Philharmonic Or-
chestra/Karajan

Deutsche Grammophon
2707 044

*Donath, Tear, van Dam/Philharmonia Or-
chestra/Frühbeck

HMV SLS 5125

Popp, Döse, Hollweg, Luxon, Moll/Brighton
Festival Chorus/Royal Philharmonic Orches-
tra/Dorati

Decca D50D2

© Trevor Harvey

Bartók   *Sonata for Two Pianos and Percussion*

ARNOLD WHITTALL

Béla Bartók is invariably cited as the composer most directly responsible for the more percussive treatment of the piano in the twentieth century; and even an early piece like the *Allegro barbaro* shows that he could make real music out of an approach in which the traditional kind of romantic lyricism finds little place. Yet with Bartók we are still a long way from the use of drumsticks on the strings and the tapping of the frame – means which more recent composers have adopted in order to transform the piano into a fully-fledged member of the kitchen department. Bartók still calls for a virtuoso brilliance in the execution of scales and arpeggios, and the richness of his textures, based on chords with many doublings and repetitions, recalls Liszt, or even Brahms. But it is to the earlier nineteenth century, to Beethoven, that we must turn for the principal influence on the form, as well as the character, of the Sonata for Two Pianos and Percussion. In works like the *Waldstein* and *Hammerklavier* sonatas, percussiveness certainly has a part to play. Yet what really matters is that forms are both elaborate and clearly defined, and the character of the music is direct and intense, whether the mood is cheerful or melancholy. Such are the qualities of Bartók's sonata: and novelties in the sphere of tone colour matter much less than the strength of the formal organization and the inventiveness of the thematic argument.

The work is far from easy to play or record. The engineers have the difficult task of providing a vivid sound which is not over resonant, and of giving the two percussionists a degree of independence without under-mining the composer's evident intention that the pianos should be very much the senior partners. In the score Bartók included a diagram which places Piano One on the left and Piano Two on the right. The percussion is placed behind and between the pianos with the pitched instruments – xylophone and timpani – at the front of the group. Bartók excluded softer pitched instruments like vibraphone or tubular bells: instead, the emphasis is on a variety of drums and cymbals, with a triangle and a tamtam. So only the xylophone and timpani have the capacity to contribute directly to the thematic and harmonic material of the sonata.

In view of the composer's declared intentions about the lay-out of the ensemble, fidelity to those intentions, and the actual quality of the recorded sound, may seem even more important than usual. The recorded quality of the five available versions on which this comparison is based certainly varies enormously, and, in the main, according to age: two of the records are more than ten years old, one is four years old, and the other two have been issued more recently. Even so, as I have already stressed, the work is much more than a mere sonic showpiece: so in the end it's the quality of the interpretation which matters most, and all but one of these performances have things to commend them. The exception is the more than twelve-year-old performance by György Sandor and Rolf Reinhardt on Turnabout, which is for the most part simply too dull and under-characterized seriously to challenge later issues.

The first of the sonata's three movements is the largest and most ambitious. It begins with a slow introduction which offers a roll-call of all the principal tone colours of the work, with the important exception of the xylophone. There is a gradual increase of weight, pace, and excitement, until the main *allegro molto* is reached and the pianos hammer out short phrases punctuated by peremptory timpani strokes. It is a powerful opening, moving steadily from brooding intensity to almost feverish activity. Its forceful concentration is very evident in the performance on DG in which the pianists are Alfons and Aloys Kontarsky with percussionists Christoph Caskel and Heinz König. The clarity and breadth of the DG sound are superb, and the interpretation is very Beethovenian, suggesting menace rather than mystery from the very outset. The vital necessity for a recording which captures the full dynamic range of the music – and, indeed, of the performance being recorded – is clearly demonstrated if the Kontarskys are compared with Dezső Ránki and Zoltán Kocsis on Hungaraton. Their performance begins in a manner which contrives to be both sluggish and lightweight; and although the interpretation improves greatly later on, the recording remains rather dry and shallow. This, too, is the only record to reverse, whether by accident or design, the stereo placing of the two pianos indicated in the score.

Once the *allegro* is launched, its basic energy and drive are rarely in doubt. Yet there is important contrasting material, with such markings as *tranquillo* and *dolce*, and the players have the difficult task of balancing these more restrained episodes, and the various crucial fluctuations of tempo, against the prevailing, hectic propulsion. Martha Argerich and Stephen Bishop-Kovacevich, on Philips, with their two Dutch percussionists, Willy Goudswaard and Michael de Roo, manage the first such transition with great skill and, when they reach the *tranquillo*, their soft, gentle tone is particularly attractive. Yet the contrast with what precedes it is not so extreme as to run the risk of disrupting the flow of the music.

A little later on, there is a passage marked *vivo*, at a faster tempo than the immediately preceding one: and the players must begin it softly, in spite of the intensity of the contrapuntal argument raging between them. The music rapidly gets louder, and there is a slight broadening of the tempo just before the abrupt climax. Then the *dolce* material returns. Somehow all these twists and turns must be conveyed without exaggeration, and the Decca recording, with Eden and Tamir, manages it successfully. This version also has the advantage of two expert British percussionists, Tristan Fry and James Holland; but the eleven-year-old recording does show its age in places. We get sharper detail from Argerich and Bishop-Kovacevich, and while the contrasts are even stronger, they seem just a little less self-conscious.

Bartók uses the all-important marking *dolce* again at the start of the slow movement where, after a short, very soft introduction by the two per-cussionists, playing cymbals and side drums, the pianos state a charac-teristic Bartók melody. It moves within a narrow compass to begin with, but expands in volume and register in its central phrases before subsiding to a very soft conclusion. The challenge here is not one of technical difficulty, but the need to strike a proper balance between expressiveness and restraint. Too much warmth is as unsatisfactory as too detached a tone; and while I find Ránki and Kocsis almost too casual and nonchalant, the Kontarskys are too loud and unyielding, sounding stern instead of restrained. Argerich and Bishop-Kovacevich strike a better balance, catching perfectly the necessary blend of mystery and magic, while on Decca Eden and Tamir also shape the phrases sensitively and expressively. The central part of the movement brings a striking contrast between slowly moving octaves in one piano and short flickering figures in the other, in which the xylophone eventually joins. It is a dramatic effect, but one which can easily be overdone by too sudden a *crescendo* and *accelerando*, so that the rest of the movement becomes something of an anticlimax. Ránki and Kocsis, for example, seem too hasty and over-excited to convey the full tension of the central episode, and in my view none of these performances manages an absolutely ideal treatment of it. The Kontarskys are nevertheless most impressive – predictably, perhaps, in view of the way in which they seize on the darkest and most disturbing aspects of the work for special emphasis. The excellent quality of the DG sound, too, ensures that the very great range of tone and touch which this otherwise quite straightforward movement requires is fully evident in the Kontarskys' version. There are passages in the Philips recording where Argerich and Bishop-Kovacevich do not seem to have been recorded with comparable sensitivity, but they nevertheless shape the slow movement with great skill. There is nothing studied about the result, yet equally clearly, nothing has been left to chance. As for the DG recording, its virtues are also very apparent at the end of the slow movement, where the long sustained chord in the first piano really does continue sounding to the very end. Then the Kontarskys proceed to launch the Finale with a formidable combination of weight and energy.

No other version quite matches the impact they make here, and one or two are distinctly tame. But of course there is more to this movement than forceful energy. As the Kontarskys proceed, it is clear that they are not as aware as Argerich and Bishop-Kovacevich of all the wit and charm with which the music abounds. Like the Kontarskys, Eden and Tamir lack some of the necessary spring and bounce, and the Decca sound does not reveal every salient detail. There is plenty of excitement, however, and the strong contribution of the percussionists makes for some lively interchanges in the more contrapuntal episodes. Ránki and Koscis also have some nice touches of characterisation in this movement, with well-balanced tempos, and the rather dry recorded sound on Hungaraton is less of a disadvantage in the Finale. Their basic tempo is if anything a little on the fast side, but no important detail gets lost. This Hungaraton recording of the sonata, coupled with the sonata for solo violin, is part of that company's complete Bartók edition, and is available at medium price. Eden and Tamir have a coupling which appeals rather less to me – Poulenc's two-piano sonata – but in any case the now rather old Decca recording cannot really be considered for a full-price recommendation today. The Kontarskys on DG are superbly recorded, and have a most generous and appropriate coupling in the Concerto and Sonata for Two Pianos by Stravinsky. Argerich and Bishop-Kovacevich on Philips are marginally less sympathetically recorded, and have a more contrasted coupling, Debussy's three pieces *En Blanc et noir*, and Mozart's Andante with five variations, K501. On grounds of interpretation, though, I have come to feel that Argerich and Bishop-Kovacevich, simply by being less predictable and more relaxed, reveal a richer range of moods and textures than the Kontarskys. So even if the work emerges as slightly less powerfully symphonic in their performance it is a marvellously responsive and authoritative interpretation ideal for repeated gramophone listening. The humour with which they point the ending of the Finale, the blend of spontaneity and control which they display, confirm Argerich and Bishop-Kovacevich as a clear first choice.

Recordings discussed

Sandor/Reinhardt/Schad/Sohn	Turnabout TV 34036S
Eden/Tamir/Holland/Fry	Decca SXL 6357
Ránki/Kocsis/Petz/Marton	Hungaraton SLPX 11479
*Argerich/Bishop-Kovacevich/Goudswaard/de Roo	Philips 9500 434
A. and A. Kontarsky/Caskel/König	Deutsche Grammophon 2530 964

© Arnold Whittall

Brahms   *Clarinet Quintet*

ANDREW KEENER

If it was the clarinettist Anton Stadler who provided Mozart with the incentive to produce his masterpieces for the instrument, then we have Richard Mühlfeld to thank for doing much the same for Brahms towards the end of his life. Brahms was fifty-eight; he had drawn up his will the previous year, and there is little doubt that he was now tending to reflect on past glories rather than future ones. It is a melancholy state of mind, accurately mirrored in the opening bars of the quintet which, by one of those unaccountable, instinctive things, we know to be in the minor key, even if the theory books tell us it could just as easily be in the relative major. This autumnal view of Brahms's Quintet does not seem to be one that's shared by everybody, though. There is little gentle reflection about the opening as Vladimir Řiha and the Smetana Quartet play it and, to my way of thinking, not a lot of magic either. If Brahms leaves out phrase marks, the players seem to say, then he must have meant *staccato*, and a pretty robust sort of *staccato* at that. It is also worth remembering that when the two violins take up the theme in octaves soon after the start, the marking is *piano espressivo* followed by a gradual *crescendo* to *forte* a few bars later, although you would never guess as much from the Czech performance; perhaps the overbright recording is partly to blame for the sense of brashness. Much more relaxed, and also more concerned with beautiful phrasing, sound-quality and range of colour are Richard Stoltzman and the Cleveland Quartet on an RCA record of unusually wide dynamic range. Immense care over detail has obviously gone into this performance. There is one unmarked drop to *pp* in the exposition which will sound inspired to some and hopelessly self-conscious to others, and the Quartet's way of squeezing notes instead of beginning and ending them cleanly could easily be dismissed as an irritating mannerism; the short notes after the rests, for instance, are really far too long. I must say, though, that I find the sincerity behind all this beautiful playing very convincing – it seems that the players feel the music this way, and so, I suggest, for the time being, does the listener. Like three of the other versions, they observe the exposition repeat in the first movement. It matters little either way, I think, although it is always nice to hear music like this a second time through. I should point out, though, that there is a good deal of sniffing during this Cleveland performance but, once again, I cannot say that it worries me. Before I leave the first movement I must refer for a moment to the performance by Gervase de Peyer with members of the Melos Ensemble on HMV. Somehow there is an instinctive 'rightness' about everything these players do; nothing is overstated, yet never is there any suspicion of dullness or routine. When clarinet and viola fine down their tone to accompany the tune on two violins, it is done quite effortlessly as if by some unspoken agreement; after all, when this version was recorded in the mid-1960s these musicians had been working together for many years and their founder-clarinettist is as much a part of the group as anyone else. Much of this movement is open to a wide variety of interpretations, and part of the reason lies with Brahms's tempo markings, which are often vague if not downright ambiguous. At the furthermost point of the development (and you cannot get much further from B minor than D flat major) the marking is *quasi sostenuto*, literally 'almost sustained'. What Brahms probably wants here is a smooth, joined approach which still allows the rhythm heard at the beginning to come over clearly. As this rhythm serves as the acommpaniment for quite some time, it is also important that it should be kept lightly sprung. The members of the Vienna Octet with Alfred Boskovsky on Ace of Diamonds also offer one of the most forthright accounts of the first movement on disc, but what saves it from the sense of ruthlessness to be found in the Supraphon account is the beauty of sound, a gentleness in the lilt and an equally gentle *rubato*. This means however, that they have little choice but to relax the tempo for this *quasi sostenuto* section, and even though they find their way back to the original speed very discreetly, and the rhythm is never overpointed, there is a noticeable loss of concentration. This Decca recording dates from the early 1960s, and it solves the tricky balance problems in this work more successfully than one or two of the more recent versions. In the same music with Karl Leister and the Amadeus Quartet on DG there is no slackening of concentration, even if the *rubato* gives the initial impression of a slower tempo, and thanks to the rhythmic life there is a sustained, relaxed feeling over the whole passage. Once again, the players make a beautiful sound. Karl Leister's rich tone is well matched with that of the Amadeus Quartet, and this is something which sounds especially good when the clarinet doubles the first violin at an octave's distance; how strange it is to think that it was this resourceful approach to sonority which once earned Brahms the label 'turgid'.

When he marked the second movement *adagio* instead of *andante*, Brahms knew what he was about. The apparently simple nature of the opening melody offers a great temptation to take it all in one breath, in both senses. Béla Kovács on Hungaraton does just that, with the exception of one rather awkward bump. His tempo is nearer to a flowing *andante* than to an *adagio*, and the result is an unfortunate squareness of phrasing. He has also reckoned without the rather complex syncopations in the quartet accompaniment, combinations of tied triplets and ordinary quavers, often set against each other, and, paradoxically, the impression left is one of confused and lumbering inner part-writing. The lines fail to flow at all at this walking pace. I also do not care for the first violin's rather weepy style of *portamento* when he takes over the melody, not for the fact that it is all very loud. Richard Stoltzman and the Cleveland Quartet play a degree or two slower, enough to avoid each of those falling patterns sounding the same as each other; enough also to phrase the opening melody as Brahms marked it, that is, with a break after each group of three notes. This takes a fair amount of skill to accompany as there are no such breaks in the string parts, but the Cleveland Quartet is very sensitive and the syncopated lines flow far more easily than on the Hungaraton disc. Stoltzman can accompany very nicely, too, and his playing is beautifully controlled. The central section of the slow movement is a rhapsodic episode in the Hungarian style; it is marked *più lento* not, I suspect, so much because Brahms wanted a greatly slower tempo, but in order to give an idea of the improvisatory feel of the music, complete with cimbalom imitations on *tremolando* strings. The Vienna Octet plays this episode very beautifully, but I am not sure if the resulting tranquillity, especially from Boskovsky, is quite what Brahms had in mind; after all, tranquility is regained with the movement's recapitulation and in the Decca performance I feel that the 'return to normal' has been too easily won. The playing is very refined but seems to miss some of the tension and drama. Yona Ettlinger and the Tel-Aviv Quartet, on the other hand, obviously relish the wild Hungarian element to the full. With agogic pauses and darting characterization of the arabesque figures it almost sounds as if they are improvising; all the more pity then, that they sound rather as if they were recorded in a padded cell.

The success of the third movement depends largely on the relationship between the opening *andantino* and the faster section which follows. In fact this is a transformation of the opening theme, and Brahms used a similar sort of device fourteen years earlier in the same movement of his Second Symphony. Here, though, the problem stems from the fact that, unlike that of the symphony, this *presto* is not a middle section at all, as there is no strict return to the theme in its opening guise, apart from the last eight or nine bars, that is. The secret, then, lies with delicacy of touch rather than with any greatly faster speed, so that when the opening version of the melody returns very briefly at the end, it is at practically the same tempo as it was before. Vladimír Říha and the Smetana Quartet, for example, end the *andantino* at a tempo light years away from what follows; any return at the end to the gracefulness of the opening must inevitably face them with a very tricky problem indeed. With Gervase de Peyer and the Melos Ensemble the playing is neat enough to be thought of as *presto* but at the same time it is steady enough for no sudden application of the brakes for the tiny coda. And once again, de Peyer proves himself an accompanist of great sensitivity; a single repeated note is all he has to play, but there is a 'presence' about each one, however quiet.

The Theme and Variations which make up the Finale are among the most tightly-knit that Brahams wrote, an impression heightened, deliberately no doubt, by the fact that only the second half of each is repeated. More striking, though, is the theme's faint resemblance to that of the first movement – no mere accident, it would seem, in the light of the work's final pages. The theme itself is played in a suitably forthright way by Karl Leister and the Amadeus Quartet. The second variation is the only really agitated one of the set, with restless syncopations and close harmony, so it is important that its disturbed nature is not underplayed. Here, I think, that for once their refinement tends to undermine the force of the music. The syncopations are smoothed out and Leister's beautiful tone seems to convey little of the stress not far below the surface. There is altogether more urgency behind the syncopations from the Cleveland Quartet for Richard Stoltzman. So far it has been the beauty of their sound that has been so impressive, but they are well aware that there are times when something more is required of them.

As I have already suggested, these variations have been leading us full circle and by the fifth, the mood is remarkably close to the melancholy opening of the work, and indeed for the first time since the first movement we are back in compound time; it is something we have been feeling in our bones for some time. The variation itself runs straight into the coda – a shadowy version of the quintet's first theme; there must not be too much preparation for this, as the whole point is to induce a faint stab of surprise. Daniel Benjamini is the distinguished viola player with the Tel-Aviv Quartet, and his playing in the fifth variation is beautifully shaped, but I think it a pity that by slowing up he warns us of the impending coda just a little too early on. Gervase de Peyer and his Melos players leave any holding back until the last minute and their account of the coda is, I think, the most poignant simply because it is the most directly stated and approached; the sense of surprise as variation moves into coda is in the music itself. As with the whole of their record, it is the sense of fine musicians who have an intimate understanding of each other's playing that seems especially suited to this work; they have no time for overstatement. There is a catch though. At the moment you can only buy their version in a box of other Melos recordings with the Mozart and Weber Clarinet Quintets, the Beethoven Septet, and the Schubert Octet. First-rate value, but you may well have some of the recordings already, so I would urge HMV to re-issue the Brahms separately. Until they do, or in case they never do, Richard Stoltzman's sensitive account with the Cleveland Quartet is available on RCA, and I would place this hardly below the Melos, even if they do sometimes get carried away by the beautiful sounds they are making.

Note
An Argo disc, issued since this review was broadcast, is by Jack Brymer
with the Allegri String Quartet. The quality of sound is beautiful and
Brymer's vibrato is gentle, and warms, but does not saturate, his tone. For
many, though, the first movement may seem over-hasty; it moves at quite a
pace, and in this movement, and elsewhere, much of the nostalgic element
of the music is lost, admirably played and consistent as it is.

Recordings discussed

Boskovsky/Members of Vienna Octet	Decca SDD 249
*De Peyer/Melos Ensemble	HMV SLS 5046
Říha/Smetana Quartet	Supraphon SUAST 50677
Leister/Amadeus Quartet	Deutsche Grammophon 139 354
Kovács/Bartók Quartet	Hungaraton SLPX 11596–600
*Stoltzman/Cleveland Quartet	RCA RL 11993
Ettlinger/Tel-Aviv Quartet	Oiseau–Lyre OLS–R 146
Brymer/Allegri Quartet	Argo ZK 62

© Andrew Keener

Brahms   *Horn Trio*

JOHN WARRACK

As a young man, Brahms played the horn; and one need only listen to the orchestration of his symphonies and concertos, not to mention the serenades, to hear what a love for the instrument he retained all his life. Traditionally it was associated in the minds of the German Romantics with the open air, with forests and the very German emotion of *Waldeinsamkeit*, solitude in the woods; so it is not surprising to learn that the opening melody of his Horn Trio came to him when he was walking in the woods one day near Baden-Baden. The gentle, lulling opening as played by the violinist Eduard Drolc and the horn player Gerd Seifert, with Christoph Eschenbach, on DG is characteristic of the smoothness and the tonal warmth of their performance, one which makes it the more extraordinary that Brahms could have accepted alternative publication of the work with viola or cello replacing horn. This is all the more surprising as he insisted on the use of the Waldhorn, the natural hand horn and not the then novel valve instrument. I think few players would now want to use the hand horn, and indeed at one of the earliest performances, with Clara Schumann playing the piano, the horn player refused to do so. Mme Schumann also left a note in her diary suggesting that this was a work that was hard to understand; and another of the recordings currectly available indicates something rather more profound and reflective at the start. This is by the Melos Ensemble, on Oiseau–Lyre, Emanuel Hurwitz, violin, and Neill Sanders, horn, with Lamar Crowson as pianist. They give a very sensitive phrasing to the simple, separated progression of chords under the melody. Those are two of the outstanding performances of the work currently available. Another, on Decca, has a distinguished team, Itzhak Perlman, Barry Tuckwell, and Vladimir Ashkenazy who also respond to the reflective, indeed elegiac opening of the work, for this was music written under the blow of the death of Brahms's mother. It is, as Clara Schumann realized, not at all a straighforward piece: for instance, Brahms does not open with a sonata form movement but with what is really a rondo, repeated statements of the opening theme with two episodes. It is essential for the players to respond to a sense of emotional growth that is expressed more by contrasted reflections upon this theme than by thematic development; and the Decca players, Perlman, Tuckwell, and Ashkenazy, are particularly good at this, when they take the music forward from its opening statement. A fourth record of particular interest is one rescued from a broadcast, one of the last made by Dennis Brain, and his partners were Max Salpeter and Cyril Preedy; without dominating the music, it is very much Brain's beautiful playing, the warmth of his artistry, and the celestial ease of his phrasing that we find at the centre of the performance.

I have now mentioned the four most rewarding performances on record of Brahms's Horn Trio: Brain, Salpeter, and Preedy (BBC); the Melos on Oiseau-Lyre; Seifert, Drolc, and Eschenbach on Deutsche Grammophon; and Tuckwell, Perlman, and Ashkenazy on Decca. I found the Decca team especially good at taking the growth of the music forward from the opening as in the second of the two episodes, in which Brahms uses the same music, as if it were also a second subject, but subtly enrichens it. The richness of the emotion in the episode makes the subsequent return of the theme more poignant in its simplicity, a contrast made effectively by Seifert, Drolc, and Eschenbach. Compared with Tuckwell, Perlman, and Ashkenazy, they are more demonstrative, more responsive to the dynamic markings, and this makes the return to the theme after the second episode still more moving. They succeed in indicating that this is a more enigmatic work than it seems. Certainly the Scherzo has caused puzzles. Four of the sleeve note writers for these records speak respectively of 'marvellous zest and nobility', 'half-revealed menace', 'Brahmsian humour', and 'thoughtfulness'; and the performers in turn seem equally divided. The Melos take it deliberately and seriously, but they are perhaps a trifle dull in their impulse. As before, this is not a straightforward scherzo, with its irregular phrase lengths and its odd secondary motives thrown into the ring; Tuckwell, Perlman, and Ashkenazy, take it much more fiercely, regarding this Scherzo as no joke at all. Better still, though, are Seifert, Drolc, and Eschenbach; they share the view that this is rather a grim Scherzo, but they are menacing rather than hectic, and later produce a beautiful balance to this in their sorrowing, lilting rhythm for the contrasting episode which Brahms inserts into the Scherzo itself. Theirs is beautiful playing of some subtle and complicated music.

With the *adagio mesto*, the mood of darkness that has produced this half-concealed complexity comes out into the open, and Brahms writes a heartfelt elegy for his mother; though even here the uneven phrase lengths, fives and fours, and their overlapping, give the music a peculiar density. The Melos players are not as fluent as they might be, and their attack is not ideal; there is a better sense of continuity, of easy movement between phrases and contrasting textures, in the Decca version, with particularly sensitive piano playing by Ashkenazy. In the disturbed middle section, moving across a number of remote keys, there is some especially fine playing from Dennis Brain in the BBC record, but the stepping up of the tempo is a little overdone – Brahms only marks it *un poco* ('a little'). Yet despite the richness and urgency of Dennis Brain's playing in particular, I feel that Seifert, Drolc, and Eschenbach control this difficult passage more effectively and with more consistency. At the end of the *Adagio*, Brahms softly interjects a version of a folksong. 'Dort in der Weiden steht ein Haus', which one feels in the context of this work, mourning his mother, must have had some personal significance, and he then turns it into the theme of his Finale. Is this last movement, I wonder, a clearing away of the previous darkness, or is it still charged with a good deal of bitterness and grief? The Brain/Salpeter/Preedy performance is very fresh and warm; that of the Melos in similar vein but not so interesting. Tuckwell, Perlman, and Ashkenazy, regard the music as very far from blowing away all those gloomy mists in an easy gesture, and they drive the music hard; it is an intelligent approach and these players offer a consistently thoughtful view of the music, responding with sensitivity to its often strange shifts of mood and its unusual structures: the unusualness of the structure is very much bound up with the expression, of course, and they have really considered the way in which the two interact. Nevertheless, some of their effects are a little overdone, almost too conscious, and I think myself that the hectic pace of that Finale is a case in point. Seifert, Drolc, and Eschenbach share their view but can still allow themselves a bit more room without losing their sense of the inexorable. They, I feel, give the fullest performance of a beautiful, elliptical work – more than their nearest rivals, Tuckwell, Perlman, and Ashkenazy, and more than the agreeable but rather too light performance by Neill Sanders, Emanuel Hurwitz, and Lamar Crowson, of the Melos Ensemble. The BBC record, by Dennis Brain, Max Salpeter, and Cyril Preedy, is in a category of its own – a warm, affectionate reading, especially valuable for its preservation of Brain's wonderful artistry, if not so well recorded, inevitably, and not so thoroughly studied as might have been the case if the artists had recorded it in studio conditions. But it is a record the collector might well like for its special qualities; as in its day, was the beautiful old record by Dennis's father Aubrey Brain with Busch and Serkin. However, of the modern selection available, the version that is the most complete in interpretation of the Trio is the one by Gerd Seifert, Eduard Drolc, and Christoph Eschenbach on Deutsche Grammophon. The trouble is that this is part of a fifteen-record set of Brahms's complete chamber music. I wish DG would issue this fine performance separately; until they do, and unless you feel like paying for a complete set, a far more practical recommendation is Tuckwell, Perlman, and Ashkenazy on Decca.

Recordings discussed

Brain/Salpeter/Preedy	BBC REB 175
*Tuckwell/Perlman/Ashkenazy	Decca SXL 6408
Melos Ensemble	Oiseau–Lyre SOL 314
*Seifert/Drolc/Eschenbach	Deutsche Grammophon 2740 117

© John Warrack

Dvořák *String Quartet in F, 'American'*

ANDREW KEENER

Dvořák never tired of pointing out that melodies in his so-called 'American' works were simply 'impressions and greetings from the New World' rather than quotations from the folk music he found there. True, there is a lot of pentatonic writing in this music, to say nothing of the 'Scotch snap' and the use of syncopation. But these characteristics are as much Slovak as American, and if we look only a little further into Dvořák's stay in America, we shall see that he was becoming more and more unhappy in the bustle of New York, finding contentment in the little Czech village settlement at Spillville in Iowa. He arrived there in June 1893, and within a few days he had sketched out the complete score for the F major Quartet. Dvořák had been writing chamber music for some time, but things had rarely gone so smoothly. 'Thanks be to the Lord God', he wrote at the end of the sketch. 'I am satisfied; it went quickly'. I have gone into all this because I think it is a state of mind that is reflected right from the quartet's opening bars – and incidentally they are modelled on the beginning of Smetana's Quartet 'From my Life'. Further proof, I think, that Dvořák was still very much a Bohemian abroad, and the Smetana coupling is one that has been taken up by two of the five available versions. So I think there is little to be gained by underplaying the bracing character at the start of the quartet where the two youngest ensembles are at opposite poles. It is not so much that the Medici Quartet on HMV ignore or distort any markings in the score, it is just that, generally, they react more acutely than anyone else to a *crescendo* here, or an accent there. They dig into the music more trenchantly, with dotted rhythms brisk and tight, and they are very sensitive to important modulations. Perhaps they are even a little over-sensitive sometimes, bringing such details to our attention when, thanks to Dvořák, we would notice them anyway. After the first loud music, for instance, the cellist and the viola player highlight the brief return to the home key with a little *portamento* as if to say 'Here we are back home again!' At the same time it is obvious that the Medici Quartet love this music – there is a real sense of joy in what they are playing which I like very much.

Equally sensitive, but less emphatic, is the young Panocha Quartet on a Supraphon disc which at the time of writing, is about to be deleted. They have been together, so the sleeve-note tells us, since 1968. They must then have been very young indeed, as we are told that six years later their average age was a little more than twenty. Their playing occupies a narrower dynamic range than that of the Medici Quartet, even though they are just as attentive to the markings themselves. Even so, I am not sure this soft-grained approach does not bring with it some lack of a strong pulse, an appropriate emphasis now and again. This is noticeable right at the start when the cellist enters with his pedal note at the end of the first bar. From the way he plays it, I doubt if you would guess that the note is written twice; it is a sturdy 'short-*long*', but he makes it glide in almost tentatively.

More generous of tone (perhaps a little too generous when, for all their beauty of sound, they should be playing *pianissimo*) is the Italian Quartet on Philips – a version which has stayed at full-price since its first release in 1968. And quite rightly too: the recording still sounds well and it is naturally balanced, which is an especially good point in a work where first violin and cello share so much of the rhythmic and melodic interest. All five quartets play the second subject of this movement quite a lot more slowly than the 'in tempo' marking implies, and this is all very well: to play this reflective music fully up to speed would sound brisk and insensitive. But there must be a reliable pulse all the way through, and if you take the exposition repeat you move with one bound from A minor back to F major. So if the return to the opening is to sound natural, the music should have regained the original speed. The Italians, with thirty-five years' experience behind them, grade this return with faultless judgement. At no point is there any sudden gear-change, yet neither is one too aware of the gradual *accelerando*. The playing is beautifully blended and they are one of the two ensembles to take the exposition repeat (the other one is the Panocha Quartet). Of the two versions on DG the one by the Prague Quartet has, I am sorry to say, been deleted, leaving the Amadeus as DG's sole representatives of this work. I must say I am rather sorry it had to be this way around, for the Amadeus strike me as being rather out of sympathy with this music – at any rate, they sound to me to be on less than top form Norbert Brainin's *vibrato* occasionally sounds overwide, his intonation even unsteady. This is a great pity when you remember how inspired a leader he can sound. Before they cross over into the development, the second subject starts off slowly, becomes slower still, and then of course has to regain the tempo pretty suddenly to meet the music on the other side of the double bar. Peter Schidlof's playing of the important viola tune a little way into the development raises a tiny problem of text. Unlike all the other appearances of that theme, where there are two short semiquavers at the end of each phrase, the viola part has a dot after the first of the pair of notes, making it slightly longer. Most versions tend to ignore this, or, as Schidlof does, they make a sort of compromise. Without becoming too academic, I would account for the difference in notation by saying that on each side of the viola's statement of the tune, the first violin and cello play it *fortissimo* and in rather troubled harmonic surroundings, whereas in between, the viola plays it to a *pianissimo* accompaniment in the relative calm of a major key. So Dvořák clearly wanted a difference in character which he emphasized by altering the rhythm just slightly where he gave it to the viola. The Medici Quartet are the only group to sound convinced by this, and their violist's legato phrasing makes the cello version of the theme just afterwards sound splendidly tough. The Medici cellist then goes on to prepare the imitative writing with tremendous conviction, although if you are annoyed by the sound of wood on string, you may want to steer clear; yet the playing is wonderfully passionate and sensitive.

The mood of the second movement takes less kindly to such vigorous treatment, and in the words of the authority, John Clapham, 'strongly suggests that Dvořák's thoughts were turning towards his homeland with those feelings of nostalgia which came upon him so frequently when he was in America'. Dr Clapham's choice of the word 'nostalgia' is significant, for true nostalgia isn't drooling or mawkish but something altogether simpler and more private. The Medici offer some beautifully refined playing, with sensitive accompaniment of the cello melody soon after the opening. Even so, I am not so convinced by the two violins' rather over-sweet sound, especially when they are playing in thirds, since if any writing needs to be simply expressed, then this does. The Italians play it all with a purity of tone that is positively breathtaking, and where necessary there is great intensity too. Their tempo is slower than most, and it is a tribute to their skill that they have no trouble sustaining the line. Even so, the measured speed brings a rather literal feeling to the opening accompaniment from second violin and viola. I for one was too conscious that it is only the viola that plays the gently rocking figure while the second violin sets up a discreetly syncopated rhythm on the one note. Played just a notch faster, I'm sure you would get the effect Dvořák intended – of *both* instruments playing the same figure in parallel; the sound is undeniably beautiful and the phrasing marvellously judged but the Janáček Quartet on Decca Ace of Diamonds, whose tempo is not too different from the Medici's, somehow draw less attention to the mechanics and manage to convey more of a relaxed sense of movement. A matched pair of violins is essential here and the two players of this Quartet sound truly one. They strike a tempo and style which seems to me just right. I had better warn you though, that if tape edits (if that's what they are) bother you, there are several dotted about.

The third movement is a vigorous Furiant with an accented second beat placed so as to sound for all the world like the first. Its five sections, which alternate two ideas, make up a rather stop-go structure which can sound a bit fragmentary – or, if the players are sensitive to the varied scoring of each section, it emerges as the lively and resourceful, even mischievous piece that it is. The Italians are ideal in this movement, with strong, firm accents and a suitably rustic sturdiness – over-refinement has little place here. What is even more impressive though, is their characterization of the quieter music. Here and there, Dvořák gives one player a slightly different dynamic marking from his colleagues; between the viola and cello in the second section, for instance, it is the cellist who has the *pianissimo* tune, but Dvořák marks the spiky viola accompaniment a degree louder at *piano*. I suspect this is not so much because he wanted the accompaniment to sound louder than the tune, but in order that the rhythm would be kept firm and prominent. I always think this movement shares a lot in common with the Scherzo of Beethoven's 'Harp' Quartet: both, it seems to me, are very much a swift journey over rugged landscapes.

In the Finale, a light touch and the ability to relax are just as important as a ready response to the more vigorous moments. The Amadeus Quartet are trenchant enough, but they completely miss the point in the gentle music after the repeated accents. Apart from a few *sforzandos*, it is marked *pianissimo*, but you would never guess this from the well-fed sound of the first violin, and there is a nasty little jab halfway through the melody. Nor, I think, would you guess from the rather sickly *vibrato* that the marking was simply *dolce* – sweetly – when the music drops unexpectedly into A flat.

The Medici players are just as exciting and altogether more buoyant; the music fairly bowls along. And the quiet sense of joy at the change of key (bar 69) is as affecting as it was when I first heard it. After a repetition of the opening theme of the Finale we come to a chorale-like episode in which, says Dr Clapham, 'We can perhaps imagine Dvořák improvising on the little organ of the St Wenceslas Church at Spillville'. The episode starts off imitatively, dissolves briefly into the busier texture preceding it, and then becomes more earnest, more expressive, and homophonic. The Medici Quartet start off without *vibrato*, then with the homophonic answer the tone suddenly becomes infused with colour, and very beautiful it sounds on this record. They show us one way of playing the 'Chorale' episode. The Janáček Quartet, more experienced and mature, add something special. They use *vibrato* for both halves of the chorale, but in the second half it is of a different, tighter kind, so that the music takes on a more private withdrawn quality.

The Janáček Quartet, on Decca Ace of Diamonds, is all you would expect in terms of naturalness, warmth of expression, and maturity. If the recording now sounds a bit dated (it was made in the early '60s, and the cello tends to boom a bit), it is nevertheless a good medium-priced bargain. I am also much taken with the Medici Quartet's HMV account – they obviously love this music, and if, at the moment, some of their responses to it sound a little over-eager, then I think it is a fault on the right side. But then I turned to the Italians again, and this really is musicianship and ensemble playing on the highest level. Stylistically it is pure without being in any way sterile, and the twelve-year-old recording still sounds as fresh as ever.

Recordings discussed

Janáček Quartet	Decca SDD 250
*Quartetto Italiano	Philips SAL 3708
Panocha Quartet	Supraphon 111 1683
Amadeus Quartet	Deutsche Grammophon 2530 994
Medici Quartet	HMV ASD 3694

Bach *Suites for solo cello BWV 1007–12*

ROBERT DONINGTON

The cello suites of Bach, it seems to me, are an extreme example, a very extreme example, of something you do find in music from time to time. I mean that kind of rarification down to the bare essentials of which the string quartet is the best and most developed type. So many different qualities can be found in a work of music. All that glamour of power and colour and kaleidoscopic richness which can go into a fine symphony or tone poem is one thing: Mahler, say, and Elgar, and above all, Richard Strauss. It is completely valid and there is no question of its being only the sauce, or the dressing, or the garnishing; it is a most moving and essential element in that kind of music, along with the themes, the harmonies, the structure, and in every sense the patterns. But in a string quartet, on the other hand, there is so very much less of this kind of exciting contrast in the actual sounds. That brings us back all the more purely to what the patterns are saying; and so far from losing anything significant, we gain another sort of musical experience which can be incredibly inward and rewarding. It is neither better nor worse but it is certainly different.

If we think of Bach's music for the unaccompanied violin, that is a vast scaling down even compared with the string quartet, but at least Bach used every possible virtuoso resource the violin is capable of, and that is quite a lot of resourcefulness. In the cello suites, he does not really do that, though I agree that they are wonderfully written for the instrument. Yet there is not one movement in the cello suites which is like that grand Chaconne in D minor for the violin, for example, where the double-stopping – multiple-stopping, I should really call it – gets so complicated. There are indeed some chords in the cello suites, but the foundation all through is really just melody with the harmony implied and not very often sounded. That is a tremendous challenge to all three partners, the composer, the performer, and the listener.

Bach the composer has given us a fantastic display of sustained melodic invention, but I do think the success of it depends in quite unusual degree on whether the performer can get it across to the listener. Apart from beauty of tone, there is really nothing left to fall back upon except an inspired sense of line: phrasing, articulation, dynamic ups and downs, and a thousand little stretchings and *rubatos* and easings of the tempo which are implied in the notes but not of course written into the notation. Those implications have got to be spotted by simple good musicianship on the one hand, and by profound sympathy for the style on the other.

In the noble batch of available recordings, I do not think there is one which does not score reasonably high on good musicianship, but when it comes to sympathy with the style, I am not so sure; in fact, I am not so sure at all. Let us take as an example the great Casals, still regarded by many people as the absolute summit, and I do not say they are wrong if we are thinking of sheer genius for the instrument. No one could equal him at his prime for greatness as a string player, excepting Kreisler on the violin. But in the matter of Bach playing, I should say that Kreisler was not really in the picture at all, and that though Casals had, and has, a great reputation for it, he was very much in the nineteenth-century tradition. Thus, with what we now understand about Bach's performing style, we may feel that the opening Prelude of the first suite played by Casals (HMV), for example, is magnificent, but it is not Bach. The same applies to the Allemande which follows.

Of course, you have to allow quite a lot for the fairly old recording, in mono, of course, and not so very hi-fi, but actually it is not the quality of the sound I am thinking of; rather, it is mainly the extreme rubatos and tempo distortions, perfectly acceptable in themselves if only they were really growing out of the music. But they are not. They are growing out of the world in which Casals himself grew up: the world of the romantic concerto. Above all, the interpretation as a whole is conceived on too big a scale. Or, if you prefer, 'big' in the wrong way: concerto 'big'. The real bigness of the music cannot get through that way; it just gets overlaid. I think you would see what I mean if you were to listen to the same passage played by Tortelier (HMV), who is certainly everything for our generation that Casals was for his. Tortelier has just the same sort of gift for sheer string-playing, and the same immense vitality and sensitive ear, and also the same sort of glow, radiance, and joy in the music. But equally to the point, so far as Bach-playing is concerned, or any baroque music-playing, come to that, Tortelier has a lightness of touch which does not overlay the music. The whole conception is best described as transparent. There are just as many bold *rubatos* and dynamic nuances, but the difference is that they grow out of the music, and that is what makes them so beautifully right. In the opening Prelude of the first suite, Tortelier gives, I think, a shining example of letting the music tell you what to do.

Casals and Tortelier are the two brightest stars of my collection, and Casals shines not at all with the right kind of light for my judgement, but Tortelier pleases me very much because of his greater sympathy with the style. However, he is not trying to reproduce a literally authentic sound as Bach might have heard it. Harnoncourt, who is, has a fine and well-earned reputation for going deeply into original sonorities and principles of style, and I attach great importance to that. But there are problems.

One is that great uncertainties inevitably remain about what it really did sound like at the time; and I have my own doubts whether the cello sounds which Harnoncourt produces on his very interesting recording entirely resemble anything which could have been normal in Bach's day. I find it quite tubby at the bottom, though it is certainly more resonant at the top; and I do just wonder how far this is likely to be authentic coming from a period so supremely successful in constructing instruments of the violin family. On the other hand Harnoncourt has a wonderful knowledge of the stylistic considerations, and a very fine feeling for them. His phrasing and his nuancing all sound so natural to the music, and though I do not think he has the genius of my two afore-mentioned stars, and though I do not myself get the same joy out of his playing as I do from Tortelier, Harnoncourt's authentically orientated performances (Harmonia Mundi) certainly deserve the most favourable consideration, and I think a very few bars of the first Prelude make my point. His tempo is faster, which I find quite agreeable, and he has also tuned down a semitone under the prevalent delusion that this was the standard pitch in Bach's day, although Arthur Mendel has amply shown that early pitch was variable and as often up as down on ours.

Yet I think Harnoncourt here makes a pretty convincing show of authenticity and is still better in the Prelude of the Second Suite, a sombre piece. And this he plays sombrely, which of course is absolutely right. Always let the music tell you what to do. The chords at the end of this particular movement, by the way, are written as such, but were meant, I think, to be played arpeggiated. There is plenty of good phrasing, too, and a very excellent consistency of mood and sound in the following Allemande, and that is one of Harnoncourt's virtues throughout his recording. The other aspect of that is just possibly an inclination to be too monotonous. When, for example, he moves from the Prelude to the Allemande in the Second Suite, there is not an awful lot of difference to contrast the two. Still, Harnoncourt livens up rather gorgeously for the ensuing Courante. Another virtue that generally obtains with him, though not always, is the excellence of the tempo. There cannot be anything more important than tempo for a good, not to mention an authentic, performance. He adopts, perhaps, a rather slow tempo, though a good lilt, for the Second Suite's Sarabande, and that is just where so many Bach performances fall down, through being too slow and too earnest in the slow movements. They sound much grander, I think, if you keep them moving on a bit. Casals with his solemn temperament had rather a failing that way, whereas Tortelier shows once more his joyful spirit.

Somewhere between Tortelier's stardom and Harnoncourt's search for authenticity, I would tend to put the fine group of cellists whose available recordings of the Bach suites I have not so far mentioned. The famous Czech virtuoso, Miloš Sádlo (Supraphon), for example, was a pupil, and remains an admirer, of Casals, though he has a very distinct individuality of his own. He is an immensely forthright player, with a tone of somewhat metallic brilliance which is intrinsically, as I think, unsuited to Bach, and makes the interpretations sound not so much of the nineteenth as of the twentieth century; and that, in my book, means taking them not nearer to but farther away from our twentieth-century appreciation. Sádlo's is very remarkable cello playing indeed, and many people will like it very much, but I do not, because it has a kind of remorselessness, an overbearing quality, which I find quite unsympathetic to Bach's spirit. If we consider the Third Suite, all the movements sound similar in this rather heavy vein, except for the Sarabande which sounds very heavy and quite beyond my tolerance, at any rate. Henri Honneger (Telefunken) is another imposing cellist broadly in the Casals tradition, but I think considerably nearer to the spirit of Bach than either Casals or Sádlo. I still do not feel that all his quite decided effects and contrasts grow very immediately out of the music. There are plenty of them, and monotony is not the problem here, but they are rather on the massive and self-conscious side, so that they sometimes seem to me to disturb rather than enhance that all-important sense of line. Honegger has a powerful manner, shown at its best in the Sarabande of the Fifth Suite.

A very sympathetic cellist in the French tradition of Pierre Fournier and Tortelier, rather than the assertive school of Casals and his followers, is Maurice Gendron (Philips), who has plenty of bite and indeed of assertiveness where required, but also a great adaptability to the genuine requirements of the music. He is heard to good advantage on a particularly well-recorded set, and he strikes me as a very fine Bach player. He is in fact my runner-up. His playing may be just one degree less sensitive and poetical, I think, when you compare it with Tortelier, yet some might well think of it as the other way round, and it is certainly a pretty fine matter of taste. Surely in Tortelier we find, particularly in the Prelude to the Sixth Suite, that same last touch of inwardness and refinement, almost a hint of tragedy, of tragic intensity in the actual sound, which so often gives to Menuhin his still unrivalled quality on the violin. Tortelier is my first choice, for that reason among others. But while I am on the subject of the actual sound, there is one odd little problem, in that the last suite (No. 6) is scored for a cello with five strings: a perfectly ordinary cello except that an extra string is requested a fifth above at the top. The suite can be managed on four strings, but it does sound quite a lot more natural on the five strings intended. A very talented young American cellist, Frederic Zlotkin, uses a five-stringed cello, but his performance is not available on disc. He also improvises a lot for free ornamentation, which is another novelty in these modern days – and this is certainly effective, for example, on the repeats of the Sarabande. Even so, I come back to the genius of Tortelier (HMV) with Maurice Gendron (Philips) a very admirable second, in fact a very near thing indeed.

Recordings discussed

*Tortelier	HMV SLS 798
Casals	HMV RLS 712
Honegger	Telefunken EX6 35345
Harnoncourt	Harmonia Mundi HM 381–3
Sádlo	Supraphon 111 1702
*Gendron	Philips 6700 005

Chopin   *Twenty-Four Preludes*

BRYCE MORRISON

Franz Liszt was, characteristically, among the first to appreciate the astonishing range and quality of Chopin's Twenty-Four Preludes. For him they were, 'quite special compositions . . . admirable in their variety, they contain the skill and substance that are appreciated only after careful study. The music is spontaneous, brilliant and fresh. They have the freedom and spaciousness characteristic of works of genius'.

Liszt's tribute at once hints at certain cardinal qualities. Chopin's audacity, for example which enabled him to write self-sufficient preludes which preface neither fugues nor anything else. He also wrote scherzos which are far from jocular, *études* which transform basic technical problems into tone poems, and sonatas which are certainly not sonatas in the under-stood sense. His waltzes and nocturnes are brilliantly imaginative reworkings of tired and flavourless forms, and his polonaises and mazurkas emerged recharged with subtle as well as fervent patriotic life.

However, few works suggest Chopin's scope, or daring, as completely as the Twenty-Four Preludes. Although many were written before 1836 the majority were composed in the years 1838–9, the time of Chopin's celebrated stay in Majorca with his mistress George Sand. Majorca proved far from an island idyll and Chopin's stormy temper was provoked by appalling weather, fraught nerves, and ill health. Visits to the island's three most celebrated doctors were not reassuring. 'The first said I was dead, the second that I'm dying and the third that I'm going to die – and I feel the same as always', wrote the irritable composer from his damp cell in the monastery of Valdemosa. Not surprisingly many have been quick to hear a morbid and feverish state of mind in the more savage or resigned numbers but it is important to realize that for every morose or ironic prelude there is at least one flight of lyric intensity, wit, and charm. Chopin's moods zig-zag from one extreme to the other and it says much for his exceptional mastery that the overall result should somehow remain clear cut and unified.

It is this coherence and unswerving sense of assurance that characterizes Maurizio Pollini's truly wonderful recording of the Preludes. Time and again he provides a new sense of possibilities, and gives a new meaning to tired terminology – to technique, for example. With Pollini you cannot separate ends and means – the technique *is* the expression. His evenness and poise remain outside the range of all but the finest artists and the poetic result is correspondingly fresh and novel in its cool perfection. In the first Prelude in C major, for example, his playing is fluent, natural yet finely detailed and shows all the ease and flexibility of a true master. All the cobwebs of tradition, of exaggeration or self-consciousness, I think, are swept aside by Pollini's refined and exhilarating yet unaggressive confidence. There is an inner serenity and calm, too, beneath such outward energy and superfine pianistic command and even Chopin's most powerful and impassioned rages never tempt this pianist into incoherence. Few could equal Pollini's massive technical resource in the boiling, glittering cascades of No. 16 in B flat minor, yet even here there is an unmistakable sense of the music's formal clarity and logic. A more dangerous and inflamed view of this same prelude, a view willing to sacrifice coherence and even accuracy for sheer spontaneity and a wild, spine-tingling bravura comes from Martha Argerich, one of the world's most impulsive, fire-eating virtuosos fully capable of changes of pace and momentum scarcely less remarkable than the music itself. However, in calmer waters such as the familiar Prelude No. 4 in E minor Miss Argerich snatches confusedly at the music's climax and, clearly, the calm and dignity of a Pollini or Murray Perahia is not for her. At the same time her reading of No. 10 in C sharp minor is as whimsical and sparkling as even the greatest Chopin lover could wish.

There is great consistency if not Martha Argerich's irresistible fire from Murray Perahia. His reading is no less characteristically poised and lucid. Perahia can be poetically evasive when confronted by Chopin's darker moods, as in No. 2 in A minor, for example, but his elegant phrasing and understatement never degenerate into indifference, and in the nocturne-like Thirteenth Prelude, he floats Chopin's *cantabile* line with fine grained tone and unfailing clarity. In the central episode of the Prelude No. 13 Alicia de Larrocha takes a bolder view of Chopin's rapidly shifting harmonic palette than Perahia. Miss de Larrocha paints in vivid primary colours and although she often fails to hold one's attention in the manner of the finest Chopin pianist such as Cortot or Pollini her pianism is pungent and of course formidably articulate and professional. At the same time in the more rapturous, passionate Preludes such as No. 17 in A flat, Alicia de Larrocha seems oddly lethargic when compared to Cortot's brilliantly coloured and ardent response. She commences No. 21 in B flat, too, in an oddly leaden manner, and at the opposite pole to Cortot. Mention of this great pianist, who died in 1962, brings me to one of the Preludes' most legendary interpreters and it is deeply gratifying to find his incomparable reading back in the catalogues once more. In the Preludes at any rate Cortot's erratic pianism (people are said to have come from miles around to hear his wrong notes!) rarely obscures his poetic intention. His *rubato* may seem more fulsome or even tear-jerking than we are accustomed to today, his de-syncronization of the hands a relic of an obsolete tradition yet in boldness, colour, and imagination he leaves most of his rivals far behind. I can think of no other pianist but Cortot who could project No. 12 in G sharp minor with such rhythmic life or catch the cross rhythm at the end so precisely. Compared to Cortot, the Czech pianist Ivan Moravec sounds neutral and lethargic in the G sharp minor Prelude (No. 12) whereas Cortot's vitality is everywhere in evidence. There is a sheer joy in recreation and a rich polyphonic sense that often seems virtually unknown to today's players. Then there is Cortot's performance of No. 16 and a unique impetus and command that will silence for ever facetious comments concerning his weak technique. To be quite candid I do not know a more rhythmically acute performance, from Joseph Lhévinne, Martha Argerich, Pollini, or anyone else. Pollini may be more technically exact, but if you are looking for the keenest sense of Chopin's brilliant fury then Cortot is your man. Certainly he gives what must be one of his most brilliant recorded performances here.

Compared to Cortot's sort of musical verve Claudio Arrau in his set of the Preludes sounds stiff and elaborate. Those Preludes such as No. 7 in A, for example, calling for the simplest lyric grace are apt to become weighty and graceless experiences indeed. He pays little court to the Gallic or Parisian side of Chopin's make up, though he is entirely authoritative and individual in No. 14 in E flat minor, that mysterious precursor of the Funeral March Sonata's finale. Ashkenazy in his recent and very distinguished set of the Preludes generates no less breadth and dignity yet his approach is altogether simpler and less emphatic. Ivan Moravec is also impressively fiery and enigmatic in the same Prelude but as I have already suggested some of his readings are oddly perverse, notably No. 9 in E where he takes a tentative and unstable view of Chopin's processional *largo*.

To consider yet another pianist, I am not convinced that Daniel Barenboim's surprisingly low-keyed performance shows him at his most commanding or stylish. Many of the more agitated numbers are bathed in a moonlit wash of sound which although beautiful in itself hardly suggests the music's urgency, its full spectrum of colours and moods. Remote and gently lulling rather than stimulating, Barenboim fails to respond to the turbulence and ardour of so many other artists. Geza Anda, too, a sophisticated stylist for whom beautiful tone matters supremely creates an increasingly tame and salonish impression in his recording though he's much more idiomatic than Rudolf Kerer whose pianism shows the Russian school at its least sensitive or subtle.

Returning to Pollini after these readings one encounters another world of musical perception and perfectly gauged responses. His performance is so unfailingly beautiful and so successfully recorded, that you hardly notice his lack of an encore. Martha Argerich, in common with Murray Perahia, Barenboim, and Arrau, offers us the little posthumous Prelude in A flat and the ravishing and isolated Prelude in C sharp minor, Op. 45. Cortot also includes the Op. 45 Prelude and Alicia de Larrocha and Ashkenazy respectively round off their recordings with the Berceuse and a Ballade and Waltz.

First choice is a hard matter and I must say that out of the versions of the Preludes at present available at least seven provide, in their entirely different ways, an individual yet authoritative sense of Chopin's genius. Of these the finest seems to be by Vladimir Ashkenazy (Decca), Alfred Cortot (World Records), Martha Argerich (DG), and Maurizio Pollini (DG) and I personally have little hesitation in saying that Pollini is the finest of all. No doubt there will be other versions of the Preludes recorded, versions from which we can all learn and profit, but I doubt whether many will provide us with such enviable finesse, such stylistic rightness or such virile sensitivity as Pollini. I continually recall No. 19 in E flat, where he beautifully conveys Chopin's flight into a cloudless azure and, in the concluding bars, subtly decreases the composer's rapidly gyrating momentum. In this classic recording Pollini suggests a harmony between composer and interpreter no less complete than that between Chopin's form and content, between his intellect and emotion.

Recordings discussed

Cortot	World Records SH 327
Anda	CFP 40284
Arrau	Philips 6500 622
Larrocha	Decca SXL 6733
*Pollini	Deutsche Grammophon 2530 550
Moravec	Supraphon 111 2139
Barenboim	HMV ASD 3254
Perahia	CBS 76422
Argerich	Deutsche Grammophon 2530 721
Ashkenazy	Decca SXL 6877

©Bryce Morrison

Beethoven   *An die ferne Geliebte*

J. W. LAMBERT

Beethoven was forty-six when, in 1861, he wrote his song-cycle *An die ferne Geliebte*, the crown of his still underrated achievement in song-writing. It is often referred to as the first song-cycle, which of course it is not, at least as the phrase is commonly used. But it is remarkable in that its six songs are contained within an unbroken musical framework. its end returning to its beginning; the whole work lasts about a quarter of an hour.

Although Beethoven's own emotional life was, and continued to be, strangely, not to say deliberately, unsatisfactory, among his eighty or so songs for voice and piano a surprising number – and several of these among his best – celebrate the joys of peaceful, fulfilled affection. On the other hand he also wrote no fewer than six songs with the title *Sehnsucht* (longing, yearning), and that is also the whole theme of *An die ferne Geliebte*.

But – and this is most important in considering its interpretation – there is nothing woebegone or self-pitying about it. Of course the romantic idiom of the words, written by a young acquaintance of Beethoven's, uses the word *Tränen* (tears), to express the ache of separation, and wistfulness creeps in as the lover keeps remembering that separation. But throughout the cycle singer and pianist must always bear in mind the lover's essential joy in the actual fact of loving, triumphantly asserted at the last by both voice and piano.

The recorded versions currently available are all by men, though no violence would be done if some of our fine contemporary women *Lieder* singers were to take the work into their repertory. Those who feel instinctively that all lovers are young, and also that all ardent young men have tenor voices, will incline towards the three tenor versions; but I shall hope to demonstrate that darker voices can express these emotions just as effectively and with just as much validity.

Our hero is discovered sitting on a hill, gazing on the misty distance and the mountains that stand between him and the woman he loves. Here Peter Anders, with Hubert Giesen at the piano, is rough-hewn, perhaps, and rather free with what we may politely call *portamento*, but still with a sense of real feeling: a burly young farmer, as it might be. On the other hand Norman Bailey, with John Constable, sings with clean, finely focused bronze tone, suggesting to me that Schubert's miller – not the boy but his genial master – is dreaming of the warm-hearted widow in the next valley but one.

Loving looks and lover's sighs are useless to bridge the distance. What shall he do to get through to her? Well, he'll sing to her, for the music of love will obliterate space and time. And at the end of the first song he announces his decision with mounting excitement, which provides the first snag for the singer. With Fischer-Dieskau and Jörg Demus (DG), for example, what I feel is not so much excitement as a suggestion of Prussian precision, a hint of clicked heels, and Peter Schreier, with Walter Olbertz (Telefunken), is positively alarming. If I were the beloved I would run a mile. It may be a matter of national temperament, but I think the British singers manage more tenderly. There is nothing militaristic or half-cracked about John Shirley-Quirk with Martin Issepp on Argo and still less about Martyn Hill, with Christopher Hogwood at a more or less contemporary fortepiano, on Oiseau–Lyre.

Next, the singer launches into four songs made for his beloved's pleasure, at least in theory, though actually, as with all lovers, for his own satisfaction. In the first of them he is still thinking of the blue mountains and then, beyond them, the valley of peace, whose spell Beethoven spins out on a single note before more agitating thoughts return. Once again Schreier makes something very violent out of the change of mood, whereas Norman Bailey, on Saga, gravely expresses a sense of awe. In this passage Fischer-Dieskau displays a caressing vitality which is beautifully sustained, if you are not irked by his rolled 'r' in *drängt*, one of several, actually. I personally could do without them: they are more a sign or relish in the singer than expressive. But I do not really mind them, any more than I mind some little mannerism in an old friend.

In the third song the mood lightens with thoughts of clouds in a bright sky, little brooks, darting birds, western zephyrs – not without a brief darkening in the middle, but ideally dancing along in a taxing mixture of *staccato* and *legato* singing which leads straight, by way of a long-held twinge of remembered pain, into the major key and the fourth song. Here the singer sets about cheering himself up again. The dancing rhythms are what one might expect to give most difficulty to Norman Bailey, and although he is perhaps a touch too sharp on his *staccato*, to my ear he admirably transmits the spirit of the piece. Shirley-Quirk, on the other hand, seems to me ill-defined and rhythmically unsteady, and he plods with a bumpy beat into the opening of the fourth song. Peter Schreier, at any rate, cannot here be accused of plodding; on the other hand he might be thought to come perilously near to mincing. I feel that on this record, unlike his splendid Schumann *Liederkreis* Op. 39, but like his earlier *Dichterliebe*, Schreier is applying his undoubted artistry from the outside, and none too comfortably at that.

In the next song Spring is bursting out all over, until the singer reminds himself that the birds have nests and mates and nestlings, but he hasn't.

Schreier seems to me to get fearfully affected as the song goes on, and he is not helped by Olbertz's thumpy, near-musical-box introduction, especially perhaps to the last verse. Martyn Hill manages this very nicely but I am not too happy, here and elsewhere, about Christopher Hogwood's fortepiano. It often sounds as though its action is excessively stiff and positively holding things up; and occasionally it sounds to me all too like the piano in one's local!

At the risk of seeming perverse, I must make exactly the opposite complaint about Shirley-Quirk's partner. Martin Isepp is a very fine accompanist, but I wish he had chosen another instrument: as it is, his piano sometimes sounds almost like a harmonium. With this and Shirley-Quirk's timbre and a plushy recording we are left with a rather overstuffed performance, too often submerging into what I have already suggested should be avoided at all costs – the woebegone. By contrast (and it is a matter of personal taste, I dare say), I find Fischer-Dieskau beautifully quickening in the way, for example, in which he breathes on *Ja, all ihr Gewinnen* (tears of regret his only consolation).

Finally, our lover turns from the songs he is, so to speak, making up and speaks directly again. Somehow, in the peaceful evening, his distant beloved will hear his songs and sing them herself. This last song makes considerable demands upon both singer and pianist. After a tender opening it evokes the evening in a rapturous *legato* passage, and this is quite a test. You may have been wondering why I have not, apart from one brief mention, referred again to Peter Anders's version. There are alas, many reasons why. Honest rusticity is simply not enough: though it is salutary to hear something really bad from time to time, I cannot imagine how a responsible firm like Telefunken came to put out this disastrous record. It is especially painful in the exquisite passage evoking the peace of the evening floated with predictable beauty by Fischer-Dieskau. Then the joyful excitement comes surging back. Distance *will* be wiped out by the music from a loving heart; the last pages of the song echo the last verse of the first song. Here Fischer-Dieskau unfortunately echoes his own heel-clicking as well.

Indeed, I have no doubt or hesitation whatever in deciding which of these singers best balances musicality and excitement, making the work's conclusion both loving and thrilling: Norman Bailey, with his pianist John Constable, who is specially successful in the surging final prelude.

Since I have to make a choice, Peter Anders is nowhere, Peter Schreier is often beautiful but sometimes strained and frequently mannered, Martyn Hill is sensitive and musicianly, but a little pallid and hampered by that fortepiano. Truth to tell, if I were determined to have a tenor version I should try somehow to find somewhere either the Gedda or the Haefliger versions, both now deleted. Among the baritones, I really cannot help finding Shirley-Quirk excessively glum and despondent. Fischer-Dieskau is, as always, marvellously full of understanding, but for me he does spoil things with that touch of the parade-ground. So I choose, for myself, for a performance in which the whole work is seamlessly knit together, that gleaming, mature yet ardent voice deployed with unassertive artistry by Norman Bailey.

Recordings discussed

Shirley-Quirk/Isepp	Argo ZRG 664
Anders/Giesen	Telefunken DP6 48064
	(2-record set)
*Bailey/Constable	Saga 5450
Fischer-Dieskau/Demus	Deutsche Grammophon
	2563 735
Schreier/Olbertz	Telefunken AP6 42082
Hill/Hogwood	Oiseau Lyre DSLO 535

© J. W. Lambert

Mahler   *Lieder eines fahrenden Gesellen*

J. W. LAMBERT

The many recordings currently available speak for the lasting appeal of Mahler's youthful heart-cry. *Lieder eines fahrenden Gesellen* is usually translated as *Songs of a Wayfarer* – though not, as *Gesellen* would normally suggest, a sociable one. Mahler's young fellow was wandering off alone because he had been crossed in love – as indeed had Mahler, shamelessly teased by a singer at the Kassel Opera, where he was deputy music director. Actually, Mahler was nearly always in love with some female singer, and often felt hard done by, expressing himself in extravagantly romantic terms in letters to friends, when not urging them to get news of his activities into the Vienna papers, or scheming to get a better job.

The mood of being shut out and of desolate parting in these four songs was not only a typical element in German romanticism (one has only to remember Schubert's two great cycles on the same themes) but a particular element in Mahler's temperament. He was apt to refer to himself as 'a wayfarer who has met adversity, setting out into the world and wandering on in solitude' – which is how, I am afraid, more people than ever must feel in the world today. So these songs, written when he was 23, were more than a sentimental response to an emotional mishap. He originally intended that there should be six. He took his title from that of a book by a contemporary minor poet – the title but not the poems; these he wrote himself in the style of that fruitful collection of folksongs and folkish poems, *Des Knaben Wunderhorn*. The first song in the cycle, in fact, takes two verses straight out of it, as Donald Mitchell has pointed out.

Though Mahler always intended to orchestrate them, the first versions were for voice and piano. I personally regret that there is no example of this form now available on record; but most people, I suppose, prefer the rich orchestral colouring. I relish it myself, come to that, so long as the looming threat of *Schmaltz* is avoided. Wayfaring *lad* or not, six out of the available recordings are by women, all but one mezzos. The exception I must alas disqualify. When Kirsten Flagstad made her record with Adrian Boult and the Vienna Philharmonic Orchestra (Decca, Eclipse) she was surely not at her best. For instance at the end of the first song Flagstad ignores all dynamic markings, and scoops along relentlessly for the rest of the cycle. In this first song the wayfarer is bewailing the fact that the girl he loves is marrying someone else. Treatment of the opening is marked by extraordinary variations of tempo. Fischer-Dieskau with Kubelik and the Bavarian Radio Orchestra on DG approach the song quite differently from Robert Tear – the only tenor on hand – with Neville Marriner and the Academy of St Martin-in-the-Fields on Argo. Dame Janet Baker, with Barbirolli and the Hallé (HMV), is if anything even slower than Tear. There is no such thing as one correct tempo, even when a composer has left a metronome marking; but to my ear Tear and Baker are uncomfortably slow. Nor does that sort of exaggeration make it easy for the conductor to hold the songs together, avoiding stops and starts as they keep changing direction, with all sorts of rhythmical and harmonic switches. A moment's brightening in the middle of the song fades into regret again at its end. I am rather surprised by the heavy weather several of the ladies make where Mahler has marked the four notes given to the word *Leide* (sorrow) with a strong stress on each. But not so strong, surely, as they are made in a recent and rather uneasy version by Marilyn Horne with Mehta and the Los Angeles Philharmonic (Decca); or come to that by Yvonne Minton, rather matronly throughout, with Solti and the Chicago Symphony (Decca). Frederica von Stade, accompanied by Andrew Davis and the Royal Philharmonic Orchestra (CBS), begins rather hard and edgy, but comes finely to the close.

In the second song the disappointed lover determines to enjoy the dew-spangled morning world in spite of everything – the birds, the flowers, the sunshine. One wants a smile in the voice here, and I do not detect it in Marilyn Horne. She sounds more like a school mistress pointing out the beauties of nature. Janet Baker seems to have a good deal of mud on her sensible shoes and there is a strange little break between 'wie' and 'mir' in the last phrase. For the true note of delight, however short-lived, we must turn to Fischer-Dieskau and to the light and sensitive voice of Mildred Miller, with Bruno Walter – another of the recordings which are now quite venerable; she makes every word dance on her lips. The last section of this song is a real killer. Already I have reproached Flagstad for not observing Mahler's markings. I must in fairness add that most of the ladies shirk them a good deal of the time, especially his above-the-ledger-lines *ppp*'s. Here, as the young man wonders whether, on the evidence of all this beauty, his luck will change, but sadly comes to the conclusion that it never will, I am a bit suspicious, too, of Robert Tear's seemingly falsetto solution to the vocal difficulty. Fischer-Dieskau, however, does manage the many changes of mood, which include an almost direct quotation from the song *Mein* in Schubert's *Schöne Müllerin*.

In the third song the mood changes drastically. It is a wild and whirling cry of rage and despair – the knife in my heart cuts deep, I see her eyes in the blue sky, her hair in the golden cornfield, her silvery laughter mocks my waking. All the singers do pretty well with this operatic outburst, though Solti gets the bit between his teeth and leads Yvonne Minton the devil of a breathless dance.

So far I have made no mention of Hermann Prey (Philips). He sings sensitively in his distinctive somewhat adenoidal way, but to my mind is too unvaryingly depressed throughout. He has the advantage of the best orchestral accompaniment, from Haitink and the Concertgebouw, and rises, even with his soft-grained voice, nobly to the nightmare vision. Some may prefer Prey's still fairly lyrical manner to Fischer-Dieskau's more openly characterized approach, but I much admire the controlled force of the latter, even when, with that silvery laughter, the music seems to look straight ahead to *Wozzeck*. Here, too, Mildred Miller's diction more than makes up for what might have been expected to be a rather light voice for the song's last page, a postlude not without its problems. Barbirolli, for example, lets Janet Baker down by allowing it to sound positively jaunty.

In the last song resignation sets in, in the shade of that familiar friend of German romantics, the *Lindenbaum* or lime-tree. This heart-rending funeral march of a song, with its relentless drums, is full of hazards arising from Mahler's demand for high-lying *pianissimos*, and once again Yvonne Minton finds herself in trouble. So does Marilyn Horne. Frederica von Stade manages to bring it off, though, compared with Mildred Miller, she makes us feel too conscious that she is doing so. Here, once more, Haitink and the Concertgebouw Orchestra shine and Prey is at his best. And then, when the lime-tree at last is reached, comes the wonderful, forgiving dying fall. Janet Baker handles it well, but unfortunately her last word virtually disappears and Barbirolli hangs all too lovingly on to the postlude. Robert Tear lapses into strained and ugly sound at the end of the song and so does Frederica von Stade; and she is not helped by Andrew Davis who fails to obtain a real *pianissimo* from the orchestra. Not so Fischer-Dieskau and Kubelik; and not so Mildred Miller and that quintessential, not at all sentimental Mahlerian Bruno Walter. How vitally she shapes and colours word and tone, with what feeling she floats her apparently effortless line of sound – exactly, I feel sure, as Irma Kurz did when she first appeared in Vienna and delighted Mahler with her singing of this cycle. It comes coupled with Mahler's Symphony No. 9 on two CBS Classics discs. You will not, by this time, need second sight to have worked out which of the nine versions under review I am going to recommend. If only to avoid the obvious I should like not to have picked Fischer-Dieskau; but for real meaning, musical and verbal communication, he seems to me unmatched among the men. His version is coupled with Mahler's Fifth Symphony in a double album in DG's mid-priced Privilege series. But my prime choice is Mildred Miller's combination of delicacy, vitality, and pure tone.

Recordings discussed

Flagstad/Vienna Philharmonic Orchestra/ Boult	Decca ECS 780
*Miller/Columbia Symphony Orchestra/ Walter	CBS 61736
Baker/Hallé Orchestra/Barbirolli	HMV SLS 5013
Minton/Chicago Symphony Orchestra/ Solti	Decca SET 469–70
Prey/Amsterdam Concertgebouw Orchestra/Haitink	Philips SAL 6500 100
Fischer-Dieskau/Bavarian Radio Orchestra/ Kubelik	Deutsche Grammophon 2530 630
Tear/Academy of St Martin-in-the-Fields/ Marriner	Argo ZRG 737
Horne/Los Angeles Philharmonic Orchestra/Mehta	Decca SXL 6895
Von Stade/Royal Philharmonic Orchestra/ A. Davis	CBS 76828

© J. W. Lambert

Delius on Record

CHRISTOPHER PALMER

The focal point of any discussion of Delius on disc must inevitably be the legacy of Sir Thomas Beecham. It must be galling and discouraging for present-day Delius conductors constantly to be compared with Beecham, generally unfavourably; but much as I sympathize I have to be honest and state that my own view is the commonplace one, namely that Beecham as a Delius interpreter was without peer. In their qualities of musicality, integrity, and poetic sensitivity his performances can surely never be equalled, let alone surpassed.

In 1948 Arthur Hutchings produced his book on Delius which is still in many ways the best critical introduction to Delius's music. As a fond Beecham admirer he has claimed in letters to me that Beecham had rather more in common with Delius than the conductor cared to admit. They were both North-of-Englanders, Delius from Bradford in Yorkshire, Beecham from St Helens in Lancashire . . . from there he went to Rossall where he learnt what Hutchings described as the 'blah-blah nil admirari manner of the ruling klarsses'.

This was all a pose, as was the mountebankery which he learnt from his mother who was a circus woman. Experience or instinct early showed him what the world does to people who make public property of their vulnerability, and all this was his defence. He showed his true feelings in his performances of Delius. Delius, too, revealed his inner nature only in his art; the world he dealt with in a spirit of North Country no-nonsenseness, and with one of the sharpest of sharp tongues. Beecham, an over-sophisticated man, responded to the other Northerner's yearning for the heart of things in nature and natural man. So much in general terms. But more specifically, one needs to discover why Delius's music lends itself so reluctantly to satisfactory performance? Much of the trouble originates with the composer himself. He was one of the truest and most natural musicians of all time, and tended to presuppose a commensurate degree of musicianship in his performers. For this reason he gave them in his printed scores the barest minimum of interpretative instruction. 'But surely', he used to say to his amanuensis Eric Fenby, 'a really musical person *must* feel it my way.' No doubt if one had had the temerity to point out that many otherwise admirable performing musicians, whether amateur or professional, are not necessarily as musical as they might be, he would have retorted that such people had no business to be playing his music in the first place. That may be true, but we have to live in the world as it is, not as it ideally should be. It was Beecham's inborn musicianship which established a performance tradition for Delius's works.

When Beecham played them Delius said simply that that was how he wanted them to sound, and we must surely respect that. The trouble is that musicianship, unlike technique, cannot be taught, and where Beecham's musical faculties came most vitally into operation was in the matter of *pacing* Delius. Delius's music is essentially a music of nature, and nature even in her deepest tranquillities is never still. In fact a paradox central to nature, and to Delius's nature-music, is that a feeling of motionlessness can be engendered only through motion: because motion, or momentum, means life and lack of momentum means death. Delius's music dies if it is not kept on the move. This does not mean that it should be played faster rather than slower. It means the player must have a feeling for its natural ebbings and flowings, for rising towards what Eric Fenby termed the 'operative note in a phrase', and then sinking back from it. He must know intuitively when in the course of a paragraph to linger, often protractedly; and when to forge ahead, often determinedly. In short he must be able to gauge the music's natural *sense of flow*, which Delius never tired of insisting upon as the most important thing in music and music-making. This is not something which can be conveyed in written symbols on a page; it can only be felt. and Beecham felt it supremely well. His readings are set about with every conceivable unpredictability and waywardness, but of the kind that turns earth into heaven. And surely a measure of their truth and rightness is the fact that every time we play one of Beecham's recordings we can be made to feel that we are hearing the piece for the first time. I suppose I must have heard *On Hearing the first Cuckoo in Spring* a few hundred times in my life, and it is certainly one of Delius's most popular works, possibly *the* most popular and the most frequently played. Yet I remember hearing a passage from it during one of Joseph Cooper's 'Face the Music' BBC television programmes, and it suddenly seemed to me that there could be no fairer music in the world. It was the Beecham performance on HMV ASD 357, a record to be recommended particularly as a sampler or introduction to Delius: it includes perennial favourites like *Brigg Fair, A Song Before Sunrise, Summer Night on the River*, and the *Fennimore and Gerda* intermezzo as well as two pieces from the early period which always fascinated Sir Thomas, the *Marche Caprice* and *Sleigh Ride*. All were made in the mid-to-late-1950s, and although that is more than twenty years ago the sound has freshness as well as that special glow which all Beecham's best recordings have about them. Yet granted that the intrinsic merit of his Delius interpretations may be unrivalled, he died in 1961, and recorded for many years before that, so inevitably we must consider the *quality* of the recorded sound. Surely Delius, a composer for whom beauty of sound was a paramount concern, cannot be best served by recordings made twenty, thirty and even forty years ago, and would benefit immeasurably from today's higher fidelity. I think the answer is not as much as might be imagined. A relevant parallel may be drawn here with personal or physical beauty. We all know about the immediate and intoxicating power of beauty in a person. But we know too that beauty which is only skin-deep can pall with alarming rapidity. What is vastly more important is personality, charisma, awareness, lovingness, and all those qualities not necessarily manifest in the form of outward glamour. Another analogy could be with the cinema. A film made in the 1930s on the small screen in black and white and with inferior sound quality may be accounted a classic and be shown everywhere. Re-made today in lavish technicolour on the Cinemascope screen and in stereophonic sound it can be forgotten in a matter of months. This *has* happened, not once but many times. The same applies to recordings. The best of Beecham's Delius has a presence, an enduring quality which utterly transcends the technical limitations of the time it was made. I am not going to be so foolish as to pretend that I get as much pleasure from listening to Beecham's 1928 recording of *Brigg Fair* as I do from the one he made thirty years later. But I do feel that the magic of nature-rhythm and muted colour he distils in the opening of *Sea Drift* is quite timeless; and this was a recording he made in 1938. It is part of the first of two boxed sets from World Records called *The Music of Delius* which gather together Beecham recordings ranging from 1927–1952, many previously unissued. These sets should form the cornerstones of any Delius record collection. There is some slight duplication between the two, for instance a 1928 *Brigg Fair* and one of 1946; but this can give you an idea of how Beecham's view of Delius changed in subtle ways over the years.

The number of Volume I is WR SHB 32. This covers primarily the pre-war years and includes a number of recordings that Delius himself knew and liked. After *Sea Drift*, major works represented are *Appalachia, Paris, Eventyr*, and *In a Summer Garden*; incidentally Beecham's later recording of *Appalachia* is available separately on CBS 61354, a record also worth having for the definitive account of the *North Country Sketches* it contains. The first boxed set also includes numerous short pieces like *Summer Night on the River*, and the *Irmelin Prelude*; excerpts from *Hassan* and *Koanga*; and a selection of songs with orchestral or piano accompaniment sung by Dora Labbette, who has the sweet innocent voice of a young girl. Beecham's own voice is also heard in an interview given at the time of the publication of his Delius biography. A paperback reissue of this comes as a bonus, complete with a new introduction by Felix Aprahamian and a Beecham-Delius discography compiled by Malcolm Walker. In a radio talk also included in Volume I Sir Thomas gives his views on *A Mass of Life*, further to which it is relevant to point out, I think, that Delius seemed to take a perverse delight in presenting quite an imposing array of negatives to the world. He had no theories, or so he said. He had no technique. He had little or no interest in any music other than his own. He was a supreme egoist and had very little regard for the feelings of others and he had no time whatsoever for religion. That, at least, is the picture he liked to present, and the source of the myths that were perpetuated about him by the credulous and unperceptive. Yet in spite of the seeming blasphemy of the very title of *A Mass of Life,* I believe that Delius was an intensely religious man. Not in the limited sense that your orthodox churchmen might understand, but then Delius had little time for orthodox churchmen; he maintained that for too many of them 'religion' meant simply the despising of the things of the earth, and a readier belief in the Devil than in God. Delius's entire life was devoted to admiring, loving, enjoying, and celebrating the things of the earth, in fact to seeing his way to spiritual things by the light of sensible things. The man who like Delius apprehends and gives expression to earthly beauties and delights does so because, whatever he may outwardly profess, he sees in them, veiled, the beauties and delights of the everlasting. If he did not he would be unable to apprehend or express them in the way he does. Delius's was one of those rare uncorrupted minds who sees the divinity that is latent in every form of life. He was a supreme egoist and like all supreme poets an ecstatic and a visionary. And nowhere does he give more splendid and intoxicating expression to his vision that in *A Mass of Life.* I can well imagine some youngster perhaps just casually tuning in to it, knowing nothing of Delius, and thinking the music the most glorious he has ever heard. In that case let him then go out and buy Sir Charles Groves's complete recording on HMV SLS 958. It may sound ungracious to say, in default of Beecham's which at present is absent from the catalogue, but Sir Charles does not flame with any great spiritual ardour in the big hymnic apostrophes and apotheoses, and the role of Zarathustra, in which the sweet melancholy of evening and the splendour of the midsummer night are incessant refrains, needs a voice of greater refinement than Benjamin Luxon's, strong, manly singer though he be. The recording is excellent and gives a faithful account of the unique sound of Delius's orchestra.

The second World Records Beecham collection which covers the years 1946–1952 includes what is surely the finest imaginable performance of *The Song of The High Hills,* one of Delius's great masterpieces; the only available version of *Songs of Sunset* with Nancy Evans and Redvers Llewellyn as soloists, unfortunately missing one song; the two Dance Rhapsodies; an early tone-poem after Ibsen called *On the Heights,* never before issued; and a truly magisterial account of *Brigg Fair* with some heart-stirring moments as Dennis Brain plays a distant solo horn in the famous Interlude. This second box of 'The Music of Delius' contains six records and the number is SHB 54. Two entire records in this second collection are devoted to the opera *A Village Romeo and Juliet,* and this is the place for a short digression on the subject of Delius's operas and their representation on record. Although he wrote a total of six he was never by nature a dramatic composer. In operatic as opposed to purely Delian terms, *Koanga* is the most successful, but that is because at the time it was written Delius was still dealing in shadows and imitations of other composers and styles. As he progressed towards maturity the area of feeling he explored became progressively more limited, until by the time he reached his last opera, *Fennimore and Gerda*, he was neither willing nor able to turn conventional techniques of operatic effectiveness to his purpose. *Koanga* can be effective on the stage, and for this reason I would recommend the complete recording under Sir Charles Groves (HMV) more to opera buffs than to Delians. Quite the best music is the closing scene which Beecham recorded separately and which is on the second record of the first boxed set.

As for *Fennimore and Gerda*, it apparently never occurred to Delius that a stageworthy libretto cannot subsist merely on a sequence of poetic moods; it needs also down-to-earth commodities like plot, incident, and fully-drawn characters if it is to serve its purpose (even *Pelléas* has both, and the poetry of Maeterlinck's French to boot). Of course the 'poetic moods' as and when they arise are beautifully rendered; but betwixt times Delius commits himself to setting long stretches of dialogue quite devoid of poetic or lyrical content, and the result is some predictably tedious music. Meredith Davies's complete recording (HMV) is admirable in almost every respect but is strictly for Delius idolaters; my greatest personal joy is in the famous intermezzo with its heart-piercingly lovely oboe song of spring and apple-blossom time, and in Sir Thomas Beecham's 1936 recording of it in the first of the World Records boxes.

A Village Romeo and Juliet is the most completely satisfactory of Delius's operas because stylistically it represents a kind of half-way house in his development: he was in the act of shedding the old self and donning the new, and in a sense combining the advantages of both. If you have the second Beecham boxed set which contains his complete recording there is no need to look farther; otherwise the opera on its own is very well served by Meredith Davies who has a fine team of soloists and the Royal Philharmonic Orchestra (HMV SLS 966). This set, incidentally, includes a lecture by Eric Fenby on the development of Delius's art, and a fascinating reconstruction of the way in which the blind and paralysed composer dictated to him the ending of *Cynara*. However my own favourite among Delius's stage works has always been his incidental music for James Elroy Flecker's *Hassan*. Its success is surely due at least in part to the fact that Delius was not hamstrung by a text as he was in the operas. True, he had a few of Flecker's exquisite lyrics to set, but these were of the kind that would spontaneously strike beautiful music from him. And what bewitching and aromatic sounds he draws from his handful of instruments in the pit! Never, surely, was there such an artist in timbre and sonority. One or two excerpts are to be found in the first Beecham boxed set, but in this instance Vernon Handley's complete recording is well worth investing in. Some of the orchestral playing could be a little more polished, but the chorus's contribution is beyond reproach. The sound of Delius's choral writing is like no other in the world, because it represents a continual attempt on his part to recapture a moment of transcendent bliss from his youth. Perhaps he rarely came closer to it than in the wordless choruses behind the scenes in *Hassan*. The Bournemouth Sinfonietta and Chorus are conducted by Vernon Handley on HMV ASD 3777.

So far I have made no mention of the Delius concertos. The third record of the second Beecham boxed collection which consists of two of them, the Violin Concerto, one of his best works, and the Piano Concerto, one of his worst. In fact some of its moments are so blatantly bad that I wonder Delius ever sanctioned its publication. It is not well played in this performance by Betty Humby Beecham, and I found that even a bright and enthusiastic modern recording by Jean Rodolphe Kars failed to rehabilitate it (Decca SXL 6435). Beecham's affection for the piece seems misplaced, but he was always drawn to the earlier Delius – I suspect largely because it evinces a certain innocence of spirit to which he, being a hypersophisticated man, would be prone to respond. Certainly this could explain the fact that though he adored *A Village Romeo and Juliet* he could never warm to *Fennimore and Gerda*, which was dedicated to him. The Violin Concerto, written for the instrument which Delius himself could play well, is another matter altogether. Of all the available versions Jean Pougnet's with Beecham seems by far the most successful in bringing out both the strength and purpose inherent in Delius's rhapsodic flights, and the poetic quietude of his withdrawals for musing. Menuhin's tone, on his more recent recording, is too wiry and uningratiating, and he seems to approach the work more as a traditional concerto than as what in fact it resembles more – a poem for orchestra with violin obbligato. His coupling, incidentally, is the Concerto for Violin and Cello, with Paul Tortelier. This is an excellent piece in substance, but its effectiveness is undermined by the uneasy relationship between the two solo instruments and the nature of the contribution they make to the overall texture. Not a priority on my list, but for those interested the number is HMV ASD 3343.

From concertos to Delius's instrumental sonatas. Deprived as he is in this context of the blandishments of orchestral colour, Delius is here critically dependent on sympathetic and idiomatic interpretation, as I discovered from listening to two versions currently listed of the Cello Sonata. After playing a short way into one of them I found myself wondering how I could ever have admired the piece. It sounded nothing but an interminable sequence of chords, all without form and void. Then I put on Julian Lloyd Webber's record with Clifford Benson at the piano, and the music immediately started to make sense – not surprisingly if you read Lloyd Webber's sleeve-notes and discover that he has a full understanding of the workings of Delius's musical mind and of the problems involved in realizing his unwritten intentions. This record comes from Discourses on ABK 17 in a series called *The Voice of the Instruments*.

I have touched on records by conductors other than Beecham, but in my view his only serious rival is Barbirolli. The difference in their approaches to Delius is surely a difference of origin and temperament. Beecham, like Delius a Northerner, tended to accentuate that strain of Nordic keenness or austerity inherent in all Delius's writing which can probably be traced back to Grieg. Barbirolli was a Southerner, Italian, a passionate and hot-blooded Latin, and he naturally responded more to the element of luxuriance and self-indulgence in Delius. Beecham's view was in essence dynamic; he kept the music in motion and in an overall perspective. Barbirolli's was more static; he loved to linger and inhale and savour to the full, and with clouds of linden blossom and honeysuckle round every corner who can blame him? Barbirolli's Delius is dear to me for its deep love and affection; Beecham can sound almost aloof by comparison. Barbirolli's tempos tend to be on the slower side, sometimes unacceptably so inasmuch as the rhythms may flag, the momentum sag, and the sense of flow be impeded. But for spaciousness and architectural grandeur, and sheer splendour of sound, I can wholly recommend his record of *Appalachia* on HMV ASD 2635. There are so many fine moments in this performance that it seems invidious to single any one out, but among my own favourite is the vision of the mighty river induced by the strumming of Negro banjos. With that and the two Beecham versions I have already mentioned I think no one need re-record *Appalachia* for a long time to come. It would be a pity if they did, because a surprisingly large number of major Delius works are not at present to be had: the *Requiem*, the *Idyll*, the complete *Songs of Sunset, Cynara,* the *Arabesque*, the *Songs of Farewell*, not to mention many fine solo songs. There is no shortage of lollipop records, but let me re-iterate that the one to go for is Beecham's HMV ASD 357. Barbirolli's anthology called *In A Summer Garden* can also be recommended without reserve and is available on ASD 2477. Other records need to be approached with some caution. Do not be too readily seduced by a cheap label; Delius is an expensive composer! Vernon Handley's Classics for Pleasure Collection is rather charmless; the climaxes in *The Walk to the Paradise Garden*, for example, sound more like a forced growth than a natural flowering of passion. Those works recorded by Anthony Collins in the 1950s, including *Paris, In a Summer Garden,* and *A Song of Summer*, are available on Decca ECS 634. Widely praised as they have been, I have always found them a shade prosaic. Ormandy and Neville Marriner should be avoided altogether, but Norman Del Mar is an experienced and reliable Delian who knows how to shape a piece and to create a rapt atmosphere. His record is called 'Miniatures' and its number is RCA RL 25079. The programme of an HMV Concert Classics Beecham reissue (SXLP 30415) is more esoteric: the *Florida Suite* (an early work with interesting pre-echoes of Gershwin), the mysterious *Dance Rhapsody No. 2,* and *Over the Hills and Far Away* which sounds like a rough and primitive forbear of *The Song of the High Hills.*

Finally, another record by the Bournemouth Sinfonietta but with an interest all its own because the conductor is Eric Fenby. For some years

Delius's amanuensis has been coming more and more to the fore as a performing musician; he and Ralph Holmes have produced a definitive account of the three violin sonatas on Unicorn UNS 258, a record which also includes a spoken account by Fenby of the calamitously unpromising start of his collaboration with the composer. Eric Fenby is, in fact, a fine all round musician, and on the Bournemouth Sinfonietta record he appears not only as conductor but also as arranger, all the music being transcriptions of works written for other media including *La Calinda* and the *Dance for Harpsichord* most winningly set for solo flute and strings. Surely Eric Fenby of all people should be invited to restore some of those missing Delius masterpieces to the catalogue.

Recordings of works discussed

Appalachia. BBC Chorus/London Philharmonic Orchestra/Beecham	World Records SHB 32
Royal Philharmonic Chorus and Orchestra/Beecham	CBS 61354
Ambrosian Singers/Hallé/Barbirolli	HMV ASD 2635
Brigg Fair. Symphony Orchestra/Beecham	World Records SHB 32
Royal Philharmonic Orchestra/Beecham	World Records SHB 54
Royal Philharmonic Orchestra/Beecham	HMV ASD 357
Hallé Orchestra/Barbirolli	HMV ASD 2635
La Calinda. Bournemouth Sinfonietta/Fenby	HMV ASD 3688
Cello Sonata. Lloyd Webber/Benson	Discourses ABK 17
Concerto for Violin and Cello. Menuhin/Tortelier/Royal Philharmonic Orchestra/A. Davis	HMV ASD 3343
Dance for Harpsichord, arr. Fenby. Bournemouth Sinfonietta/Fenby	HMV ASD 3688
Dance Rhapsodies: Nos. 1 and 2. Royal Philharmonic Orchestra/Beecham	World Records SHB 54
Eventyr. London Philharmonic Orchestra/Beecham	World Records SHB 32
Fennimore and Gerda (complete). Söderström/Danish Radio Symphony Orchestra and Chorus/M. Davies	HMV SLS 991
(Intermezzo). Royal Philharmonic Orchestra/Beecham	HMV ASD 357
Florida Suite. Royal Philharmonic Orchestra/Beecham	HMV SXLP 30415
Hassan (complete). Bournemouth Sinfonietta and Chorus/Handley	HMV ASD 3777
(excerpts), Royal Opera Chorus/London Select Choir/London Philharmonic Orchestra/Beecham	World Records SHB 32
In a Summer Garden. London Philharmonic Orchestra/Beecham	World Records SHB 32
Irmelin (prelude). London Philharmonic Orchestra/Beecham	World Records SHB 32
Royal Philharmonic Orchestra/Beecham	World Records SHB 54

Koanga (complete). Holmes/Alldis Choir/ London Symphony Orchestra/Groves	HMV SLS 974
(excerpts). London Philharmonic Orchestra/ Beecham	World Records SHB 32
Marche Caprice. Royal Philharmonic Orchestra/ Beecham	HMV ASD 357
Eine Messe des Lebens. Harper, Watts, Tear, Luxon/London Philharmonic Choir/Royal Philharmonic Orchestra/Groves	HMV SLS 958
North Country Sketches. Royal Philharmonic Orchestra/Beecham	CBS 61354
On Hearing the First Cuckoo in Spring. Royal Philharmonic Orchestra/Beecham	HMV ASD 357
On the Heights. Royal Philharmonic Orchestra/ Beecham	World Records SHB 54
Over the Hills and Far Away. Royal Philharmonic Orchestra/Beecham	HMV SXLP 30415
Paris: The Song of a Great City. London Philharmonic Orchestra/Beecham	World Records SHB 32
Piano Concerto. Humby Beecham/Royal Philharmonic Orchestra/Beecham	World Records SHB 54
Kars/London Symphony Orchestra/Gibson	Decca SXL 6435
Sea Drift. Brownlee/London Select Choir/ London Philharmonic Orchestra/Beecham	World Records SHB 32
Sleigh Ride. Royal Philharmonic Orchestra/ Beecham	HMV ASD 357
Song before Sunrise. Royal Philharmonic Orchestra/Beecham	HMV ASD 357
Song of the High Hills. Hart, Jones/Chorus/ Royal Philharmonic Orchestra/Beecham	World Records SHB 54
Songs of Sunset. Evans, Llewellyn/Royal Philharmonic Orchestra/Beecham	World Records SHB 54
Summer Night on the River. London Philharmonic Orchestra/Beecham	World Records SHB 32
Royal Philharmonic Orchestra/Beecham	HMV ASD 357
A Village Romeo and Juliet (complete). Dowling Sharp/Royal Philharmonic Orchestra/ Beecham	World Records SHB 54
Luxon, Mangin/Alldis Choir/Royal Philharmonic Orchestra/M. Davies	HMV SLS 966
Violin Concerto. Pougnet/Royal Philharmonic Orchestra/Beecham	World Records SHB 54
Menuhin/Royal Philharmonic Orchestra/A. Davis	HMV ASD 3343
Violin Sonatas Nos. 1 and 2. Holmes/Fenby	Unicorn UNS 258
The Walk to the Paradise Garden. London Philharmonic Orchestra/Handley	CFP 40304

© Christopher Palmer

Grainger on Record

CHRISTOPHER PALMER

Not many years ago Percy Grainger's reputation as a composer to be taken seriously was almost non-existent. In the minds of most people he was just the composer of *Country Gardens*, *Molly on the Shore*, and *Handel in the Strand*. But latterly much has changed for the better. In 1970 Londoners were given the chance to hear a number of Grainger's major compositions during the course of a Grainger Festival held on the South Bank. In 1976 John Bird's magnificent biography was published. But as far as the record-buying public is concerned I imagine that a great many people were first made aware of Grainger, as I myself was, by another composer, Benjamin Britten. Britten really inaugurated the Grainger revival in this country, just as he did more than anyone else to rehabilitate Frank Bridge. Britten's 'Salute to Percy Grainger' (Decca) still cannot be bettered as an introduction to Grainger. Its contents are exquisitely chosen: they remind one of Britten's faultless taste in the selecting of poems for his own vocal anthologies such as the *Serenade*, the *Spring Symphony*, or the *Nocturne*. Admittedly none of the larger works is represented but neither are the pot-boilers, with the exception of *Shepherd's Hey*. But even this is given in the much sunnier, friskier chamber-orchestra version as opposed to the rather brash and boisterous full-orchestra setting.

For the rest, every facet of Grainger's unrivalled art as a transcriber and arranger of folk, traditional, and popular music is illustrated. As early as 1933 we find Britten writing in his diary that he had just heard on the radio two brilliant Percy Grainger folksong arrangements 'knocking all the Vaughan Williams and R. O. Morris arrangements into a cocked hat', and Grainger's settings for solo voice and instrumental accompaniment clearly reveal that when a tune took his fancy he was not content merely to try to preserve it in what we might term a 'non-contributory' setting. He attempted always to realize the latent implications of melody and text, and it is something of a creative miracle that however sophisticated Grainger's settings may be from a harmonic and textural point of view, they always respect the integrity of the given tune. In *Willow, Willow*, for example, Grainger opens the floodgates of chromatic harmony really only in the last verse and so creates an overwhelming impression of the love-lorn singer, in this case the incomparable Peter Pears, abandoning himself to his grief.

John Shirley-Quirk is another distinguished soloist on this record (in the sea-shanty *Shallow Brown*, for example). Britten himself is heard with Viola Tunnard playing a piano duet arrangement of a racy piece called *Let 's Dance Gay in Green Meadow*, a folkdance from the Faeroe Islands. It certainly makes a difference having an artist of Britten's calibre in charge. Many of these small pieces could have sounded trivial in the hands of a non-creative conductor or soloists of suspect musicianship, as indeed they do on some of the other Grainger anthologies still to be discussed. But this is without question the record to start out from (Decca SXL 6410).

No less definitely the one to proceed with is 'Salute to Percy Grainger' Vol. 2. This was to have been conducted by Britten, but at the last minute illness intervened and his Aldeburgh deputy Steuart Bedford stepped very capably into the breach. However Britten was present at all the sessions and approved the 'takes', and so it is not surprising to find that volume 2 bears the same imprint of excellence as volume 1. This is nowhere more in evidence than in the singing of Peter Pears. Grainger himself loved Pears's voice. He once wrote: 'He has the sweetest voice which grows falsetto-ish as he rises into the higher notes, which is much more lovable than the Caruso method of forcing a mad-bull-type of tone into what Stokowski called ''Purdah''.' Pears, with the Linden Singers, is especially fine in *Brigg Fair*, a tune collected by Grainger in Lincolnshire and set by him for tenor solo and unaccompanied chorus, but better known in the form of Delius's orchestral rhapsody which came later. 'Salute to Percy Grainger' Vol. 2 is on Decca SXL 6872. However, the undoubted high point of the disc for me is the magnificent *Passacaglia on Green Bushes* which is one of Grainger's finest works: astonishing to think that this should be its first commercial recording. Grainger loved this tune with what he called its 'raciness, its fresh grace, its manly clear-cut lines', and it is hard to think of a form better suited than the passacaglia to conveying that feeling of foot-stamping primitiveness and what Grainger termed the 'unbroken keeping-on-ness of the dance'. Debussy described Stravinsky's *The Rite of Spring* as 'primitive with every modern convenience' and the phrase could appositely be applied to Grainger's *Green Bushes*, yet we are conscious neither of primitiveness nor modernism as we listen. The blend is exquisite and perfect, and all we hear is wonderful music: folk music enhanced by culture and not emasculated by civilization. The record is a real treasure-trove. *The Three Ravens* for instance: one falls to musing as to what long-forgotten medieval tragedy inspired this folk-poem and Grainger's poignant setting of it. *The Power of Love* I shall be returning to later in another context. You will also find the *Irish Tune from County Derry*, not the familiar Grainger diatonic harmonization but a more oozily chromatic version scored for the same combination as the Mozart G minor symphony. The reason is not given in the notes but is unusual enough to be worth mentioning. The session involved should have been devoted to Britten conducting the symphony. When he was unable to, it was decided to use the session to record more Grainger, and so this string arrangement of the *Irish Tune* was expanded on the spot so as to accommodate the extra instruments. Inasmuch as this was Grainger's own practice in setting his tunes and the basis of his system of 'elastic' scoring, we may be sure he would have been delighted.

These two Aldeburgh 'Salute to Percy Grainger' anthologies I can recommend without reservation. Others are less good, but two records call for consideration first, each showing Grainger painting on a rather larger canvas than usual. Both are central to a representative Grainger collection. The first comes from HMV and has Neville Dilkes conducting the English Sinfonia in the *Danish Folk-music Suite* and the *In a Nutshell Suite*. Neither had been recorded before, but if you know Grainger's *Colonial Song* you will recognize it in the last movement of *In a Nutshell*, as a subsidiary theme in the 'Gumsuckers' March'. I am surprised, incidentally, that this march has never become popular for it has got one of Grainger's catchiest tunes. However from an objectively musical point of view the most interesting movement of *In a Nutshell* is certainly the 'Pastoral' in which members of the orchestra detach themselves rhythmically and metrically from their colleagues and do their own independent things in a way very reminiscent of the music of Ives. An astonishing fact about Grainger is that there was hardly a single aspect of twentieth-century musical development that he failed to touch on at one time or another, but always quite independently of anyone else. The *Danish Folk-music Suite* is really first-class. Few are as familiar with the flavour of Danish folksong as with English, but Grainger is an accomplished ambassador. He creates unusual and attractive textures in both 'Lord Peter's Stable-boy' and the 'Jutish Medley', but the real jewel is 'The Power of Love'. Peter Pears recorded this on the Decca 'Salute' volume 2, but that need in no way deter anyone from listening to its orchestral counterpart. It is perhaps the most gloriously full-blooded folk-music setting Grainger ever devised. At its climax the expressive burden is carried by all the strings in unison instead of by the voice, with a horn counter melody marked characteristically, 'hugely to the fore'; the effect is overwhelming. The title of the records is 'Grainger on the Shore' and the number is HMV ASD 3651. *The Power of Love* is a good example of what Grainger termed his principle of 'elastic' scoring. By this he meant that his settings were so conceived as to be playable by a variety of instrumental combinations, the substance of the music being in all cases the same. By this token the Britten 'Salute' Vol. 1 will make you familiar with two movements – 'Lisbon' and 'The Lost Lady Found' – of one of Grainger's most admired works, the *Lincolnshire Posy* for military band. These settings of 'musical wild-flowers', as Grainger called them, each have the dramatic self-sufficiency and emotional concentration of a Wolf song; at the same time each contrives to be a portrait of the singer who sang the original tune. Again for all their technical sophistication these settings still leave a taste in the mouth as of something quite pure and whole, no sugar or preservatives added. If you have ever heard Britten's Suite on English Folktunes you will recognize 'Lord Melbourne' because Britten borrowed the tune in Grainger's original transcription from the *Lincolnshire Posy*. But 'Rufford Park Poachers', as far as I know, is not to be found anywhere else, and the setting is one of Grainger's most powerful. Incidentally the original singer of this song was Joseph Taylor, the source of 'Brigg Fair' and many of Grainger's other treasurable finds. The title of this record is 'By Plane from Paris' on account of the other side which contains works by Milhaud and Poulenc both entitled Suite Française; incidentally the Milhaud Suite Française was a particular favourite of Grainger's and when you hear its delightful and utterly idiomatic treatment of French folktunes it's easy to see why. It is an enjoyable record; the performers are the London Wind Ensemble, conductor Denis Wick, and the number is Enigma K 53574.

I want to turn now to what I might term my 'B' category. All the records I have so far recommended have their share of the Grainger 'pop classics'; but in the two remaining miscellanies, neither of which merits unqualified praise, we begin to run into duplication problems. The trouble is that both contain a certain amount of music not to be found elsewhere, so that if you have acquired a taste for Grainger you will want to have them, warts, duplications, and all. First, a record from Australia, 'Country Gardens – The Orchestral Works of Percy Grainger', with John Hopkins conducting the Sydney Symphony Orchestra. This shares a good deal of material with the Decca 'Salutes', but in no cases are the performances comparable, and the sound is on the dim side. On the other hand definitely worth hearing are the two versions of the *Harvest Hymn*, the arrangement for tuneful percussion of 'La Vallée des cloches' from Ravel's *Miroirs*, and, most interestingly, a strange and lovely piece called *The Lonely Desert Man sees the Tents of the Happy Tribes* for wordless solo voices and instrumental accompaniment with prominent marimba and guitar. This record also includes the luscious *Colonial Song* and the children's march *Over the Hills and Far Away*. The number is HMV 5514. The Bournemouth Sinfonietta under Kenneth Montgomery has brought out an album called 'Percy Grainger: Free Rambles, Room Music Titbits, And . . .'. I wish I could be more positive about it, but the general quality of the playing is strait-laced, civilized, and English in a way that is totally opposed to the Grainger ethos. It scarcely sounds as though anybody was really having fun, and as the Bard said, 'where no pleasure is, there is no profit taken'. However, no other record has *Spoon River*, the Bach paraphrase *Blithe Bells*, the *Walking Tune*, and an early piece for solo cello and orchestra called *Youthful Rapture*, a title which is certainly an improvement on the original which was 'A Lot of Rot'. An earlier generation of critics might have described the piece as 'tumescent', and it is interesting to hear the sort of music the young Grainger was writing before his life-changing encounter with folksong.

One other orchestral record will certainly appeal to Graingerites,

Grieg-lovers, and those interested merely in the popular Grainger. One side has Grainger playing the Grieg Piano Concerto on a piano roll with the orchestral accompaniment realized by John Hopkins and the Sydney Symphony Orchestra. The other side is a re-issue of a recording of Grainger favourites made in the early '50s by Stokowski for which the composer provided a set of brand-new arrangements. Even for Grainger these are unusually extravagant and colourful and well calculated to bring out the best in the conductor. Grainger himself plays solo piano in *Handel in the Strand* and orchestral piano elsewhere. The number is RCA RL 10168 and should on no account be missed. Grainger made 'dish-ups' as he called them of nearly all his instrumental works for solo piano, and if the idea appeals to you invest in a record called 'Room Music Tit-bits and Other Tone-Stuffs' played by the young Australian pianist Leslie Howard who is joined on one side by David Stanhope. Theirs is a nice programme, unadventurous perhaps but enjoyably played; it includes one item not available elsewhere, namely the 'English Waltz' from the *Youthful Suite* which is one of the movements not recorded on the Bournemouth Sinfonietta collection. The record is worth buying just to hear it because it represents Grainger at his most fun-loving and irresistible. The record number is HMV HQS 1402.

There is also a solo piano record by Daniel Adni, but it gave me little pleasure. The playing is often more heavy-handed than dynamic, and things like the Gershwin transcriptions just lie outside the pianist's ken altogether. What we are still lacking is a complete record devoted to Grainger's own interpretation of his works. By and large, however, he is quite well provided for now. Of course there are still lacunae – we are still missing the *English Dance* for orchestra and organ, the *Hill Song* No. 1, by which Grainger set such store, the *Marching Song of Democracy*, the *Tribute to Foster* which is an immensely likeable work, and the choral settings of Kipling which spanned nearly half a century of Grainger's creative life. The most glaring omission of all is *The Warriors*, perhaps Grainger's most complex and controversial score and certainly one which could gain from the repeated hearings that only the gramophone can provide.

No doubt the time will come when all these will be made available to us. Meanwhile I find myself impelled to reinforce my recommendation of Britten's Grainger, and to single out 'Lord Maxwell's Goodnight' (Vol. I) as the epitome of Grainger's recreative art at its best, a setting quite heart-stilling in its simplicity – solo voice and solo strings only, and the accompaniment seems hardly to exist as an entity at all, so apt and subtle are the shifting shades of emotion it conveys from one verse to the next, so naturally do the strings seem to serve as an expressive complement to or extension of the singing voice. Pears commits to record one of his finest performances, and the result to me is very moving: the work of a composer who really cared for the voice, for words, and for a great heritage of music which he helped preserve and bring to life again for our delight.

Recordings of works discussed

Blithe Bells. Bournemouth Sinfonietta/Montgomery	RCA RL 25198
Brigg Fair. Pears/Linden Singers/Bedford	Decca SXL 6872
Colonial Song. Sydney Symphony Orchestra/Hopkins	HMV EMD 5514
English Waltz. Howard/Stanhope	HMV HQS 1402
Green Bushes, passacaglia. English Chamber Orchestra/Bedford	Decca SXL 6872
Handel in the Strand. Grainger/Symphony Orchestra/Stokowski	RCA RL 10168
Harvest Hymn. Sydney Symphony Orchestra/Hopkins	HMV EMD 5514
In a Nutshell, suite. English Sinfonia/Dilkes	HMV ASD 3651
Irish Tune from County Derry. English Chamber Orchestra/Bedford	Decca SXL 6872
Let's Dance Gay in Green Meadow. Britten/Tunnard	Decca SXL 6410
Lord Maxwell's Goodnight. Pears/English Chamber Orchestra/Britten	Decca SXL 6410
Lincolnshire Posy. London Wind Ensemble/Wick	Enigma K 53574
Over the Hills and Far Away. Sydney Symphony Orchestra/Hopkins	HMV EMD 5514
The Power of Love. Pears/English Chamber Orchestra/Bedford	Decca SXL 6872
Shallow Brown. Shirley-Quirk/Ambrosian Singers/English Chamber Orchestra/Britten	Decca SXL 6410
Spoon River. Bournemouth Sinfonietta/Montgomery	RCA RL 25198
Suite on Danish Folksongs. English Sinfonia/Dilkes	HMV ASD 3651
The Three Ravens. Pears/Ambrosian Singers/members of English Chamber Orchestra/Bedford	Decca SXL 6872
Walking Tune. Bournemouth Sinfonietta/Montgomery	RCA RL 25198
Willow, willow. Pears/English Chamber Orchestra/Britten	Decca SXL 6410
Youthful Rapture. Welsh/Bournemouth Sinfonietta/Montgomery	RCA RL 25198

Rubbra on Record

A prolific composer, now in his late seventies, Edmund Rubbra has never suffered from being over-recorded. Thanks to Lyrita and RCA, some important items have become available in recent years, but the present list is still woefully inadequate. For instance, apart from one comparative trifle, the chamber music, a major branch of Rubbra's work, is totally unrepresented, and only three of the ten symphonies are recorded. All of which is a reflection of two related facts: Rubbra has never been a fashionable composer and he has never gone with the fashions. From a 'modernist' point of view, his is traditional music; and yet traditionalists, if lazy-minded, or simply inattentive, may well find the thread of his musical thought elusive. So in recommending records, I want to try and clarify the nature of Rubbra's traditionalism, which is to say, his independence.

First, two very general points: whatever its resources, Rubbra's music is invariably vocal in feeling, and his textures have a natural leaning towards counterpoint. What better beginning, then than one of his madrigals to words by Campion? This is a four-part setting of 'It fell on a summer's day', one of two madrigals by Rubbra, sung by the Alban Singers directed by Peter Hurford, on a miscellaneous record called 'Songs of Leisure and Love': the number is Argo ZRG 833. Also on this record are some madrigals from around 1600, which underline the reality of Rubbra's roots in the music of that period. And we find the same affinity, in a very direct and engaging way, in one of his earlier orchestral works. This is the suite of five *Improvisations on Virginal Pieces by Giles Farnaby* played by the Bournemouth Sinfonietta under Hans Hubert Schönzeler on RCA RL 25027, an important record which also includes *A Tribute* written for the seventieth birthday of Vaughan Williams, and – the main work – the Symphony No. 10, which I shall be returning to, for it is very much the culmination of Rubbra's development.

Before turning to the symphonies, I should like to recommend another RCA record, this time of some choral music. The principal works are the *Missa Cantuariensis* and the *Missa in honorem Sancti Dominici*. These are two very different settings, the one expansive, written for double choir, the other a masterly piece of concision, economical at every stage. The latter, the *St Dominic Mass*, in particular, has much to tell us of Rubbra's basic musical values. For example, the 'Laudamus te' section of the Gloria relies upon the plainest stepwise motion in all four parts, and at 'Domine Deus' there is an equally characteristic key change. The beginning of the 'Agnus Dei' is a simple, telling example of common chords in uncommon relationships. As Rubbra himself has put it, 'All the chords . . . are plain unvarnished consonances: but for me they live in a new way because of the light thrown on them by unusual neighbours.' However, there is a semitonal clash of the two middle parts at the word 'miserere', and for a moment the prevailing chordal writing gives way to counterpoint. This is music in which the slightest deviation from an established norm is felt to be significant. The *St Dominic Mass* is sung by the St Margaret's Westminster Singers conducted by Richard Hickox on RCA LRL1 5119. The other works are the *Canterbury Mass* and two short carols, one of which, 'Dormi Jesu', was the first piece by Rubbra to be published. This is an indispensable record, the sole representation of one of the most important aspects of Rubbra's works. For he is nothing if not a religious composer in much the same way as Messiaen is. Even if he is writing a dance-like piece or setting a secular text, his basic orientation is still evident.

Of the first four symphonies completed in close succession during the years 1937–42, only the Second is recorded. This is a mine of basic imagery, and basic working, an excellent starting-point for anyone who wants to come to grips with Rubbra's symphonism at a stage when the composer himself was first exploring its possibilities. Growth rather than pattern is the guiding principle: that is to say, thematic and textural growth. The slow movement, for example, begins with a contemplative theme on the strings – a good deal of stepwise motion again – followed by some distinctive wind chords; and from this material the whole slow movement evolves. Much is derived from both the wind chords and the characteristic intervals of the string theme. The ultimate climax and fulfilment begins with a typical Rubbra *crescendo* over an insistent pedal-note, and also typical is the way he returns to his original statement.

This symphony, together with the Festival Overture, one of only two concert overtures by Rubbra, is played by the New Philharmonia Orchestra under Vernon Handley on Lyrita SRCS 96, and it offers many insights into the composer's symphonism in general, for over the years his thinking has not so much changed fundamentally as developed an increasing subtlety and inner strength. As I have said earlier, growth, as distinct from pattern, has remained the guiding principle, but growth from a tiny melodic germ or cell, perhaps of only two or three intervals, rather than from an identifiable theme. This is what baffles the casual or inattentive listener who, because the musical surface is deceptively 'easy on the ear', expects to be able to nod in and out. That is something you can seldom do with Rubbra. When he begins with some seemingly inconsequential little figure, the merest opening gambit apparently, the chances are that every interval is significant, and that the consequences will in fact prove far-reaching. In other words, we are expected to listen, to listen actively, following a line of thought. There is no better example than the Tenth Symphony (*Sinfonia da camera*), a one-movement work for chamber orchestra written in 1974. Virtually the whole of this is derived from the rising, stepwise figure of five notes played by a solo cello at the outset. These five notes span the interval of a tritone (B – F), in steps of tones and semitones, two of each. It is Rubbra's way so to reflect upon and absorb the intervallic content of his material that everything that follows will be germane. In these opening bars we can feel him doing precisely that. He 'tries out' the seconds, and the tritone, and in only the third bar postulates a descending version of the germinal idea. The Tenth Symphony is played by the Bournemouth Sinfonietta under Hans-Hubert Schönzeler on RCA RL 25027 – the same record as the one containing the *Farnaby Improvisations*. The Tenth confronts us with the uniqueness of Rubbra's symphonic writing, his very personal re-creation of tradition, in the most direct and concentrated way. The slow tempos; the tone that is neither abrasive nor ingratiating, but serious, contemplative, absorbed; the expectation that the listener will really listen – these are typical. They are further exemplified in the passacaglia Finale of the Seventh Symphony, which is the other at present on record. The middle movement is an extended scherzo with two trios, for after stressing the more demanding aspects of Rubbra's musical thinking there is a tune that breaks spontaneously into the first part of the movement and is not heard again. It is that sort of movement – Rubbra at his most prodigal – but the whole expression is closely held together by a recurring rhythmic idea. Rubbra's Seventh Symphony is played by the London Philharmonic Orchestra under Sir Adrian Boult on Lyrita SRCS 119. It is coupled with Rubbra's *Soliloquy* for cello and orchestra played by Rohan de Saram with the London Symphony Orchestra conducted by Vernon Handley.

Another shortish work of a soloistic nature that is well worth investigating is the *Improvisation* for violin and orchestra, which is coupled with Britten's Violin Concerto on RCA GL 25096. The sound is 'electronically processed stereo', but any shortcomings are more than offset by the intense playing of Sidney Harth and the Louisville Orchestra conducted by Robert Whitney.

The concept of improvisation is found again in Rubbra's Piano Concerto, a work dedicated to and in some degree inspired by the Pakistani musician, Ali Akbar Khan. Commissioned by the BBC in the mid '50s, but still, I suspect, little known, this concerto could yet become Rubbra's most popular work. It is played by Denis Matthews with the BBC Symphony Orchestra conducted by Sir Malcolm Sargent. It is an old recording which still sounds well, and we are lucky to have it. Unfortunately, though, this is only available in a boxed set of four records, 'Twentieth-Century British Piano Concertos', HMV SLS 5080. The other works are by Ireland, Bliss, Rawsthorne, Tippett, Britten, and Williamson. It is a very worthwhile package, but uneven in quality of sound.

In concentrating so much on the music, I have seldom remarked on performance or recording. This was deliberate, for in no case is there an alternative version. However, be assured that everything I have mentioned stands up well in both categories, and the best – the two symphonies on Lyrita, for instance – are of outstanding quality.

Recordings of works discussed

Dormi Jesu. St Margaret's Westminster Singers/Hickox	RCA LRL1 5119
Festival Overture. New Philharmonia Orchestra/Handley	Lyrita SRCS 96
Improvisation for violin and orchestra. Harth/Louisville Orchestra/Whitney	RCA GL 25096
Improvisations on Virginal Pieces by Giles Farnaby. Bournemouth Sinfonietta/ Schönzeler	RCA RL 25027
'It fell on a summer's day'. Alban Singers	Argo ZRG 833
Missa Cantuariensis. St Margaret's Westminster Singers/Hickox	RCA LRL1 5119
Missa in honorem Sancti Dominici. St Margaret's Westminster Singers/Hickox	RCA LRL1 5119
Piano Concerto. Matthews/BBC Symphony Orchestra/Sargent	HMV SLS 5080
Soliloquy for cello and orchestra. R. de Saram/ London Symphony Orchestra/Handley	Lyrita SRCS 119
Symphony No. 2 in D. New Philharmonia Orchestra/Handley	Lyrita SRCS 96
Symphony No. 7 in C. London Philharmonic Orchestra/Boult	Lyrita SRCS 119
Symphony No. 10 (*Sinfonia da camera*). Bournemouth Sinfonietta/Schönzeler	RCA RL 25027
A Tribute. Bournemouth Sinfonietta/ Schönzeler	RCA RL 25027